Probabilistic Approaches for Social Media Analysis

Data, Community and Influence

East China Normal University Scientific Reports
Subseries on Data Science and Engineering

ISSN: 2382-5715

Chief Editor
Weian Zheng
Changjiang Chair Professor
School of Finance and Statistics
East China Normal University, China
Email: financialmaths@gmail.com

Associate Chief Editor
Shanping Wang
Senior Editor
Journal of East China Normal University (Natural Sciences), China
Email: spwang@library.ecnu.edu.cn

This book series reports valuable research results and progress in scientific and related areas. Mainly contributed by the distinguished professors of the East China Normal University, it will cover a number of research areas in pure mathematics, financial mathematics, applied physics, computer science, environmental science, geography, estuarine and coastal science, education information technology, etc.

Published

Vol. 11 *Probabilistic Approaches for Social Media Analysis:*
         Data, Community and Influence
         by Kun Yue (Yunnan University, China), Jin Li (Yunnan University, China), Hao Wu (Yunnan University, China), Weiyi Liu (Yunnan University, China) and Zidu Yin (Yunnan University, China)

Vol. 10 *Clustering and Outlier Detection for Trajectory Stream Data*
         by Jiali Mao (East China Normal University, China), Cheqing Jin (East China Normal University, China) and Aoying Zhou (East China Normal University, China)

Vol. 9   *Concurrency Control and Recovery in OLTP Systems:*
         High Scalability and Availability
         by Peng Cai (East China Normal University, China), Jinwei Guo (East China Normal University, China) and Aoying Zhou (East China Normal University, China)

More information on this series can also be found at https://www.worldscientific.com/series/ecnusr

(Continued at end of book)

East China Normal University Scientific Reports | **Vol. 11**

Subseries on Data Science and Engineering

Probabilistic Approaches for Social Media Analysis

Data, Community and Influence

Kun Yue

Jin Li

Hao Wu

Weiyi Liu

Zidu Yin

Yunnan University, China

World Scientific

EW JERSEY · LONDON · SINGAPORE · BEIJING · SHANGHAI · HONG KONG · TAIPEI · CHENNAI · TOKYO

Published by

World Scientific Publishing Co. Pte. Ltd.

5 Toh Tuck Link, Singapore 596224

USA office: 27 Warren Street, Suite 401-402, Hackensack, NJ 07601

UK office: 57 Shelton Street, Covent Garden, London WC2H 9HE

Library of Congress Cataloging-in-Publication Data
Names: Yue, Kun, author.
Title: Probabilistic approaches for social media analysis : data, community and influence /
    Kun Yue, Jin Li, Hao Wu, Weiyi Liu, Zidu Yin, Yunnan University, China.
Description: New Jersey : World Scientific, [2020] | Series: East China
    Normal University scientific reports, 2382-5715 ; vol. 11 |
    Includes bibliographical references and index.
Identifiers: LCCN 2019052216 | ISBN 9780000987709 (paperback) |
    ISBN 9789811207372 (hardcover) | ISBN 9789811207389 (ebook)
Subjects: LCSH: Social media--Data processing. | Text processing (Computer science) |
    Quantitative research--Statistical methods. | Machine learning. |
    Content analysis (Communication)--Data processing.
Classification: LCC HM742 .Y85 2020 | DDC 302.23/1--dc23
LC record available at https://lccn.loc.gov/2019052216

British Library Cataloguing-in-Publication Data
A catalogue record for this book is available from the British Library.

For any available supplementary material, please visit
https://www.worldscientific.com/worldscibooks/10.1142/11476#t=suppl

Desk Editor: Herbert Moses

Typeset by Stallion Press
Email: enquiries@stallionpress.com

Printed in Singapore

East China Normal University Scientific Reports

Preface

Social media plays increasingly important roles in relevant fields of big data and artificial intelligence, with the popularity of social networks and Web 2.0 applications. In both academic and industry paradigms, the acquisition, modeling, analysis, and utilization of social media are paid much attention. Following the tendency of data socialization, computational or intelligent social science has been developed rapidly in recent years. Social media analysis facilitates knowledge discovery, behavioral preference/profile modeling, personalized services, sentiment monitoring, society governance, etc. The methodology of social media analysis also accelerates the improvement of research and development of traditional social science.

From the engineering perspective, the following two aspects constitute a system of social media analysis: methods for social media data acquisition and those for application-oriented social media analysis or knowledge discovery. Leveraged by the properties of social media and ideas of probabilistic models, we present a series of probabilistic approaches in the lifecycle of social media analysis. From social behavioral interactions, we establish our methods by adopting Markov network (MN) and Bayesian network (BN), two classic probabilistic graphical models, to represent associations with uncertainties. Also, from the local structure of social networks and records of influence spread, we establish our methods by the graph model with state probabilities and random walk with transition probabilities to fulfill containment of social influence and location of influence sources.

In this book, we consider the following issues and present our research findings:

- **Acquisition of social media data from online big graphs:** We adopt the ideas of Quasi-Monte Carlo and branch and bound methods to give an adaptive Web-scale sampling algorithm for parallel data collection implemented upon Spark. Then, given the collected online big graph data, we present the method for parallel incremental maintenance based on entropy and Poisson process.

- **Incremental learning of probabilistic graphical models:** To make the knowledge model, like BN and MN for association representation, up to date in response to the newly generated social media data, we consider measurement of the coincidence between the original BN structure and new data. According to the influence of new data on the original model from the structural perspective, and probabilistic conditional independencies from the semantic perspective, we give the hierarchical method for incremental learning of probabilistic graphical models through various cases.

- **Discovering user similarities in social behavioral interactions:** We adopt BN as the underling framework and propose a data-intensive approach for discovering user similarities. A BN is constructed to describe user similarities by a graphical model with probabilistic properties called user Bayesian network (UBN). To measure the indirect similarities between users, we give the method for measuring the closeness of user connections and the MapReduce-based algorithm for measuring the dependence degrees by probabilistic inferences of UBN.

- **Associative categorization of frequent patterns in social media:** We illustrate the idea of MN-based representation of mutual dependences of frequent patterns. We then give the algorithm to construct an item association Markov network (IAMN) and discuss its chordal property theoretically. To fulfill hierarchical associative categorization, we transform the IAMN into a join tree, by which the hierarchical classes of nodes could be obtained.

- **Latent link analysis and community detection from social media:** We consider discovering latent links implied in social interactions from the perspective of participants' behaviors instead of social network structures. We construct an IAMN to represent both observed and latent links without regard for the topological structures of social networks. We then differentiate social links with strengths on edges of the IAMN to extend the concept of k-clique. By incorporating the concepts of the nearest neighbor and association degree, we give the method to detect overlapping communities via latent links described by IAMN.

- **Probabilistic inferences of latent entity associations:** We propose entity association Bayesian network (EABN), in which entities are regarded as variables, edges describe the associations between entities, and conditional probability tables (CPTs) quantify the dependencies. We employ self-organizing map to divide a dataset of textual Web contents into several subsets and construct the EABN efficiently. To rank the entities for the given specific entities, we use probabilistic inferences of EABN to evaluate the associations quantitatively.

- **Containment of influence spread on social networks:** We consider containing influence spread and locating influence sources, respectively. For the first strategy, we extend the classic linear threshold model to establish the diffusion–containment model. Then, we give a greedy algorithm to approximately solve the problem of competitive influence containment maximally. For the second strategy, we give a Bayes backtracking model (BBM) to identify the possible node which spreads influence to other nodes with a partial observation of propagation results in big online social networks. Then, we give a random walk based backtracking algorithm (RWBA) to locate the source nodes via posterior probabilities in BBM.

Kun Yue
Kunming, China

About the Authors

 **Kun Yue**, born in 1979, is a professor of Computer Science at Yunnan University and the vice dean of School of Information Science and Engineering at Yunnan University. He received the M.S. degree in computer science from Fudan University in 2004 and received the Ph.D. degree in computer science from Yunnan University in 2009. He is leading the innovative research team "Massive Data Analysis and Services" of Yunnan University. His research interests include massive data analysis, knowledge engineering, and service computing. He has been in charge of more than 20 research grants, including the Key Program of Natural National Science Foundation of China, Science Foundation for Distinguished Young Scholars of Yunnan Province, Foundation for Key Program of Ministry of Education of China, etc. He has published more than 100 papers in academic journals, including *IEEE Transactions on Cybernetics, IEEE Transactions on Services Computing, Information Sciences, Knowledge-Based Systems, Neurocomputing, Applied Soft Computing, Applied Intelligence, Chinese Journal of Computers, Journal of Software*, and conferences including DASFAA, CIKM, BigData, etc. He has published four monographs on data management and analysis in World Scientific Publishing, Science Press, and Tsinghua University Press. He received the first prize and the second prize in Yunnan Province's Nature Science Award in 2009

and 2019, respectively, and the Science & Technology Award for Young Talents of Yunnan Province in 2015. He was awarded the Young Academic and Technical Leader of Yunnan Province in 2016. He is the director of Chinese Association for Artificial Intelligence (CAAI), the vice-chairman of CAAI Uncertainty in Artificial Intelligence Society, and the member of CCF Database Society.

Jin Li, born in 1975, is an associate professor of computer science at Yunnan University. He received the B.S. degree in computer science, M.S. degree in computational mathematics, and Ph.D. degree in telecommunication and information system from Yunnan University in 1998, 2004, and 2012, respectively. His current research interests include machine learning, data mining, and social media analysis. He has been in charge of more than 10 research grants, including the Natural National Science Foundation of China and Natural Science Foundation of Yunnan Province. He has published more than 40 papers in academic journals, including *Future Generation Computer Systems and Knowledge-Based Systems*, and conferences, including WISE, APWeb, TAMC, etc.

Hao Wu, born in 1979, is an associate professor of computer science at Yunnan University. He received the M.S. degree and Ph.D. degree in computer science from Huazhong University of Science and Technology in 2004 and 2007, respectively. He finished his postdoctoral position research at Yunnan University in 2018. His research interests include knowledge discovery, information retrieval, and service computing. He has been in charge of more than 10 research grants, including the Natural National Science Foundation of China, China Postdoctoral Science Foundation, Natural Science Foundation of Yunnan Province, etc. He has published more than 70 papers in academic journals, including *IEEE Transactions on Services Computing, Knowledge-Based Systems, Personal and Ubiquitous Computing, Scientometrics, Journal of the American Society for*

Information Science and Technology, and conferences, including CollaborateCom, CIKM, BigData, etc. He served as the editorial member of *International Journal on Advances in Software*.

Weiyi Liu, born in 1950, is a professor of computer science at Yunnan University. He graduated from Huazhong University of Science and Technology in 1976. His research interests mainly include artificial intelligence, data, and knowledge engineering. He has been in charge of 15 research grants, including the Natural National Science Foundation of China and Natural Science Foundation of Yunnan Province. He has published more than 100 papers in academic journals, including *IEEE Transactions on Systems, Man and Cybernetics (Part B)*, *IEEE Transactions on Fuzzy Systems*, *Information Sciences*, *Fuzzy Sets and Systems*, *Applied Soft Computing*, *The Computer Journal*, and *Journal of Computer Science and Technology*. He has published two monographs on data modeling and analysis in the Science Press. He received the first prize in Yunnan Province's Nature Science Award in 2001 and 2009.

Zidu Yin, born in 1990, is a Ph.D. candidate of computer science at Yunnan University. He received the M.S. degree in computer science from Yunnan University in 2016. His research interests mainly include Web data management and knowledge engineering with big data. He has published eight papers in academic journals and conferences, including *Journal of Software*, *Neurocomputing*, *International Journal of Uncertainty, Fuzziness and Knowledge-Based Systems*, *DASFAA*, etc. He has obtained an invention patent authorization on personalized recommendation of Web pages.

Acknowledgments

The research in this book was supported by the National Science Foundation of China (Nos. U1802271 and 61472345), Science Foundation for Distinguished Young Scholars of Yunnan Province (No. 2019FJ011), Young Top-Notch Talent in 10,000 Talent Program of Yunnan Province (No. C6193032), and Program for Donglu Scholar of Yunnan University.

We thank all friends, Aoying Zhou, Xiaodong Fu, Liang Duan, Mingliang Yue, Zhengbao Sun, Zhijian Zhang, Xinran Wu, Jixian Zhang, Lei Li, and Jie Li, without whom the technical contributions of this book cannot be worked out.

We would like to express our sincere thanks and appreciation to the people at World Scientific Publishing and East China Normal University for their generous help throughout the publication process.

Contents

East China Normal University Scientific Reports   v

Preface   vii

About the Authors   xi

Acknowledgments   xv

1. Introduction   **1**

   1.1   Background   1

   1.2   Challenges and Basic Ideas   3

       1.2.1   Acquisition of social media data
from OBGs   3

       1.2.2   Incremental learning of probabilistic graphical
models   3

       1.2.3   Discovering user similarities in social
behavioral interactions   5

       1.2.4   Associative categorization of frequent patterns in
social media   6

       1.2.5   Latent link analysis and community detection
from social media   6

       1.2.6   Probabilistic inferences of latent entity
associations   7

1.2.7   Containment of influence spread on social
          networks   8
1.3   Organization   9

**2. Adaptive and Parallel Acquisition of Social Media
    Data from Online Big Graphs**   **11**
2.1   Motivation and Basic Idea   11
2.2   Related Work   14
2.3   Adaptive Data Collection Based on
      QMC Sampling   16
      2.3.1   Basic idea and algorithm   16
      2.3.2   Analysis   19
2.4   Updating Sampling Results by Incremental
      Maintenance   23
      2.4.1   Overview of incremental maintenance   23
      2.4.2   Entropy-based data updating   24
2.5   Experimental Results   26
      2.5.1   Experiment setup   26
      2.5.2   Effectiveness   27
      2.5.3   Efficiency 30
2.6   Summary   34
References 36

**3. A Bayesian Network-Based Approach for Incremental
    Learning of Uncertain Knowledge**   **39**
3.1   Motivation and Basic Idea   39
      3.1.1   Motivation   39
      3.1.2   Ideas and contributions   41
3.2   Related Work   43
3.3   Influence Degree of BN Nodes   46
3.4   Incremental Learning of BNs   50
      3.4.1   Markov equivalence and its properties   50

3.4.2 A scoring-based algorithm for BN's
incremental learning 54

3.5 Experimental Results 59

3.5.1 Correctness of influence degree 59

3.5.2 Effectiveness of revised BNs 62

3.5.3 Efficiency of incremental learning 63

3.6 Summary 67

References 67

4. **Discovering User Similarities in Social Behavioral
Interactions Based on Bayesian Network**   **71**

4.1 Motivation and Basic Idea 71

4.2 Related Work 75

4.3 Bayesian Network Based Measurement of User
Similarities 78

4.3.1 Definitions and problem statement 78

4.3.2 Constructing user Bayesian network based
on MapReduce 80

4.4 Deriving Indirect Similarity by Probabilistic
Inferences 84

4.4.1 Graphical structure-based indirect
similarities 85

4.4.2 Probabilistic inference-based indirect
similarities 87

4.4.3 Combining structure-based and inference-based
indirect similarities 89

4.5 Experimental Results 92

4.5.1 Experiment setup 92

4.5.2 Efficiency of UBN construction and inferences 93

4.5.3 Effectiveness of UBN and its inferences 100

4.5.4 Effectiveness of UBN-based user similarity . . 101

4.6 Summary 104

References 105

5. **Associative Categorization of Frequent Patterns
    in Social Media Based on Markov Network**   **109**

    5.1   Motivation and Basic Idea   109
    5.2   Constructing Item-Association Markov Network
          from Behavioral Interactions in Social Media   114
    5.3   IAMN-Based Hierarchical Categorization   122
    5.4   Experimental Results   127
          5.4.1   Experiment setup   127
          5.4.2   Efficiency of IAMN construction   128
          5.4.3   Effectiveness of IAMN   131
          5.4.4   Effectiveness of associative categorization . . .   132
    5.5   Empirical Study on Hierarchical Categorization of
          Microblog Users   135
          5.5.1   Basic idea   135
          5.5.2   Graph model of microblog users   137
          5.5.3   Hierarchical categorization of microblog users .   141
          5.5.4   Performance studies   144
    5.6   Summary   148
    References   149

6. **Markov Network Based Latent Link Discovery
    and Community Detection in Social Behavioral Interactions 153**

    6.1   Motivation and Basic Idea   153
    6.2   Related Work   157
    6.3   Community Detection from IAMN-based
          Latent Links   160
          6.3.1   Definitions   160
          6.3.2   Algorithm for community detection   162
          6.3.3   Community combination   165
    6.4   Experimental Results   168
          6.4.1   Experiment setup   168
          6.4.2   Effectiveness   168
          6.4.3   Efficiency   175

6.5   Summary   176

References   176

7. **Probabilistic Inferences of Latent Entity
    Associations in Textual Web Contents**   **179**

7.1   Motivation and Basic Idea   179
7.2   Related Work   182
7.3   Definitions and Problem Formalization   183
7.4   Generating Samples of EABN Nodes   184
7.5   Learning an EABN and Ranking EAs   186
    7.5.1   BIC metric and division of TWC dataset   186
    7.5.2   Scoring-based construction of EABN   190
    7.5.3   Ranking EAs by probabilistic inferences of EABN   193
7.6   Experimental Results   195
    7.6.1   Experiment setup   195
    7.6.2   Effectiveness   196
    7.6.3   Efficiency   199
7.7   Summary   201
References   202

8. **Containment of Competitive Influence Spread
    on Social Networks**   **205**

8.1   Motivation and Basic Idea   205
8.2   Related Work   208
8.3   Diffusion–Containment Model   211
    8.3.1   Graph model   211
    8.3.2   Interaction strategy   212
    8.3.3   D-State probability and C-State probability   . .   213
    8.3.4   Influence propagation rules   215
8.4   Propagation of Vertex Activation Probabilities   216
8.5   Finding C-Seeds for D-Influence Minimization   219
8.6   Experimental Results   224
    8.6.1   Experiment setup   224
    8.6.2   Feasibility   225
    8.6.3   Functionality and relationship of relevant
        parameters   230

8.7   Summary   231
References   232

9. Locating Sources in Online Social Networks
    via Random Walk   **235**

9.1   Motivation and Basic Idea   235
9.2   Related Work   238
9.3   Influence Propagation Model and Source Location
       Problem   239
       9.3.1   Influence propagation model   239
       9.3.2   Source location problem   240
9.4   Bayes Backtracking Model   241
9.5   Random Walk Based Sources Location   244
9.6   Experimental Results   247
       9.6.1   Experiment setup   247
       9.6.2   Performance studies   248
9.7   Summary   255
References   255

10. Conclusion   **259**

Index   263

Chapter 1

Introduction

1.1 Background

With the rapid development of data acquisition and IT infrastructures, as well as the popularity of social networks and Web 2.0 applications, social media plays increasingly important roles in relevant fields of big data and artificial intelligence. In both academic and industry paradigms, the acquisition, modeling, analysis, and utilization of social media are paid much attention due to the indispensable requirements of research and applications of computational and intelligent social science.

From the engineering perspective, the following two aspects constitute a system of social media analysis: methods for social media data acquisition and those for application-oriented social media analysis or knowledge discovery.

For the former, most user behavioral data are generated by Web applications or social activities called user-generated data (UGD). Specifically, users' behavioral interactions, an important part of UGD, embody many unobservable but critical properties other than their demographic descriptions if we could find associations, latent links or categorizations among them. The knowledge implied in UGD and unveiled by association analysis is useful for user behavior/profile modeling, personalized recommendation, decision-making, event tracking, etc.

Meanwhile, social network is an important medium for information propagation among its members. With the increasing popularity of social media, such as Facebook, Twitter, LinkedIn, etc., ideas, opinions, news, and product information are spread across online social networks. The discipline or tendency of social influence spread or network evolution is important for several social network-based applications, such as blocking e-commerce opponents, attracting public attention, monitoring social sentiment, etc.

For the latter, associations among users or entities are preliminary for behavior modeling. To this end, frequent patterns and the consequent association rules are effectively used to search for their interesting association relationships from the given database transactions. However, complex associations among behaviors (i.e., frequent items) cannot be represented globally by means of $X \rightarrow Y$ manner, where X and Y are frequent itemsets. The associations among users or entities are not "linear" and the "if-then" representation is not always appropriate. In the context of massive social media data, the associations are always uncertain, but not either exactly associative or not. On the other hand, the spread of influence or transition of states on social networks are also not linear with uncertainties in general situations.

Therefore, leveraged by the properties of social media and ideas of probabilistic models, we present a series of probabilistic approaches in the lifecycle of social media analysis by focusing on social behavioral data acquisition and knowledge discovery. By acquiring UGD from social networks, an important type of online big graph (OBG), we establish the repository of social media data. We also give the generic ideas for acquiring other OBGs, such as linked Web pages and knowledge graphs. Then, from social behavioral interactions, we establish our methods by adopting Markov network (MN) and Bayesian network (BN), two classic probabilistic graphical models, to represent associations with uncertainties. Also, from the local structure of social networks and records of influence spread, we establish our methods by the graph model with state probabilities and random walk with transition probabilities to fulfill containment of social influence and location of influence sources.

1.2 Challenges and Basic Ideas

1.2.1 *Acquisition of social media data from OBGs*

In terms of the inherent properties of OBGs like social networks, data acquisition will have to solve the following challenges. First, many petabytes of data stream are collected from millions of users per day by some e-commence platforms to build an innovative smart business. In large-volume and high-velocity social media data on the Web, connections among objects or entities are represented by graphical structures. The massive data volume with graphical connections should be considered. Second, the availability of a search engine's database is guaranteed by continuous tracking of billions of independent URLs or updating of crawled data for maintenance of related services and datacenters. The tracking process should be adaptive to fulfill updating and keep the result up to date according to the online property of OBGs. Third, the global topology of an OBG is unknown during data acquisition, and the graphical structures of the currently collected data should be used to crawl more. The optimal selection of successive nodes should be made to acquire as much as possible information with as less as possible nodes in a social network.

In response to the massive, heterogeneous, dynamically evolving properties of OBGs with unknown global topological structures, we give an adaptive and parallel approach for effective data acquisition from OBGs. First, we adopt the ideas of Quasi-Monte Carlo (QMC) and branch and bound to give an adaptive Web-scale sampling algorithm for parallel data collection implemented upon Spark. Then, given the collected OBG data, we present the method for parallel incremental maintenance based on entropy and Poisson process.

1.2.2 *Incremental learning of probabilistic graphical models*

Given a dataset, the knowledge framework could be learned, or there has been a knowledge framework specified by experts. In social network-based applications, newly generated social media data imply new knowledge that may not be included in the existing framework, which makes it necessary to keep the corresponding knowledge up to date with respect to the new data and thus refine the original knowledge framework. Learning the knowledge again completely on receiving the new data is straightforward but quite impractical, since the original data may be missing, or the knowledge framework was specified by experts without regard for any prior data. Even if the original data are available, the efficiency cannot be guaranteed due to the large size of the whole dataset. Moreover, data in general real applications are often updated periodically in a batch mode and expired data will not be preserved accordingly. In particular, knowledge discovered from data streams should be up to date according to the evolving nature of data streams, and the knowledge framework should be constructed by means of incremental strategies consequently.

BN is the well-adopted framework for uncertainty representation and inferences. A BN is a directed acyclic graph (DAG), where nodes represent random variables and edges represent dependencies among these variables. Each variable in a BN is associated with a conditional probability table (CPT) to give the probability of each parent state. By combining the graph theory and probability theory, uncertainties can be represented straightforwardly and inferred effectively. The incremental learning of a BN concerns the incremental learning of DAGs and CPTs.

First, we will have to determine the subgraphs that need to be revised in response to the new data. For this purpose, we consider measuring the coincidence between the original BN structure and the new data. According to the influence of new data on the CPTs or DAGs from the structural perspective, and probabilistic conditional independencies from the semantic perspective, we consider the incremental learning by various cases. If the DAG of the original BN is coincident with the new data, then we only need to update the CPTs easily. If the variation of new data influences the DAG of the original BN but does not influence the implied conditional independencies, then we replace the original structure by its equivalent structure with equivalent independence relationships. If the variation of new data influences the conditional independencies in a local structure of the original BN, we revise the BN's substructures. In the incremental revision, we emphasize the preservation of probabilistic conditional independencies implied in the BN as a probabilistic graphical model based on the concept and properties of Markov equivalence.

1.2.3 *Discovering user similarities in social behavioral interactions*

User similarities could be obtained by analyzing their behavioral interactions other than directly from users' demographic properties. However, the similarity between two users, say A and B, may depend on the behavioral interactions of several users other than just these two ones, which means that the similarities among social users are not linear and the "if-then" representation is not always appropriate. The similarity between two users depends on the mutual interactions rather than those just from A to B or those just from B to A in general situations. Whether two users are similar or not is generally uncertain but not either exactly similar or dissimilar, which is more obvious when confronted with massive social behavioral interactions. To solve these challenges, a global graphical model to represent user similarity should be constructed, in which directed edges are used to represent orientation (a.k.a. direction) aware similarities of pairs of two users. User similarities should be represented not only by the assertion that A is similar to B but also the uncertain dependence degree of how much A is similar to B in the universe of all concerned users. More importantly, it is desirable and challenging to discover the indirect similarities between two users without connections by direct edges in the graph model, which makes the inferences of similarities indispensable.

Therefore, we adopt BN as the underling framework and propose a data-intensive approach for discovering user similarities. A BN is constructed to describe user similarities by a graphical model with probabilistic properties called user Bayesian network (UBN). To measure the indirect similarities between users, we give the method for measuring the closeness of user connections in terms of the UBN's graphical structure, and the MapReduce-based algorithm for measuring the dependence degrees by UBN's probabilistic inferences.

1.2.4   *Associative categorization of frequent patterns in social media*

From the perspective of representing behavior associations, frequent patterns (i.e., items) and the consequent association rules are effectively used. However, complex associations among behaviors (i.e., frequent items) cannot be represented globally by means of $X \to Y$ manner, where X and Y are frequent itemsets. Also, the uncertainties of the association rules, measured by confidence and support, cannot be inferred, which is actually critical in decision-making on indirect behaviors.

Associative categorization is to discover the hierarchical structures of different granularities of behavior classes. For example, the relevant classes of participants could be discovered by means of grouping their behaviors in coauthored publications or co-operated projects. By aggregating finer granularities of classes level by level, higher granularities of classes could be generated pertinent to the practical requirements of various abstraction degrees. Actually, ultimate classes dependent on associations greatly, which could not be well incorporated if we used the classic algorithms of clustering, associative classification, and associative clustering, in data mining paradigms.

From the object-behavior point of view, it is natural to describe the relationships among behaviors by an undirected graph, where the nodes represent objects and edges represent connections among them. Therefore, we discuss MN-based mutual dependences of frequent patterns instead of the BN-based influence, since MN focuses on mutual dependence while BN focuses on causal relationships. Thus, we give the algorithm to construct an item association Markov network (IAMN). An MN, as an undirected graph, could be transformed into a tree (called join tree) if the MN satisfies the specific condition (called chordal), by which the hierarchical classes of nodes could be obtained. This is the basic idea of IAMN-based hierarchical associative categorization.

1.2.5   *Latent link analysis and community detection from social media*

From the perspective of user behaviors, some associations among users in social networks are latent (i.e., implied in social behaviors and inferred from the existing links), such as the indirect friendships among microblog users or paper authors. Latent links are implied in behavior interactions of users and correspondingly reflect their behavioral pattern or preference. We consider discovering latent links implied in social interactions from the perspective of participants' behaviors instead of social network structures. To overcome the deficiency of association rules to describe user links, we construct an IAMN to represent both observed and latent links without regard for the topological structures of social networks.

The community structure of social network means that the distribution of edges is often inhomogeneous, with high concentrations in special groups of participant users and low concentrations between these groups. Community reflects social relationships of the concerned participant users, and we detect overlapping communities upon discovered behavior relationships from a novel perspective of social behavioral data analysis. Accordingly, latent link-based community detection is different from the classic associative classification on association rules, as well as that in the context of topological structures of social networks. The classic k-clique algorithm finds all complete subgraphs with k vertices that are not the parts of larger complete subgraphs, on which communities could be found from complex networks. The prerequisite of k-clique is too strict for social media analysis, and thus we quantitatively differentiate social links with strengths on edges of the IAMN to extend the concept of k-clique. By incorporating the concepts of nearest neighbor and association degree, we give the method to detect overlapping communities via the latent links described by IAMN.

1.2.6 *Probabilistic inferences of latent entity associations*

Textual Web contents (TWCs) in social media data include words that describe entities. Entity associations (EAs) could be divided into two categories: direct EAs and latent EAs. The former represents that two entities co-occur in the same TWC document, while the latter represents that two entities associate with each other indirectly through other intermediate entities in different TWC documents. To infer EAs in practical applications, several critical challenges are confronted. Latent

EAs are uncertain in general cases. For example, whether "Microsoft" is associative with "GitHub" is uncertain unless all co-occurrences are discovered already. Latent EAs are likely to exist between two arbitrary entities. So, we will have to construct a global model that contains most entities in TWC documents while efficiently fulfilling the evaluation of co-occurrences on large volume entities. Ranking of latent EAs is significant, since not all latent EAs are useful for subsequent tasks, especially for the situations with massive TWCs and massive entities.

By using BN as the knowledge framework, we propose entity association Bayesian network (EABN), in which entities are regarded as variables, edges describe the associations between entities, and CPTs quantify the dependencies. Self-organizing map (SOM) is a type of artificial neural network trained using unsupervised learning to produce a low-dimensional (typically two-dimensional) and discretized representation of the input space of training samples. We employ SOM to divide a TWC dataset into several subsets and construct the EABN from TWC efficiently. To rank the entities based on latent EAs for the given specific entities, we use probabilistic inferences of EABN to evaluate the association quantitatively.

1.2.7 Containment of influence spread on social networks

In view of the situations with positive and negative influence simultaneously, the influence maximization problem is more challenging but frequently experienced in the real world, where how to limit the misinformation spread or maximize the overall influence is paid much attention. For this purpose, we consider the following two strategies: containing influence spread and locating influence sources.

With respect to the first strategy, each rational one of the competing participants is to make its influence spread as maximal as possible and make that of its opponents as minimal as possible. A straightforward idea is to block the spread of its opponents' influence. But it does not always make sense in realistic situations, since one enterprise finds it impossible to interfere with the legal marketing strategies of others in online social networks. Meanwhile from the perspective of underlying techniques, this strategy is not always feasible, since it will take great computation cost when confronted with the large number of opponent seeds. The challenge is how a participant could use its influence spread strategy to contain and thus minimize the spread of its opponents' influence. Therefore, we focus on finding a seed set such that its influence spread contains the spread of the competing influence maximally and breaks the rules of the opponent influence propagation. We first extend the classic linear threshold model to establish the diffusion–containment model. Then, we discuss the influence spread mechanism, and give a greedy algorithm to approximately solve the problem of competitive influence containment maximally.

With respect to the second strategy, the problem of source location is to locate possible source nodes of influence spread based on an observation about network structure and diffusion details. In realistic social networks, there may be more than one source node frequently, which could not be well addressed by many state-of-the-art methods. However, it is impossible to obtain the complete information about the network structure and diffusion details due to the large-scaled online social networks. Therefore, we consider the strategy to locate multi-source nodes of influence diffusion with a partial observation of propagation results in big online social networks. That is, we are to find possible source nodes after the diffusion has occurred. This motivates us to propose a Bayesian backtracking model (BBM) to identify the possible node which spreads influence to other nodes in the activation process. Then, we give a random walk based backtracking algorithm (RWBA) to locate the source nodes via posterior probabilities in BBM.

1.3 Organization

The remainder of this book is organized as follows:

In Chapter 2, we first give the parallel and adaptive method for data acquisition of OBGs to acquire users' behavioral interactions for data-intensive analysis of social media data.

In Chapter 3, we give the method for incremental learning of BN, as the framework for representing and inferring uncertainties implied in social media data, which also provides a general idea for incremental revisions of knowledge discovered from social media data.

In Chapter 4, we give the data-intensive method for discovering similarity users by incorporating behavioral associations and local topological structure of social networks.

In Chapter 5, we give the method for constructing an MN from frequent patterns and bridge the gap between frequent patterns, association rules, and probabilistic graphical model.

In Chapter 6, we give the Markov network-based method for latent link discovery and community detection in social behavioral interactions.

In Chapter 7, we give the method for probabilistic inferences of latent entity associations in TWCs to find latent entity associations.

In Chapter 8, we give the probabilistic method for containment of competitive influence spread on social networks.

In Chapter 9, we give the probabilistic method for locating sources in online social networks via random walk.

Finally, in Chapter 10, we present the summary and discuss future work.

Chapter 2

Adaptive and Parallel Acquisition of Social Media Data from Online Big Graphs

Acquisition of contents from online big graphs (OBGs) like linked Web pages, social networks and knowledge graphs is critical as data infrastructure for Web applications and massive data analysis. However, effective data acquisition, including collection and updating, is challenging due to the massive, heterogeneous, dynamically evolving properties of OBGs with unknown global topological structures. In this chapter, we give an adaptive and parallel approach for effective data acquisition from OBGs. First, we adopt the ideas of Quasi-Monte Carlo (QMC), and branch and bound methods to propose an adaptive Web-scale sampling algorithm for parallel data collection implemented upon Spark. Then, given the collected OBG data, we propose the method for parallel incremental maintenance based on entropy and Poisson process. Experimental results show the effectiveness and efficiency of our method.

2.1 Motivation and Basic Idea

Many data-intensive or data analysis research and development are established upon enormous and fast-changing Internet contents and social media, which could be text, picture, video and user actions, such as user behaviors in a social network and ratings in a shopping site. The contents cannot be processed directly due to the unknown global topological structures and access speed limitation, although critical for both analysis as a service and data as a service [4]. In view of the infrastructure of knowledge engineering systems, data acquisition including collection and updating has gained great attention accordingly for Web search, massive data analysis [25], data integration [26], knowledge extraction and fusion [17], etc.

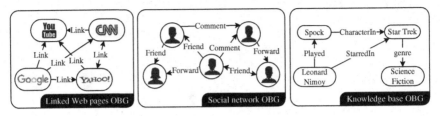

Fig. 2.1. Typical OBGs.

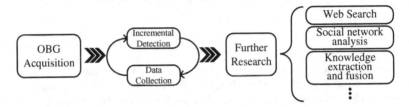

Fig. 2.2. OBG acquisition.

Regarding the organization of Internet contents and social media, graphical structure is an essential feature represented by online big graph (OBG), such as linked Web pages, social network and knowledge base, as shown in Fig. 2.1. An OBG consists of objects and connections, varying with respect to different kinds of specific contents. For example, linked Web page OBGs consist of Web pages and hyperlinks; social network OBGs consist of user-generated contents and corresponding social connections; knowledge base OBGs consist of entities and their mutual relations. Represented as OBGs without knowing the global topological structures, data are massive, distributed, heterogeneous and fast-changing [19]. Given online property of OBG data acquisition, it begins with an empty set without prior knowledge, and the OBGs could be meanwhile explored gradually during the process of acquisition [27]. This is exactly the focus of this chapter, where we discuss the effective and generic method for online data acquisition from OBGs to establish the basis for Web-scale data analysis, as shown in Fig. 2.2.

In terms of the inherent properties of OBGs themselves, data acquisition from OBGs will have to solve the following challenges:

(1) **Data volume:** Alibaba collects many petabytes of data stream in real time from more than 100 million users per day to build an innovative "smart" business.[a] Meanwhile, many data-centric applications are established upon quick analysis over large volume and high velocity streaming data [4], where graphical structures to represent connections among objects or entities are highlighted for Internet data specifically.

(2) **Data updating:** Google tracks more than 30 billion independent URLs per day to guarantee the availability of the database and will cost much for the maintenance of related services and datacenters. In particular, the online property makes the tracking process adaptive to fulfill updating and keep the result up to date.

In view of the online property of OBGs without knowing the global topologies, we make use of graphical structures of the currently collected data to crawl more. OBG data with a high importance degree are data with much information or concerned contents, which are expected to be selected and collected. Moreover, we make incremental updating to keep the results up to date. Our work in this chapter includes the following two aspects.

Sampling has been widely used in statistic machine learning [24], signal and graphic processing [7], by which the global outline shaping for a certain process could be done without much effort. Thus, using OBG's graphical structures, we adopt the ideas of Quasi-Monte Carlo (QMC) sampling [8], and branch and bound to propose the online algorithm, called BB-QMC. By this algorithm, we split the currently considered OBG recursively and hierarchically, and calculate the importance of its subsets called areas. Then, we find the most important area adaptively for successive data collection. We further give the theoretic analysis of BB-QMC from effectiveness, complexity, standard error estimation, iteration bound, and conflict efficiency. By our BB-QMC, the importance of objects in an area could be measured in a scalable way, which makes it possible to parallelly acquire the data in that area, and the importance degree of areas could be ordered consequently. From the perspective of

---

[a] Alibaba's double 11 event information. *MIT Technology Review*. https://www.tech nologyreview.com/s/602850/big-data-game-changer-alibabas-double-11-event-raises-the -bar-for-online-sales/, 2016.

real applications upon OBGs, less important objects with low importance degrees could be discarded intuitively, which decreases the total cost of data acquisition correspondingly.

The changing possibility of a certain area in an OBG could be obtained, although the changes could not be found directly, which facilitates finding OBG updates. To this end, we propose an entropy-based method to describe the changing possibility of an area within a past period of time and then employ Poisson process to estimate the area's current status. Further, we give an online algorithm, called EPP, to find OBG updates adaptively and implement incremental updating of the collected data. By means of EPP, "dirty" data are likely to be detected to a great extent, which is useful for on-demand or temporal-sensitive applications upon compact and valid data.

Meanwhile, focusing on the iterations during online data acquisition in response to the fast-changing contents, our algorithms are implemented upon Spark. Finally, we illustrate performance studies of our algorithms for online collection and incremental updating, respectively by experiments upon three typical kinds of OBGs, including BerkStan, Facebook and Wikidata, as well as Weibo and LFR. Experimental results show the effectiveness and efficiency of our method.

The remainder of this chapter is organized as follows. In Section 2.2, we introduce related work. In Section 2.3, we give the algorithm for adaptive data collection based on QMC sampling. In Section 2.4, we give the algorithm for updating the sampling results by incremental maintenance. In Section 2.5, we show experimental results and performance studies. In Section 2.6, we summarize our work in this chapter.

2.2 Related Work

Previous approaches for data collection from OBGs can be categorized into the following three categories: universal crawlers, hidden Web crawlers, and preferential crawlers [11].

First, universal crawlers primarily depend on local graph structures, such as the classic breadth-first [18] and deep-first methods [21]. The fact that all areas are treated with the same importance degree is not consistent with the intuition in realistic situations [16], since only some important parts are required rather than the whole OBG. The methods in [11, 22] are different from our method, by which the areas could be collected from a much broader range and important areas could be collected prior to others instead of one-by-one access along the graph structure.

Second, hidden Web crawlers use keyword query, attribute and label extraction, and form-based approaches to find information hidden behind search engines [11].

Third, preferential crawlers include topical crawler and focused crawler. Topical crawler or topic-specific crawler is used to search information from Web for a given specific topic [15]. Chakrabarti *et al.* [3] proposed the crawling method that selectively seeks out webpages relevant to a predefined set of topics. By using the application-based [1], link-based [23], and semantic-based [2] approaches, focused crawler gives priority to those URLs during crawling and achieves a high probability such that the found information satisfies user interest.

The concepts of sampling were introduced for data collection [16], by which sub-areas of data with different importance degrees could be revealed. In particular, the concept of importance sampling was incorporated into data collection by a semi-auto way [14] due to its ability to find important parts in a global graph structure. Recently, adaptive methods [5] reinforced online data collection in terms of the massive and rapidly evolving characteristics.

Change or update detection was discussed to maintain the valid state of acquired data. To reduce the expensive cost when revisiting all massive data sources, simple statistic methods were given [22]. With respect to the complexity of real data environments, structure-based methods to detect updates in a graph were given by using graph patterns to determine whether the area is likely to change [10], but failure may occur, since specific structures could not indicate all correct changes.

It is difficult to use current methodologies and data mining tools on a single computer to efficiently deal with very large volume of data [20]. Many distributed systems and methods were introduced to solve OBG operations, and many parallel systems and problems for online data collection were built [6]. However, the online, fast-changing characteristics of OBGs have not been incorporated in these methods.

2.3 Adaptive Data Collection Based on QMC Sampling

2.3.1 *Basic idea and algorithm*

Definition 2.1. An OBG is a directed graph $G_{ON} = \{O, E, R\}$, where $O = \{o_1, \ldots, o_s\}$ and $E = \{e_1, \ldots, e_t\}$ constitute the set of objects and connections, respectively. Let $R = \{r_1, r_2, \ldots, r_v\}$ be the set of connection types in an OBG. Each connection in G_{ON} corresponds to an edge connecting two different objects with a type of connection, i.e., $e = (o_i, o_j, r_k)$, $e \in E$, $o_j, o_j \in O$, $i \neq j$.

Different types of OBGs can be represented by G_{ON} with different O and R. For example, R is a set including forwarding, comment, etc. in social network OBGs. It is expected to collect data from OBGs with priority to the most important areas, where the importance of an area is determined by the volume of contained information. For this purpose, we consider splitting G_{ON} into K areas and selecting the most important area by employing the idea of sampling. Areas are denoted as $\{A_1, A_2, \ldots, A_K\}$, where $A_i \subseteq G_{ON}$, $i = 1, 2, \ldots, K$. By repeating this process recursively and hierarchically, if there are more than K objects in an area, a K-fork tree will be built finally with a height of $\log_K |O|$, where $|O|$ is the number of objects in G_{ON}.

By modeling adaptive data collection as an optimization problem, we employ the branch and bound technique to obtain the importance degree of different scaled areas in every fork structure in the K-fork tree. This will be fulfilled by executing several iterations of QMC sampling, in each of which branch and bound is incorporated. The BB-QMC algorithm is proposed to denote the whole process, which speeds up QMC sampling and gathers each area's density as importance degree in parallel.

In the following, we further sketch the idea of BB-QMC by illustrating the two stages of every iteration, as shown in Fig. 2.3. Selected sampling points in each area will be visited and collected implicitly while an estimated density will be generated by QMC sampling. Then, the density information of each area will be added into a candidate pool, and the

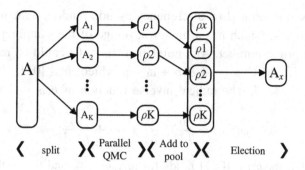

Fig. 2.3. A single iteration of BB-QMC.

density-based election method will be used to choose the most important area adaptively for the next iteration.

In the first stage, the importance degree of each area is measured by gathering its density. Let $A = \{A_1, A_2, \ldots, A_K\}$ be K areas, and the density of an area A_i is

$$\rho_{A_i} = \frac{\sum_{o \in A_i} D(o)}{|A_i|} \qquad (2.1)$$

where $D(o)$ represents the connections of o pointing to other objects in an OBG.

Now, we consider the idea to obtain ρ_{A_i}. Monte Carlo (MC) sampling [9] basically uses values of few sampling points to estimate the value of the whole area, and the results will become more and more accurate with the increase of sampling points. For a given h-dimensional space D, a subset of real space R_m, the integration (or mass) of target function $f(X)$ can be represented as I, where X is a set of points in D, and I could be calculated by $\int_D f(X)dX$. The volume of D is $\int_D 1 dX$, denoted as Z. Given n randomly selected sampling points $\{x_1, x_2, \ldots, x_n\} \in D$, the approximation of I is

$$I \approx MC_n \equiv Z \frac{1}{n} \sum_{i=1}^{n} f(x_i) \qquad (2.2)$$

By MC sampling, generated points may be too close to each other to be distinguished, while random point generation is also costly. Frequently used with Halton sequence, QMC sampling [8] adopts deterministic approaches to generate low-discrepancy pseudo-random sequences as the sampling points, which has a higher coverage of the sampling area. Let b denote a prime number. Any number w ($w > 0$) could be represented as $d_j b^j + d_{j-1} b^{j-1} + \cdots + d_1 b + d_0$, in which $d_i \in \{0, 1, \ldots, b-1\}$, and $i = 0, 1, \ldots, j$. The radical inverse function of b is

$$\phi_b(w) = \frac{d_0}{b^1} + \frac{d_1}{b^2} + \cdots + \frac{d_j}{b^{j+1}} \qquad (2.3)$$

Note that $\phi_b(w) \in [0, 1]$ holds for any $w \geq 0$, and the w-th element in a Halton sequence is $\phi_b(w)$. In particular, if $b_1, \ldots, b_d$ are d different prime numbers, then a d-dimensional Halton sequence with m length is represented as $\{\vec{x}_1, \ldots, \vec{x}_m\}$, where the w-th element $\vec{x}_w$ is described by

$$\vec{x}_w = [\phi_{b_1}(w-1), \ldots, \phi_{b_d}(w-1)]^T, \quad w = 1, \ldots, m \qquad (2.4)$$

This does make sense for OBG sampling, since OBG information could be gained comprehensively by QMC while avoiding the uneven sampling by random selection. Suppose n is the number of sampling points in area A_i, $n = |A_i| \cdot R_{\text{samp}}$, where R_{samp} is the sampling rate and $O_1, \ldots, O_n \in A_i$ is the object generated by the Halton sequence corresponding to sampling points. By the QMC sampling of n objects, the approximation of ρ_{A_i} is calculated as

$$\rho_{A_i} \approx \frac{1}{n} \sum_{i=1}^{n} D(o_i) \qquad (2.5)$$

In the second stage, we use a candidate pool to record the density of visited areas, denoted as $C = \{\rho_{A_1} \rho_{A_2}, \ldots, \rho_{A_k} \rho_x\}$, where ρ_x denotes the density of visited areas in previous iterations. Area election is fulfilled by an election criterion, adopted as the bounding function, and the area with the maximal density will be collected next. Thus, the algorithm can acquire the important area adaptively. According to the fact that some parts without much information, like shattered isolated parts of an OBG, are unnecessary to collect, we give the following termination condition:

$$\frac{\sum_{o \in \Delta o^c} D(o)}{|\Delta o^c|} < \rho_{\min} \qquad (2.6)$$

where Δo^c is the set of acquired objects by the latest iteration, and $\rho_{\min}$ is the minimum acceptable density to make the collection process continue.

When almost all objects with dense connections are acquired, other objects will contribute less to the connections, and $\frac{\sum_{o \in \Delta o^c} D(o)}{|\Delta o^c|}$ will be decreased with the increase of acquired objects. If $\frac{\sum_{o \in \Delta o^c} D(o)}{|\Delta o^c|}$ is finally less than $\rho_{\min}$, then the collection process will be terminated.

Now, we give Algorithm 2.1 to summarize the above ideas to select fork structures in the K-fork tree of the original OBG.

2.3.2 *Analysis*

Effectiveness: The effectiveness of Algorithm 2.1 in a given area A is described as

$$S_A = \sum_{i=1}^{|A|} \sum_{j=1}^{i} D(o_j^c) \tag{2.7}$$

where $|A|$ is the number of objects in area A. The more the early important objects are found and acquired, the larger the value S_A will be.

Complexity: In realistic situations, the most time-consuming step in Algorithm 2.1 is the data collection by visiting the Internet. We introduce the probability distribution of collection time while acquiring objects from an OBG. By experiments, we found that all the collection time satisfies normal distribution, denoted as D_{CT}. If we suppose that μ is the expectation of D_{CT}, then the average execution time of Algorithm 2.1 will be μn, which means that the complexity of Algorithm 2.1 is $O(n)$. Thus, we conclude that the execution time of Algorithm 2.1 is linear to the scale of an OBG, which will be verified later by experiments in Section 2.5.

Standard error estimation: The standard error of sampling in BB-QMC is different in terms of the number of sampling points in each iteration. In view of the density of an area in Eq. (2.5), the standard error estimation can be inferred as $|A_i| \frac{\sigma_n}{\sqrt{n}}$, where $\sigma_n = \sqrt{\frac{1}{n-1} \sum_{i=1}^{n} \left(D(o_i) - \frac{1}{n} \sum_{i=1}^{n} D(o_i) \right)^2}$. This means that the standard error estimation of Algorithm 2.1 will nonlinearly decrease with the increase of sampling points.

Algorithm 2.1 BB-QMC

Input:

A, *area range* from A_1 to A_n

R_{samp}, sampling rate

D_{obj}, empty data container

P_{cand}, empty candidate pool

Output:

$D_{obj} = \{ODC_1, ODC_2, \ldots, ODC_n\}$

Steps:

If $A.start \neq A.end$ And $\frac{\sum_{o \in \Delta o^c} D(o)}{|\Delta o^c|} \geq \rho_{min}$ Then

  $S \leftarrow$ divide(A, K) // split A into K areas

  For each s in S Do // s is the range of area

    $mass \leftarrow 0$, $H \leftarrow$ HaltonSeq(s, R_{samp}) // generate sampling objects

    For each e in H Do

      If $D_{obj}.find(e)$ is NULL Then

        $ODC \leftarrow$ collect(e) // collect objects in OBG

        $D_{obj}.add(ODC)$

        $mass \leftarrow mass + ODC.numConnection$

      Else

        $ODC \leftarrow D_{obj}.find(e)$

        $mass \leftarrow mass + ODC.numConnection$

      End If

    End For

    If $|s| > 1$ Then

      $density \leftarrow mass/|H|$

      $P_{Cand}.add([s, density])$// add range with density

    End If

    $A \leftarrow P_{Cand}.findMax()$ // choose an area with the maximum density

    BB-QMC() // next iteration

  End For

End If

Iteration bound: The number of iterations of QMC sampling in Algorithm 2.1, denoted as N_{iter}, is determined by the number of areas (i.e., K) and that of objects (i.e., n). Following, we give the iteration bound by Theorem 2.1.

Theorem 2.1. *Given n objects and K areas $(n > 0, K > 1)$, the N_{iter} can be obtained as*

$$N_{iter} = \begin{cases} 1 & 0 < n < K \\ n - K^{m-1} + \sum_{j=0}^{m-1} K^j & K^m \le n \le 2K^m \\ \sum_{j=0}^{m} K^j & 2K^m < n < K^{m+1} \end{cases} \tag{2.8}$$

where $m = \lfloor \log_K n \rfloor$, $m \in Z^+$.

Proof.

(1) For the first case, the number of areas is less than the maximum to be sampled, so all areas will be sampled within a single iteration.

(2) For a K-fork tree, the leaf nodes represent objects, and every non-leaf node will be an iteration node. If $K^m = n$, which means a full complete K-fork tree, then there are $\sum_{j=0}^{m-1} K^j$ leaf nodes. Once an object is added, some leaf will become an iteration node, and the original and newly added objects will become its children. Thus, there are $n - K^{m-1}$ newly added nodes. Accordingly, the leaf nodes will lie in different levels as shown in Fig. 2.4(a).

(3) The process will be continued until all previous leaf nodes become non-leaf iteration nodes, and then the newly added objects would not lead to generation of any new iteration node before reaching another full complete K-fork tree with a height increased by 1. The number

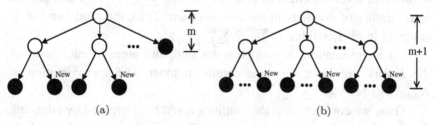

Fig. 2.4. Iterate cases (white: non-leaf node, black: leaf node): (a) Leaf node in different levels; (b) Leaf node in the same level.

of iteration nodes is constantly $\sum_{j=0}^{m} K^j$, and all leaf nodes are in the same level, as shown in Fig. 2.4(b). $\square$

Conflict efficiency: Sampling points in different iterations of Algorithm 2.1 may be overlapped and cause conflicts, which are sampling points in the current iteration but already sampled in the previous iterations. The conflict efficiency, denoted as E_{conf}, is

$$E_{\text{conf}} = 1 - \frac{N_{\text{conf}}}{N_{\text{iter}} \cdot K \cdot |A_i| \cdot R_{\text{samp}}} \tag{2.9}$$

where $|A_i| \cdot R_{\text{samp}}$ is the number of sampling points in every sub-area A_i of the iteration and N_{conf} is the total number of conflicts that occurred in the entire process.

In the following, we give the measurement of total conflicts in Theorem 2.2.

Theorem 2.2. *Given an OBG with n objects, the total number of conflicts is*

$$N_{\text{conf}} = \sum_{i=1}^{N_{\text{iter}}} \sum_{j=1}^{m_i} P_{ij} \tag{2.10}$$

where N_{iter} is obtained by Theorem 2.1, $m_i = \lfloor \log_K |A_i| \rfloor$, A_i is the sampling area of the i-th iteration and P_{ij} is the number of non-overlapping conflicts in the j-th level of children areas of A_i.

Proof. When sampling is fulfilled in a top-down manner, conflicts begin to occur from the first level of children areas of A_i during the execution of Algorithm 2.1. By summing the number of non-overlapping conflicts in different levels of children areas of A_i, i.e., $\sum_{j=1}^{m_i} P_{ij}$, we can get the total number of conflicts in the i-th iteration. Thus, the total number of conflicts in all iterations is $\sum_{i=1}^{N_{\text{iter}}} \sum_{j=1}^{m_i} P_{ij}$.

For simplification, we suppose the sampling areas in each level of the K-fork tree have the same conflict number. The approximation of N_{conf} will be $N_{\text{iter}} \cdot \sum_{j=1}^{m_1} P_{ij}$.

Thus, we conclude that the conflicts could be decreased by adjusting K and R_{samp}. E_{conf} could be small by adjusting the values of K and R_{samp}. $\square$

2.4 Updating Sampling Results by Incremental Maintenance

2.4.1 *Overview of incremental maintenance*

Definition 2.2. Let $G_{ON} = \{O, E, R\}$ be an OBG at time T and $G'_{ON} = \{O', E', R'\}$ be the same OBG at time $T'(T' > T)$. Updates of G_{ON} from T to T' are denoted as

$$\Delta G_{ON} = \{\text{DIFF}(O', O), \text{DIFF}(E', E), \text{DIFF}(R'R)\} \qquad (2.11)$$

where $\text{DIFF}(O'O)$ refers to $[O'\backslash(O' \cap O)] \cup \overline{O\backslash(O' \cap O)}$ describing the union of newly added and previously deleted objects as the difference between the objects in G'_{ON} and those in G_{ON}. ΔG_{ON} with respect to E and R can be described analogously.

Definition 2.3. The set of update operations U includes addition and deletion represented by u and $\bar{u}$, respectively. U_O, U_E, and U_R denote the set of update operations on O, E, and R, respectively. Thus, $\Delta G_{ON} = \{U_O, U_E, U_R\}$.

Similar to the process of data collection in Section 2.3, the process of incremental maintenance also includes two stages, as shown in Fig. 2.5.

In the update prediction stage concerning collected data, we use the Poisson process to estimate the changing possibilities of all areas as prior for update detection by making use of the data that has been collected. Thus, the volume of updates in ΔT $(\Delta T = T' - T)$ can be predicted by the acquired data in a statistic window, and the possibilities will be quantified and converted into the update densities of splitted areas.

In the update searching stage, we regard the new data as acquisition target, analogous to those in Algorithm 2.1, but we differently give a method to combine the densities by sampling on the new data and those obtained in the first stage.

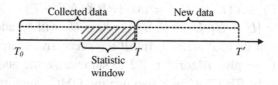

Fig. 2.5. Process of incremental maintenance.

2.4.2 Entropy-based data updating

Definition 2.4. The range of statistic window is a portion of acquired data starting from T_0 to T, defined as $\alpha(T - T_0)$, where α is called window factor $(0 < \alpha \leq 1)$.

Let B denote the set of currently acquired data in the statistic window. We split B into K areas and $B = \{B_1, B_2, \ldots, B_K\}$, each of which will be updated independently. To predict the updates during ΔT, we give the entropy-based average self-information to measure the information volume of each area.

Definition 2.5. Given the probabilities $P(o_i)$, $P(e_i)$, and $P(r_i)$ of O, E, and R from an OBG, respectively from T_0 to T, the average self-information is $H(O) = E[I(o_i)]$, $H(E) = E[I(e_i)]$, $H(R) = E[I(r_i)]$, where $I(o_i) = -\log P(o_i)$, $I(e_i) = -\log P(e_i)$, and $I(r_i) = -\log P(r_i)$. The information volume of area B_j is $Y_j = |O_j| * H(O) + |E_j| * H(E) + |E_j| * H(R)$, where O_j and E_j denote the set of objects, connections with a connection type in B_j, respectively, and $o_i, e_i \epsilon B_j$, $j = 1, 2, \ldots, K$.

Incremental maintenance is to predict the updates of areas in ΔT from T to T'. Actually, data arrival in B_j in the statistic window satisfies the Poisson process [13].

Definition 2.6. Let $\lambda = \frac{Y_j}{\alpha(T-T_0)}$ be the mean value of Poisson distributions. Suppose the volume of updates in ΔT is τ starting from T, and the update possibility of τ in ΔT is

$$P\{X(\Delta T + T) - X(T) = \tau\} = e^{-\lambda \Delta T} \frac{(\lambda \Delta T)^\tau}{\tau} \qquad (2.12)$$

where X denotes the Poisson process and $\tau = 0, 1, \ldots$.

The volume of updates in B_j is predicted by U_j that satisfies $P\{X(\Delta T + T) - X(T) = U_j\} = \max\{P\{(X(\Delta T + T) - X(T) = \tau\}\}$. Then, we have $\{U = U_1, U_2, \ldots, U_K\}$, where U_j will be adopted as the initial density of divided areas to fulfill the successive searching for the updates. Next, we give Algorithm 2.2 to summarize the above ideas.

Analogous to BB-QMC, we also use the QMC sampling to find all the updates, including new objects, connections, and connection types.

Algorithm 2.2 EPP

Input:

A, area range from A_1 to A_n

N_{split}, number of areas to be divided

R_{samp}, sampling rate

ODC_{old}, acquired data container

ODC_{new}, empty data container

P_{cand}, empty candidate pool

Output:

$ODC_{\text{new}} = \{ODC_1, ODC_2, \ldots, ODC_n\}$

Steps:

If $A.start \neq A.end$ And Not $\frac{\sum_{o \in \Delta o^u} D(o)}{|\Delta o^u|} < \rho_{\min}$ Then

$\quad S[] \leftarrow \text{divide}(A.start, A.end, N_{\text{split}})$ // K sub-areas

$\quad$ For each s in S Do

$\quad\quad vol \leftarrow 0, H[] \leftarrow \text{HaltonSeq}(s, R_{\text{samp}})$

$\quad\quad$ For e in H Do

$\quad\quad\quad ODC_{\text{new}} \leftarrow \text{collect}(e), ODC_{\text{old}} \leftarrow OD_{\text{obj}}.\text{find}(e)$

$\quad\quad\quad$ If $ODC_{\text{new}} \neq ODC_{\text{old}}$ Then

$\quad\quad\quad\quad vol \leftarrow vol + \text{InfoVol}(ODC_{\text{new}}, ODC_{\text{old}})$// obtain informa-
$\quad\quad\quad\quad$ tion volume

$\quad\quad\quad$ End If

$\quad\quad$ End For

$\quad\quad$ If $|s| > 1$ Then

$\quad\quad\quad density \leftarrow (1 - \beta) * vol/|H| + \beta * \text{ParentAreaDensity}$

$\quad\quad\quad P_{\text{Cand}}.\text{add}([s, density])$

$\quad\quad$ End If

$\quad$ End For

$\quad A \leftarrow P_{\text{Cand}}.\text{findMax}()$ // choose the next area

$\quad \text{EPP}()$ // next iteration

End If

As the preprocessing of Algorithm 2.2, the information volume of split areas is calculated. Δo^u is the set of collected updates from the latest iteration. *InfoVol* in Algorithm 2.2 will calculate the volume of updates by comparing the new and acquired data. Specifically, the density of updates in an area of B_j is denoted by V_{jl} as follows:

$$V_{jl} \approx \frac{1}{n} \sum_{\varepsilon=1}^{n} \left[N_\varepsilon \frac{H(O)}{N_\varepsilon + 1} \right] + N_\varepsilon * H(E) + N_\varepsilon * H(R) \qquad (2.13)$$

where N_ε is the number of new connections of sampled objects and n is the number of sampling points.

Compared with the volume of sampled data, U_j obtained from B may better reflect the real volume of updates. Thus, a fusion ratio β is introduced to adjust the sampling results and information density of the area is $V_{jl} = (1 - \beta)V_{jl} + \beta(U_j/|B_j|)(0 \leq \beta \leq 1)$. Children areas will be influenced iteratively. The time complexity of Algorithm 2.2 is $O(n)$, the same as that of Algorithm 2.1.

2.5 Experimental Results

2.5.1 Experiment setup

To test the performance of our proposed methods, we implemented our algorithms and tested the effectiveness and efficiency. We adopted the test datasets listed in Table 2.1, including BerkStan, Facebook, and Wikidata for data collection, and Weibo and LFR for data updates.

Table 2.1. Description of datasets.

Test type	Dataset	$|O|(\times 10^3)$	$|E|(\times 10^4)$	$|R|$
Collection	BerkStan[b]	15	150	1
	Facebook[c]	4	88	4
	Wikidata	10	49	2900
Updating	Weibo	11	45	4
	LFR	15	16	4

---

[b]http://snap.stanford.edu/data/web-BerkStan.html.
[c]http://snap.stanford.edu/data/egonets-Facebook.html.

Our experiments were fulfilled upon a Spark cluster with six workers (each has a $4 \times 3.6\,$GHz CPU and $128\,$GB RAM) sharing a Gigabit Ethernet switch. The version of Spark and HDFS is 1.6.1 and 2.5.2, respectively. Network speed is limited to $2\,$Mb/s.

2.5.2 *Effectiveness*

We selected BerkStan, Facebook, and Wikidata as typical linked Web page OBG, social network OBG, and knowledge base OBG, respectively, to test the effectiveness of Algorithm 2.1. In our experiments, we used first 10,000 entities in Wikidata on the Wiki website, while simulating the environment of data crawling on BerkStan and Facebook benchmark datasets available in local disk.

To test the effectiveness of Algorithm 2.1 for data collection, we used connection coverage to measure the ratio of acquired edges to those actually existing in the OBG. It is calculated by $(\sum D(o^c))/|E|$, where $\sum D(o^c)$ is specified in Eq. (2.7). We compared the connection coverage and S_A (in Section 2.3) by Algorithm 2.1 (BB-QMC), sequence collection (Sequence), broad-first strategy (BFS), snowball sampling (Snowballing), random selection (Random), and MC without using low-discrepancy sequence (BB-MC), shown in Fig. 2.6 on BerkStan, Facebook, and Wikidata, respectively. It can be seen that the connection coverage of Snowballing, Sequence, and BFS is close to that of Random with the increase of collected objects, since these methods do not consider the area importance. Both the connection coverage of BB-MC and BB-QMC increased more considerably with the increase of collected objects, while the latter is better than the former. Given a certain ρ_{min}, BB-QMC is terminated earlier than other methods and achieves the smallest $|O^C|$. This means that the acquisition cost of BB-QMC is much lower than that of the other methods under the same termination condition. Upon the three types of OBGs, BB-QMC can make all connections in the original OBGs that have been acquired efficiently.

We then tested the influence of R_{samp} (R) on connection coverage when using BB-QMC as shown in Fig. 2.7. It can be seen that better collection results have been achieved when R_{samp} is larger than 0.05 upon the three datasets. Meanwhile, we tested the influence of division

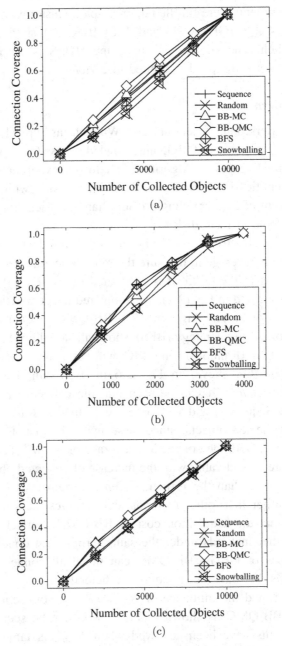

Fig. 2.6. Connection coverage of different methods for data collection: (a) BerkStan; (b) Facebook; (c) Wikidata.

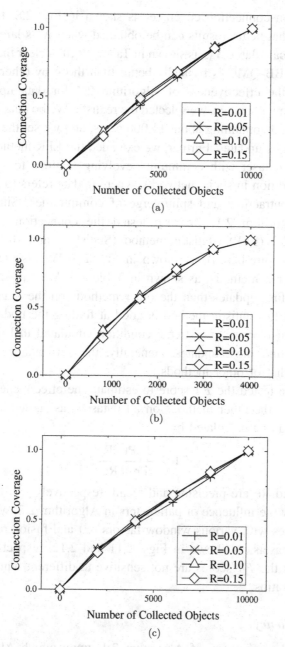

Fig. 2.7. Connection coverage of BB-QMC with different values of R_{samp}: (a) BerkStan; (b) Facebook; (c) Wikidata.

number K on connection coverage, as shown in Fig. 2.8, from which we can see that better results can be obtained when K is larger than 30.

We also calculated S_A, as shown in Table 2.2. It is clear that the result obtained by BB-QMC is basically better than those by other methods.

To test the effectiveness of Algorithm 2.2 for data updating and incremental maintenance, we selected the realistic Weibo dataset covering two weeks and containing about 11,000 users, and we set the data of the second week as updates. Further, we extended the LFR method [12] and generated a dataset with community evolving features to simulate the extreme condition in social networks, where update refers to birth/death, expansion/contraction, and split/merge of communities. Similar to the tests of Algorithm 2.1, we also tested the connection coverage of Algorithm 2.2 (EPP), statistic method (Statistic), and structure-based method (Structure-based), as shown in Fig. 2.9. We also tested S_A of the above three methods, as shown in Table 2.3. We can see that EPP is better to find updates than the other methods on the realistic Weibo datasets, but the statistic method is good at finding the updates in LRF datasets. Considering the extreme condition simulated in LFR datasets, EPP could find most updates. Generally, the performance of EPP is better than that of other methods.

Next, we tested the $F1$ score to estimate the effectiveness and EPP is better than the other methods on all datasets, as shown in Fig. 2.10, where $F1$ can be calculated by

$$F1 = \frac{2 \cdot \text{Pr} \cdot \text{Re}}{\text{Pr} + \text{Re}} \tag{2.14}$$

where Pr and Re are precision and recall, respectively.

To show the influence of parameters in Algorithm 2.2, we compared the $F1$ scores with various window factors (α) and fusion ratios (β) on different datasets, as shown in Figs. 2.11 and 2.12, respectively. It can be seen that the $F1$ scores are not sensitive to different window factors and fusion ratios.

2.5.3 Efficiency

We tested the efficiency of Algorithm 2.1, upon which Algorithm 2.2 was established, by execution time, speedup, and parallel efficiency, as

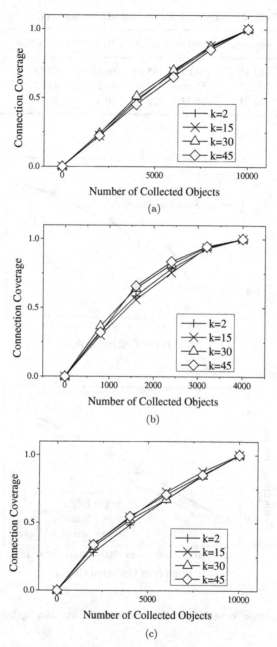

Fig. 2.8. Connection coverage of BB-QMC with different values of K: (a) BerkStan; (b) Facebook; (c) Wikidata.

Table 2.2. S_A of different methods for data collection.

Dataset	Sequence	Random	MCS	BFS	Snowballing	BB-QMCS
Wikidata	53.45	50.02	55.65	50.66	49.59	56.45
BerkStan	49.99	51.06	53.46	46.27	43.05	56.44
Facebook	21.51	18.23	22.77	20.40	20.19	22.83

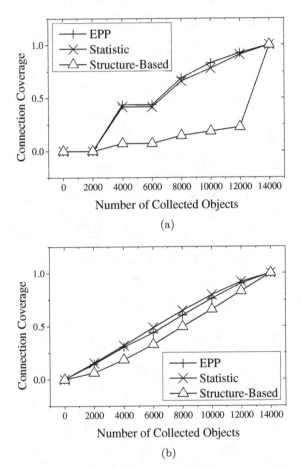

(a)

(b)

Fig. 2.9. Connection coverage of different methods for data updating: (a) Weibo; (b) LFR.

Table 2.3. S_A of different methods for data updating.

Dataset	Statistic	Structure base	EPP
Weibo	41.03	10.99	42.17
LFR	115.62	90.49	109.72

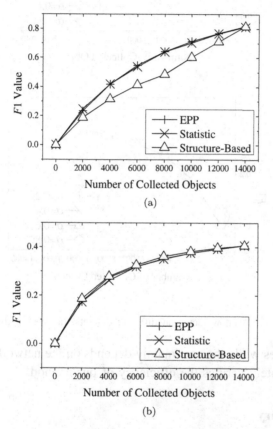

Fig. 2.10. $F1$ scores of different methods for data updating: (a) Weibo; (b) LFR.

shown in Figs. 2.13–2.15, respectively. It can be seen that the execution time of data acquisition is linearly increased with the increase of OGBs, and the more the workers, the less the time and the higher the speedup. Speedup and parallel efficiency become stable quickly and are basically

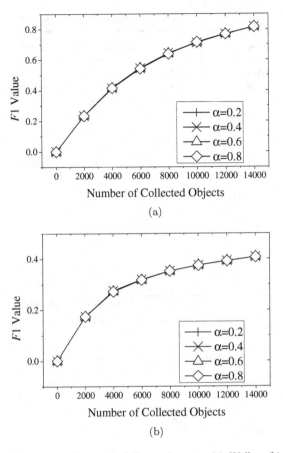

Fig. 2.11. Window factor on different datasets: (a) Weibo; (b) LFR.

the ideal cases while the cost mainly depends on the network bandwidth, which ultimately verifies the efficiency of our method.

2.6 Summary

We explore parallel and adaptive data acquisition, including collection and updating from massive social media represented as OBGs. Our method adopts adaptive QMC sampling with importance degrees of different areas and uses the entropy and Poisson process to predict and obtain the updates in different areas. Our method predominates in data collection and incremental maintenance from OBGs in most situations compared

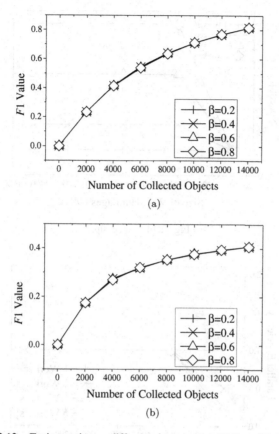

Fig. 2.12. Fusion ratio on different datasets: (a) Weibo; (b) LFR.

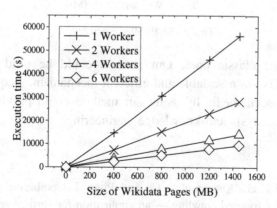

Fig. 2.13. Execution time.

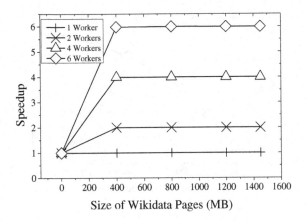

Fig. 2.14. Speedup.

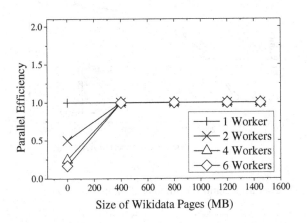

Fig. 2.15. Parallel efficiency.

with the other classic ones. Our method could be used for various kinds of OBGs via a scalable and efficient mechanism. Acquired online contents of social media by using our method could provide the basis for big data analysis and knowledge engineering.

References

1. Almpanidis, G., Kotropoulos, C., and Pitas, I. Combining text and link analysis for focused crawling — an application for vertical search engines. *Information System*, 2007, **32**: 886–908.

2. Batzios, A., Dimou, C., Symeonidis, A., and Mitkas, P. BioCrawler: An intelligent crawler for the semantic web. *Expert Systems with Applications*, 2008, **35**(1–2): 524–530.

3. Chakrabarti, S., Berg, M., and Dom, B. Focused crawling: A new approach to topic-specific Web resource discovery. *Computer Networks*, 1999, **31**: 1623–1640.

4. Chen, L., Li, X., Sheng, Q., Peng, W., Bennett, J., Hu, H., and Huang, N. Mining health examination records — A graph-based approach. *IEEE Transactions on Knowledge Data Engineering*, 2016, **28**(9): 2423–2437.

5. Dong, H. and Hussain, F. Self-adaptive semantic focused crawler for mining services information discovery. *IEEE Transactions on Industrial Informatics*, 2014, **10**(2): 1616–1626.

6. Dong, X., Gabrilovich, E., Heitz, G., Horn, W., Lao, N., Murphy, K., Strohmann, T., Sun, S., and Zhang, W. Knowledge vault: A web-scale approach to probabilistic knowledge fusion. *Proc. KDD*, 2014, pp. 601–610.

7. Fatemi, M., Granström, K., Svensson, L., Ruiz, F. J., and Hammarstrand, L. Poisson multi-bernoulli mapping using gibbs sampling. *IEEE Transactions on Signal Processing*, 2017, **65**(11): 2814–2827.

8. Faure, H. and Lemieux, C. Improved Halton sequences and discrepancy bounds. *Monte Carlo Methods Applications*, 2010, **16**(3): 1–18.

9. Hammersley, J. and Handscomb, D. Monte Carlo methods. *Applied Statistics*, 1964, **14**(2/3): 347–385.

10. Huang, W., Wang, T., Chen, W., and Wang, Y. Category-Level transfer learning from knowledge base to microblog stream for accurate event detection. *Proc. DASFAA*, 2017, pp. 50–67.

11. Kumar, M., Bhatia, R., and Rattan, D. A survey of Web crawlers for information retrieval. *WIREs Data Mining and Knowledge Discovery*, 2017, **7**(6): 1–45.

12. Le, B. D., Nguyen, H. X., Shen, H., and Falkner, N. GLFR: A Generalized LFR benchmark for testing community detection algorithms. *Proc. ICCCN*, 2017, pp. 1–9.

13. Mahmud, T., Hasan, M., Chakraborty, A., and Roy-Chowdhury, A. K. A Poisson process model for activity forecasting. *Proc. ICIP*, 2016, pp. 3339–3343.

14. Raufi, B., Ismaili, F., Ajdari, J., and Zenuni, X. Knowledge-base harvesting for user-adaptive systems through focused crawling and semantic Web. *Proc. CompSysTec*, 2016, pp. 323–330.

15. Ren, X., Qin, S., and Zang, P. The discovery and identification of video page based on topic web crawler. *Proc. ICIS*, 2016, pp. 1–4.

16. Sanjeev Arulampalam, M., Evans, R. J., and Letaief, K. B. Importance sampling for error event analysis of HMM frequency line trackers. *IEEE Transactions on Signal Processing*, 2002, **50**(2): 411–424.

17. Sharma, A. and Baral, C. Automatic extraction of events-based conditional commonsense knowledge. *Proc. AAAI Workshops*, 2016, pp. 527–531.

18. Stivala, A., Koskinen, J., Rolls, D., Wang, P., and Robins, G. Snowball sampling for estimating exponential random graph models for large networks. *Social Networks*, 2016, **47**: 167–188.

19. Surendran, S., Prasad, D., and Kaimal, M. A scalable geometric algorithm for community detection from social networks with incremental update. *Social Network Analysis and Mining*, 2016, **6**(1): 90.

20. Tsai, C., Lin, W., and Ke, S. Big data mining with parallel computing: A comparison of distributed and MapReduce methodologies. *Journal of Systems and Software*, 2016, **122**: 83–92.

21. Urbani, J., Dutta, S., Gurajada, S., and Weikum, G. KOGNAC: Efficient encoding of large knowledge graphs. *Proc. IJCAI*, 2016, pp. 3896–3902.

22. Vidal, M., Silva, A., Moura, E., and Cavalcanti, J. GoGetIt!: A tool for generating structure-driven web crawlers. *Proc. WWW*, 2006, pp. 1011–1012.

23. Wu, C., Hou, W., Shi, Y., and Liu, T. A Web search contextual crawler using ontology relation mining. *Proc. CISE*, 2009, pp. 1–4.

24. Wu, X., Chen, H., Wu, G., Liu, J., *et al.* Knowledge engineering with big data. *IEEE Intelligent Systems*, 2015, **30**(5): 46–55.

25. Xi, S., Sun, F., and Wang, J. A cognitive crawler using structure pattern for incremental crawling and content extraction. *Proc. ICCI*, 2010, pp. 238–244.

26. Yang, D., Xiao, Y., Tong, H., Zhang, J., and Wang, W. An integrated tag recommendation algorithm towards weibo user profiling. *Proc. DASFAA*, 2015, pp. 353–373.

27. Yin, Z., Yue, K., Wu, H., and Su, Y. Adaptive and parallel data acquisition from online big graphs. *Proc. DASFAA*, 2018, pp. 323–331.

28. Zhang, Z., Dong, G., Peng Z., and Yan, Z. A framework for incremental deep Web crawler based on URL classification. *Proc. WISM*, 2011, pp. 302–310.

Chapter 3

A Bayesian Network-Based Approach for Incremental Learning of Uncertain Knowledge

Bayesian network (BN) is the well-accepted framework for representing and inferring uncertain knowledge. It is necessary to learn the BN-based uncertain knowledge incrementally in response to the dynamically changing social media. In this chapter, we give an approach for incremental learning of BNs by focusing on the incremental revision of BN's graphical structures. First, we give the concept of influence degree to describe the influence of new data on the existing BN by measuring the variation of BN's probability parameters with respect to the likelihood of the new data. Then, for the nodes ordered decreasingly by their influence degrees, we give the scoring-based algorithm for revising BN's subgraphs iteratively by hill-climbing search for reversing, adding, or deleting edges. In the incremental revision, we emphasize the preservation of probabilistic conditional independencies implied in the BN, based on the concept and properties of Markov equivalence. Experimental results show the correctness, precision, and efficiency of our approach.

3.1 Motivation and Basic Idea

3.1.1 *Motivation*

Generated and collected data have been increased rapidly with the development of Web-based applications and more and more data acquisition strategies. To discover the knowledge implied in the data is undoubtedly the subject of great importance and wide applications. Given a dataset, the knowledge framework can be learned, or there is a knowledge framework specified by experts. Generally, in a specific domain, more and more new data are generated gradually and imply new knowledge that may not be included in the existing framework, which makes it necessary to keep the corresponding knowledge up to date with respect to the new data and thus refine the original knowledge framework. Learning the knowledge again completely on receiving the new data is straightforward but quite impractical, since the original data may be missing, or the knowledge framework may be specified by experts without regard to any prior data. Even if the original data are available, the efficiency cannot be guaranteed in general situations due to the large size of the whole dataset. Moreover, data in general real applications are often updated periodically in a batch mode and expired data will not be preserved accordingly. In particular, knowledge discovered from data streams should be up to date in terms of the evolving nature of data streams, and the knowledge framework should be constructed and preserved by means of incremental strategies consequently [3]. Therefore, it is necessary and practical to explore the incremental learning of the knowledge framework by incorporating the original one and new data, which we will discuss in this chapter.

As a graphical representation of uncertain knowledge, Bayesian network (BN) is an effective and widely used model [25]. In this chapter, we adopt BN as the underlying framework and discuss the incremental learning of uncertain knowledge, where we suppose that there exists an original BN and the size of new data is much smaller than those of the whole dataset if the previous data are available. BN's incremental learning is to revise the existing BN efficiently in response to the increasingly new data, which is able to avoid retraining all sample data and also makes it possible to refine the original BN given by experts [23]. From the semantic point of view, BN describes the probabilistic conditional independences implied among random variables by a Directed Acyclic Graph (DAG), in which there is a conditional probability table (CPT) for each node to describe the quantitative dependences. Thus, BN's incremental learning should also preserve the conditional independencies as much as possible when the original BN is revised to guarantee the effectiveness of the uncertain knowledge theoretically. When using this method for BN's incremental learning from data streams, the current BN could be revised upon the previous one and data in the current synopsis or sliding window [3].

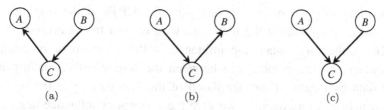

Fig. 3.1. Different levels of BN's incremental learning: (a) A BN fragment; (b) BN fragment by DAG revision; (c) BN fragment by conditional-independency revision.

BN could be constructed by statistical learning form data [10, 14], including the learning of the graphical structure and that of corresponding CPTs. Structure learning is more important and challenging than CPT learning, since CPTs can be refined gradually by BN inferences [35]. Various approaches for structure learning have been proposed recently [7, 9] as the basis of BN-based modeling and inferences, as well as the prerequisite of BN's incremental learning. Consistently, we should also consider the influence of new data on the original BN from the following different levels: CPTs, DAG structures, or even the conditional independencies. For example, upon the BN fragment (ignoring CPTs) shown in Fig. 3.1(a), if the new data influences the DAG structure but not the conditional independencies, the fragment may be changed like Fig. 3.1(b) which is probably equivalent to that in Fig. 3.1(a), while if the new data influences the conditional independencies, the fragment may be changed like Fig. 3.1(c) which is not equivalent to that in Fig. 3.1(a). The probabilistic equivalence of two DAGs will be introduced later in Theorem 3.1.

3.1.2 *Ideas and contributions*

In line with the general idea of incremental mining or incremental learning [15, 18, 29, 31, 41], it is necessary to find the influence of new data or requirements on the original model to determine the range of revisions constrained locally. Specifically, to incrementally revise the original BN, we will have to determine the subgraphs that need to be revised in response to new data. For this purpose, we consider measuring the coincidence between the original BN structure and the new data. First, we obtain the influence of the variation of the probability parameters of each node by comparing the CPTs in the original BN and those computed by the new data with respect to the original BN's DAG. Further, we obtain the influence of the variation of probability parameters on the coincidence between the original BN structure and new data by means of the likelihood of the new data upon the original BN structure. Consequently, we give the concept of influence degree as well as the efficient computation strategy.

As shown in Fig. 3.1, the incremental learning of a BN may include the following cases in a hierarchical manner:

Case 1. If the DAG of the original BN is coincident with the new data, then we only need to update the CPTs.

Case 2. If the variation of new data influences the DAG of the original BN but does not influence the implied conditional independencies of the original BN, then we replace the original structure by its equivalent structure with the equivalent independence relationships.

Case 3. If the variation of new data influences the conditional independencies in a local structure of the original BN, then we revise the BN's substructures.

Clearly, Case 1 could be fulfilled easily by re-computing the relevant CPTs directly from the new data and then replacing the original CPTs. It is known that the concept of Markov equivalence [2, 38] describes the equivalent conditional independencies in different BN structures, and the concept of consistent extension [12, 13] gives the idea for obtaining equivalent BN structures in an equivalence class. Thus, Case 2 could be fulfilled directly by considering Markov equivalence [2, 37] and the method of consistent extension [12, 13]. So, we discuss a gradual method for incremental learning of BNs by focusing on the underlying techniques for Case 3.

First, we identify the nodes influenced by the new data using the proposed concept of influence degree, by which we could sort these nodes decreasingly and regard them as "centers" of the subnetworks that need to be revised. Starting from the node with the largest influence degree, the revision could reduce the cost of incremental learning greatly, since all the nodes will not be revised if the new data have been already coincident with the local structure centered on this node.

Further, inspired by the likelihood-based Cooper–Herskovits scoring function [14], we give the scoring criterion to measure whether the current BN structure coincides with the new data. To uniquely represent the probabilistic conditional independences in a BN and then check whether the current BN structure is satisfactory, we consider its consistent extension based on the concept of Markov equivalence and its relevant properties [2, 12, 13, 38]. The Markov blanket [29] of node X in a BN includes X's direct parents, X's direct successors, and the other direct parents of X's direct successors, by which we can obtain the directly dependent nodes of X. Thus, we take the node with the largest influence degree as the "center" and select its Markov blanket as the "radius" to revise the substructure of the original BN. Finally, we give the scoring-based algorithm to revise the subgraphs iteratively by hill-climbing search for reversing, adding, or deleting edges.

To test the feasibility of our method, we conduct a series of experiments and make corresponding performance studies on manual and benchmark data. Experimental results show the correctness, precision, and efficiency of our method.

The remainder of this chapter is organized as follows. In Section 3.2, we introduce related work. In Section 3.3, we give the concept of influence degree. In Section 3.4, we give the approach for BN's incremental learning. In Section 3.5, we show experimental results and performance studies. In Section 3.6, we summarize our work in this chapter.

3.2 Related Work

BN has become an established framework for representing and inferring uncertain knowledge [27, 32]. It has been widely used in many different perspectives of intelligent applications [39]. Many algorithms have been proposed to induce BN structures from various perspectives or based on various underlying techniques. For example, Cheng *et al.* [10] and Cooper and Herskovits [14] gave the classical dependency-analysis-based and scoring & search-based algorithms, respectively. Recently, focusing on structure learning as well, Bouhamed *et al.* [6] gave the learning structure heuristic of BNs from data. Brenner and Sontag [7] gave a new scoring function that is computationally easier to maximize as the amount of data increases. Compos and Ji [9] gave a branch-and-bound algorithm for structure learning by integrating structural constraints with data in a way to guarantee global optimality. Madsen *et al.* [24] gave the parallel algorithm for BN structure learning from large datasets. Yang *et al.* [40] proposed the method for learning sparse Gaussian BN structure by variable grouping. However, when the network structure is given and all variables' values are fully observed in the training data, learning CPTs is straightforward [32].

The idea of incremental learning arose from the observation that most part of human learning can be viewed as a gradual process of concept formation or as the human ability for incorporating knowledge from new experiences into already learned concept structures [15]. Režňáková *et al.* [31] gave the incremental similarity for real-time on-line incremental learning systems. Incremental learning approaches have been widely used [5], since these approaches tally with the process of human cognition and the realistic situations of data generation or mining.

The field of data mining and knowledge discovery in databases is concerned with very large data that do not fit in long-term storage and has spawned interest in incremental methods [29]. For example, Pratama *et al.* [28] proposed the incremental classifier from data streams.

From the perspective of uncertain knowledge representation and inferences, fuzzy sets were widely used to describe the uncertain knowledge with implicit events, and evolving fuzzy systems were used for uncertain knowledge learning from evolving data, such as data streams [21, 22]. Differently, the implied and evolving dependencies among relevant explicit events or attributes were highlighted in this chapter.

In the BN community, incremental learning methods have been followed with great attention by researchers as well. Specifically, Huang *et al.* [18] pointed out that the most challenging step for BN's incremental learning is the incremental revision of the structures. Krauthausen and Henebeck [19] used incremental gradient ascent algorithm to learn network's parameters upon the given structure. Buntime [8] proposed an algorithm to yield a set of alternative networks, which could be used to revise the set of BNs in the light of new data. Flores *et al.* [16] proposed the method for incremental compilation of BNs based on maximal prime subgraphs concerning BN inferences. Lam and Bacchus [20] proposed an algorithm that can be used to revise parts of the BN that have been already learned when the new data about a subset of variables were available. Friedman and Goldszmidt [17] proposed three different approaches to sequentially learn BNs, actually the MAP-based algorithm that does not have to keep all possible data samples. Shi *et al.* [34] discussed the incremental Bayesian Ying Yang learning and dynamic rule construction.

In addition, many researchers gave different algorithms for incremental learning of BNs under specific conditions or situations. For example, Alcobé [1] gave an incremental algorithm for learning tree-shaped BNs. Shi and Tan [35] proposed a polynomial-time constraint-based technique for incremental learning of BN structures by hill-climbing search on candidate parent sets. Thibault *et al.* [36] discussed the feature-selection oriented incremental learning of BNs by reducing the search space based on the concept of Markov boundary. Ratnapinda and Druzdzel [30] discussed the discrete BN parameter learning from continuous data streams. Specifically in the privacy-preserving paradigm, Samet *et al.* [33] gave a new version of sufficient statistics based on the K2 algorithm with respect to newly coming sensitive data. Yasin and Leray [41] transformed the local structure identification part of MMHC algorithm into an incremental fashion by using heuristics and applied incremental hill-climbing to learn a set of candidate–parent–children for a target variable. Zhu *et al.* [43] gave the method for incremental learning of BNs based on the chaotic Dual-Population evolution strategies. Yue *et al.* [42] proposed the data-intensive method for parallel and incremental learning of BNs from massive and changing data by extending the classic scoring and search based learning algorithm.

The aforementioned methods for incremental learning of BNs just considered the revision from the characteristics of BN as a graphical model instead of the characteristics of BN as a probabilistic model. This makes the effectiveness of the resulting uncertain knowledge after revision unable to be guaranteed theoretically, and thus the effectiveness of the corresponding inferences or predictions cannot be guaranteed accordingly.

Meanwhile, this can also lead to unnecessary revisions since the new data may not have influenced the inherent conditional independencies implied in the original BN, although the graphical structure may be different.

It is known that equivalent conditional independencies may be implied in different DAGs [38]. The revision of BN structures should consider whether the variation of new data actually influences the inherent independencies in the original BN. Therefore, in particular from the probabilistic-semantics perspective to guarantee the correct probabilistic inferences upon the incrementally revised BN, the revision of the independence structures should be considered other than the graphical characteristics. This differentiates our work in this chapter from the above ones.

Two BNs may imply the same independence constraints, although their graphical structures may be different. Verma and Pearl [38] showed that any two DAGs imply the same independence constraints if and only if they contain the same V-structures and have the same skeleton. Partially directed acyclic graphs (PDAGs), containing both directed and undirected edges, were used to represent equivalent classes of BN structures. PDAGs were widely studied from various perspectives [2, 12, 13, 25, 38]. For example, Andersson *et al.* [2] gave the characterization of Markov equivalence classes for DAGs, and pointed out that the equivalence class of a given DAG can be uniquely represented by transforming a PDAG into the corresponding completed PDAG (CPDAG), and proved the soundness and completeness of the transformation. The concept of Markov equivalence and the relevant properties of CPDAGs were used in model selection and network aggregation in the real world [2, 38]. Nevertheless, to the best of our knowledge, Markov equivalence and the relevant properties have not been incorporated into the incremental revision of BN's independence structures. In our work, we take Markov equivalence as the basis for regulating the original subnetwork to preserve the maximal equivalent-independency information in response to the new data.

3.3 Influence Degree of BN Nodes

In this section, we discuss the influence of parameter variations of a node on the likelihood of the new data given the original BN structure. First, we give the definition of BN as the basis of later discussions.

Definition 3.1. A BN is a DAG in which the following holds [27]:

(1) A set of random variables make up the nodes of the network.
(2) A set of directed edges connect pairs of nodes. An arrow from node X to node Y means that X has a direct influence on Y. Each node X is independent of its non-descendants given its parents.
(3) Each node has a CPT that quantifies the effects that the parents have on the node. The parents of node X are all those that have arrows pointing to X.

A BN represents the joint probability distribution (JPD) in products, and every entry in the JPD can be computed from the information in the BN by the multiplication $P(x_1, \cdots, x_n) = \prod_{i=1}^{n} P(x_i | Pa(x_i))$, where x_i is the value of node X_i and $Pa(x_i)$ is the value of the parent nodes of X_i.

Intuitively, the new dataset (denoted as D_n) may be inconsistent with the original BN's representation. Given the graphical structure of the original BN (denoted as G_o), a new set of CPTs can be easily obtained corresponding to D_n. To define the influence degree, we suppose a new BN (denoted as G_n), consisting of the same DAG with that of G_o and new CPTs, can be obtained. To reflect the degree of the variation with respect to the likelihood of D_n and the original BN's graphical structure, for each node we obtain the proportion of the variation of probability parameters from the CPTs of G_o and G_n. Following, we give the definition of variation degree to describe the parameter variation of node X.

Definition 3.2. The proportion of X's probability parameters with variations is called the variation degree of the parameters of node X, denoted as $\Delta(P(X | Pa(X)))$, and

$$\Delta(P(X | Pa(X))) = \sum_{u_{ij} \in U} |u_{ij}^o - u_{ij}^n| / k \tag{3.1}$$

where

(1) U is the set of probability parameters of X in G_o and G_n, $U = U_o \cup U_n = \{u_{ij} \in U_o \text{ or } u_{ij} \in U_n\}$. U_o and U_n is the set of probability parameters of X in G_o and G_n, respectively.

(2) $u_{ij} \in U$ denotes the conditional probability that X will take on the value $X = x_i$ given its immediate parents $Pa(X)$ that take on the value $Pa(X) = v_j$. The discriminators 'o' and 'n' in u_{ij}^o or u_{ij}^n denote the original and new situation, respectively.

(3) k is the number of probability parameters in U and $k = |U|$.

(4) u_{ij}^o is assumed to be 0 if u_{ij} is not in U_o, and u_{ij}^n is assumed to be 0 if u_{ij} is not in U_n.

Example 3.1. Figure 3.2 shows the structure of a simple BN. Suppose U_o and U_n for node X is shown in Tables 3.1 and 3.2, respectively.

By Definition 3.2, we have $\Delta(P(X|Pa(X))) = (0.3 + 0.3 + 0.3 + 0.3 + 0.2 + 0.1 + 0.3 + 0.3 + 0.3 + 0.3 + 0.8 + 0.9)/12 = 0.37$.

It is worth noting that G_o and D_n may be still coincident even if there is great variation of the corresponding probability parameters. Thus, we further discuss the influence of parameter variations on the coincidence between G_o and D_n, which we represent by the probability

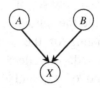

Fig. 3.2. Structure of a simple BN.

Table 3.1. U_o of node X.

$P(X|AB)$	$v_1 = a_1b_1$	$v_2 = a_1b_2$	$v_3 = a_2b_1$	$v_4 = a_2b_2$
x_1	$u_{11}^o = 0.9$	$u_{12}^o = 0.8$	$u_{13}^o = 0.7$	$u_{14}^o = 0.6$
x_2	$u_{21}^o = 0.1$	$u_{22}^o = 0.2$	$u_{23}^o = 0.3$	$u_{24}^o = 0.4$

Table 3.2. U_n of node X.

$P(X|AB)$	$v_1 = a_1b_1$	$v_2 = a_1b_2$	$v_3 = a_2b_1$	$v_4 = a_2b_2$	$v_5 = a_3b_1$	$v_6 = a_3b_2$
x_1	$u_{11}^n = 0.6$	$u_{12}^n = 0.5$	$u_{13}^n = 0.4$	$u_{14}^n = 0.3$	$u_{15}^n = 0.2$	$u_{16}^n = 0.1$
x_2	$u_{21}^n = 0.4$	$u_{22}^n = 0.5$	$u_{23}^n = 0.6$	$u_{24}^n = 0.7$	$u_{25}^n = 0.8$	$u_{26}^n = 0.9$

of observing D_n upon g_o, denoted as $P(D_n|g_o)$, where we use g_o to denote the graphical structure of G_o.

Intuitively, the larger the value of $P(D_n|g_o)$, the better the coincidence between D_n and g_o will be. The total influence of the new data on g_o consists of all variations of $P(D_n|g_o)$ with respect to all the variations of u_{ij}. This means that the expression $\int_{u_{ij}^o}^{u_{ij}^n} \frac{\partial P(D_n|g_o)}{\partial u_{ij}} du_{ij}$ describes the influence of u_{ij}'s variation on $P(D_n|g_o)$. Thus, for each node X, we use the average influence of all X's parameter variations on $P(D_n|g_o)$ to describe the influence of X's parameter variations on $P(D_n|g_o)$, defined as follows.

Definition 3.3. $\frac{1}{k}\sum_{u_{ij}\in U}\int_{u_{ij}^o}^{u_{ij}^n} \frac{\partial P(D_n|g_o)}{\partial u_{ij}} du_{ij}$, denoted as $\mathrm{ID}(X)$, is called the influence degree of parameter variations of node X on $P(D_n|g_o)$.

It can be seen from Definition 3.3 that the computation of the influence degree concerns many difficult integral calculations. Thus, we give a linear approximate expression based on the variation degree in Definition 3.2 to compute the influence degree of node X efficiently. We replace $P(D_n|g_o)$ by the log-likelihood, $\ln P(D_n|g_o)$, since the increase in the log-likelihood is proportional to that in the likelihood. Russell and Norvig [32] showed that each of these derivatives could be calculated as

$$\frac{\partial \ln P(D_n|g_0)}{\partial u_{ij}} = \sum_{d\in D_n} \frac{P(x_i v_j|r)}{u_{ij}} \tag{3.2}$$

where r is a sample in D_n.

Thus, we have the following linear approximation expression:

$$\int_{u_{ij}^o}^{u_{ij}^n} \frac{\partial \ln P(D_n|g_o)}{\partial u_{ij}} du_{ij} \approx \frac{\sum_{d\in D_n} P(x_i v_j|r)}{u_{ij}^o}|u_{ij}^o - u_{ij}^n| \tag{3.3}$$

Note that $\sum_{d\in D_n} P(x_i v_j|r) = m_{ij}$, where m_{ij} is the number of samples in D_n satisfying $X = x_i$ and $Pa(X) = v_j$. Then, we have

$$\frac{1}{k}\sum_{u_{ij}\in U}\int_{u_{ij}^o}^{u_{ij}^n} \frac{\partial P(D_n|g_o)}{\partial u_{ij}} du_{ij} = \frac{1}{k}\sum_{u_{ij}\in U} \frac{m_{ij}}{u_{ij}^o}|u_{ij}^o - u_{ij}^n| \tag{3.4}$$

This means that $\frac{1}{k}\sum_{u_{ij}\in U}\int_{u_{ij}^o}^{u_{ij}^n}\frac{\partial P(D_n|g_o)}{\partial u_{ij}}du_{ij}$ can be approximately represented as

$$\frac{1}{k}\sum_{u_{ij}\in U}\frac{m_{ij}}{u_{ij}^o}|u_{ij}^o - u_{ij}^n| \qquad (3.5)$$

Based on the influence degree given in Eq. (3.5), the nodes influenced by the new data can be identified and sorted. By the decreasing order of the influence degrees, we can consider revising the original BN centered on the node with the currently-largest influence degree, similar to the node selection strategy adopted in the classical scoring and search based BN learning algorithm. Moreover, the revision centered on the currently largest influence degree is useful to greatly reduce the cost of the thorough learning process, since all the nodes will not be revised if the new data has been already coincident with the local structure centered on this node. By giving a threshold of the influence degree, we can consider revising the original BN centered on the nodes whose influence degree is larger than the threshold.

3.4 Incremental Learning of BNs

3.4.1 *Markov equivalence and its properties*

We take Markov equivalence as the basis for regulating the old subnetwork to preserve the maximal equivalent conditional independencies with respect to the new data. Some relevant concepts and conclusions will be introduced at first.

The skeleton of any DAG is the undirected graph resulting from ignoring the direction of every edge. The V-structure in a DAG G is an ordered triple of nodes (X, Y, Z) such that G contains the directed edges $X \to Y$ and $Z \to Y$, and X and Z are not adjacent in G [27]. Two DAGs (i.e., BN's graphical structures) are graphically equivalent if and only if they define the same probability distribution. The equivalence can be determined by the following theorem [38].

Theorem 3.1. *Two DAGs are equivalent if and only if they have the same skeletons and the same V-structure.*

A directed edge $X \to Y$ is compelled in DAG g if $X \to Y$ exists in g' for every DAG g' equivalent to g. For any edge e in g, if e is not compelled in g, then e is reversible in g. From Theorem 3.1, we know that any edge participating in a V-structure is compelled [13].

A partially directed acyclic graph, or PDAG for short, is a graph that contains both directed and undirected edges. The completed PDAG, or CPDAG for short, corresponding to an equivalence class is the PDAG consisting of a directed edge for every compelled edge, and an undirected edge for every reversible edge in the equivalence class [2, 13, 25]. A CPDAG for a given equivalence class of BN structures is unique [12]. We use g^* to denote the CPDAG of DAG g. For a CPDAG g^*, every DAG contained in the equivalence class of g^* is a consistent extension of g^*.

Example 3.2. Let us consider the graphs in Fig. 3.3 to illustrate the above concepts.

(1) By the concept of Markov equivalence, we know that G_1 and G_2 are equivalent, since they have the same skeleton and the same V-structure.
(2) By the concept of CPDAGs, we know that G_3 is the CPDAG of G_1 and G_2.
(3) By the concept of consistent extensions, we know that G_1 and G_2 are the consistent extension of G_3.

Andersson *et al.* [2] gave the sufficient and necessary condition to decide whether a PDAG is a CPDAG of some DAG.

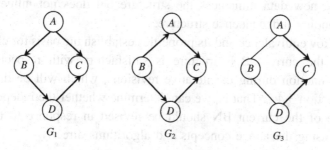

Fig. 3.3. Illustrating graphs.

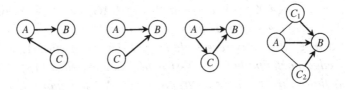

Fig. 3.4. Strongly protected configurations.

Theorem 3.2. *Let g^* be a graph that is the CPDAG for some DAGs if and only if g^* satisfies the following four conditions*:

(1) *g^* is a partially directed graph.*
(2) *Every undirected chain component of g^* is chordal.*
(3) *The configuration $A \to B \to C$ does not occur as an induced subgraph of g^*.*
(4) *Every directed edge $A \to B$ is strongly protected in g^*.*

An undirected graph is chordal if every cycle of length $n \geq 4$ possesses a chord [2, 27]. A directed edge $A \to B$ is strongly protected in g^*, if $A \to B$ is at least one of the four configurations shown in Fig. 3.4 as the induced subgraph of g^*.

Meek [25] gave the rule-based algorithm, DAG-TO-CPDAG, to transform a DAG into its CPDAG. We adopt this algorithm to obtain the unique representation of independencies implied in a DAG. Chickering [12] gave the algorithm PDAG-to-DAG to obtain the consistent extension of PDAGs. We adopt this algorithm to obtain the ultimate BN structure when the new data influences the structure but does not influence the corresponding independence structure.

Markov equivalence and its properties establish the basis for checking whether the current BN structure is satisfactory with respect to the scoring function during the iterative revisions, which will be discussed in Subsection 3.4.2. That is, we can determine whether the independence structure of the current BN should be revised in response to the new data by using the above concepts and algorithms directly.

Algorithm 3.1 DAG-TO-CPDAG

Input: DAG g

Output: CPDAG g^*

Steps:

1. Transform all directed edges into undirected edges except those in V-structures Let g^* be the derived PDAG

2. While g^* contains any undirected edges satisfying the following rules Do

3. Rule 1: If $\textcircled{A} \rightarrow \textcircled{B} - \textcircled{C}$ and $A \ldots C \notin g^*$ Then make $B \rightarrow C$ be oriented in g^*

4. Rule 2: If $\begin{smallmatrix} & \textcircled{B} & \\ \textcircled{A} & - & \textcircled{C} \end{smallmatrix}$ Then make $A \rightarrow C$ be oriented in g^*

5. Rule 3: If $\begin{smallmatrix} & \textcircled{B} & \\ \textcircled{A} & | & \textcircled{C} \\ & \textcircled{D} & \end{smallmatrix}$ Then make $B \rightarrow D$ be oriented in g^*

6. End While

7. Return g^*

Algorithm 3.2 PDAG-To-DAG

Input: PDAG $\mathcal{P}$

Output: DAG g

Steps:

1. $g \leftarrow \mathcal{P}$
2. For each component[a] K in $\mathcal{P}$ Do
3.   mark "un-processed" on all nodes in K
4. End For
5. While there are un-processed nodes in K Do
6.   select an un-processed node X with the most parents

---

[a] A component is the connected subgraph generated by removing the orientations in a DAG.

Algorithm 3.2 (Continued)

 7. For each undirected edge $X - Y$ Do
 8.   make $X \to Y$ be oriented, mark "processed" on X
 9. End For
10. End While
11. Return g

3.4.2 *A scoring-based algorithm for BN's incremental learning*

In real applications, the variation generated from the new data often influences the local independence structure of the original BN. It is necessary to partially revise the substructure of the original BN when the independence structures need to be revised. We take the node with the largest influence degree as the "center" and select a "radius" (i.e., range) to revise the substructure of the BN.

We first check the reversible edges in CPDAG g^* of a subnetwork g and decide the direction of each edge by comparing the scores of different directions of every reversible edge. If the obtained consistent extension g' of g^* does not satisfy the coincidence condition, then we use the hill-climbing search [14] to make revisions on g' by reversing, adding, or deleting edges. Thus, in the revision process of the BN structure, the following two problems are to be addressed:

- How to select the radius to revise the substructure of the BN?
- How to measure the coincidence between the original BN's independence substructure and the new data?

For the first problem, we select the Markov blanket [27], denoted as $MB(X)$, of node X as the radius, since $MB(X)$ in a BN is the subset S $(X \notin S)$ of nodes where X is independent of $V - S - X$ given S (suppose V denotes the set of all nodes in the BN). Pearl [27] pointed out that in any BN, the union of the following three types of neighbors is sufficient for forming a Markov blanket of node X: the direct parents of X, the direct successors of X, and all direct parents of X's direct successor. The substructure centered on X is composed by the nodes and the relevant edges of $MB(X) \cup \{X\}$.

For the second problem, we measure the coincidence by a scoring measure. It is well known that Cooper and Herskovits [14] proposed the measure for BN learning based on searching for a BN structure with the maximum value of the CH scoring function. The BN learning algorithm is based on the enumeration of all possible acyclic network structures, and the optimal structure achieves the greatest value of the scoring function, which actually provides a measure for the coincidence between the testing BN structure and the given sample data. Therefore, we adopt the CH scoring function to measure whether the variation of the new data influences the independence structure of the current BN.

The CH scoring function of a certain BN structure g for a given dataset D is denoted as $P(D/g)$. To avoid the factorial calculation of $P(D/g)$, we revise the widely used logarithmic CH function [31]:

$$P(D/g) = \prod_{i=1}^{n} \prod_{j=1}^{q_i} \frac{\Gamma(\alpha_{ij}^*)}{\Gamma(\alpha_{ij}^* + N_{ij}^*)} \prod_{k=1}^{r_i} \frac{\Gamma(\alpha_{ijk} + N_{ijk})}{\Gamma(\alpha_{ijk})} \qquad (3.6)$$

where $\Gamma(\cdot)$ is the Gamma function and $\Gamma(n) = (n-1)!$, if n is a positive integer.

Let $\{x_i^1, x_i^2, \cdots, x_i^{r_i}\}$ be the set of values of node X_i and $\{v_i^1, v_i^2, \ldots, v_i^{q_i}\}$ be the set of values of the parents $Pa(X_i)$ of X_i. N_{ijk} is the number of samples satisfying $X_i = x_i^k$, $Pa(X_i) = v_i^j$ and $N_{ij}^* = \sum_{k=1}^{r_i} N_{ijk}$. α_{ijk} is called hyper parameter, which is the product of the equivalent sample size and the parameter of a prior structure, and $\alpha_{ij}^* = \sum_{k=1}^{r_i} \alpha_{ijk}$. For computation convenience, Cooper and Herskovits [14] supposed that the prior distribution is a homogeneous distribution and thus $\alpha_{ijk} = \alpha_{ij}^* = 1$, where the log-likelihood was used to improve Eq. (3.6), and gave the scoring function $CH(g|D)$ as follows:

$$CH(g|D) = \sum_{X_i \in g} \sum_{j=1}^{q_i} \left[\log \frac{\Gamma(\alpha_{ij}^*)}{\Gamma(\alpha_{ij}^* + N_{ij}^*)} + \sum_{k=1}^{r_i} \log \frac{\Gamma(\alpha_{ijk} + N_{ijk})}{\Gamma(\alpha_{ijk})} \right]$$

$$(3.7)$$

For the original BN structure g, new data D_n, and the node with the largest influence degree, denoted as X_i, we use S, g_s, g_s', and D_s to denote $MB(X_i) \cup X_i$, the corresponding substructure, the substructure's consistent extension, and the observation data on S, respectively. To revise the BN structure incrementally, if $CH(g|D_n) \geq \varepsilon$, then g is coincident with D_n, that is, g is satisfactory with respect to D_n, where ε is the given threshold of the CH scores. Then g is coincident with D_n, so we do not need to make any revision on g. Otherwise, g may need to be revised by considering the following different cases:

- If $CH(g_s|D_s) \geq \varepsilon$, then the substructure centered on node X_i does not need to be revised, and consequently the substructures centered on all the other nodes will not be considered any more.
- If $CH(g_s|D_s) < \varepsilon$ and $CH(g'_s|D_s) \geq \varepsilon$, then the new data do not influence the independence substructure centered on X_i. Thus, we only need to replace the original substructure by its consistent extension with the equivalent independencies based on the concepts and properties presented in Subsection 3.4.1.
- If $CH(g_s|D_s) < \varepsilon$ and $CH(g'_s|D_s) < \varepsilon$, then the new data do influence the independence substructure centered on X_i. In this case, we need to revise the independence substructures by reversing, adding, or deleting edges. The revision is based on the hill-climbing search [14], where we select the structure revised by one of edge reversal, addition, or deletion provided that the largest CH score can be achieved.

Based on the above idea, we give the algorithm to incrementally revise the original BN.

Algorithm 3.3 BN's incremental revision

Input:

    G: the original BN

    D_n: the set of new data

    ε: the threshold of CH scores

Output: The new BN

Local variables:

    g_o: the DAG of G

    X_i: a node in g_o

    O: the decreasing order set of nodes in g_o

Algorithm 3.3 (Continued)

g: the DAG of the original BN

$MB(X_i)$: the Markov blanket of X_i

S: the subset of nodes in g

S': the set of nodes in $MB(S) \cup S$

D_s: the set of observed data on S

g_s: the substructure of g on the nodes in S

g_s^*: the CPDAG of g_s

g_s': the consistent extension of g_s^*

$CH(g|D)$: the CH scoring function of g given the observed
   data D

Steps:

Calculate the influence degree for each node in G and sort them in
decreasing order to obtain $O = \{X_1, X_2, \ldots, X_n\}$ //By Definition 3.3

Select X_i as the center and $MB(X_i)$ as the radius to revise the
   substructure of g_o

$g \leftarrow g_o$

While $CH(g|D_n) < \varepsilon$ Do //g needs to be revised

   Select the first node X_i from O //With the largest influence
      degree

   $S \leftarrow MB(X_i) \cup X_i$

   $g_s \leftarrow$ the substructure of g on the nodes in S

   $D_s \leftarrow$ the set of observed data on S

   $S' \leftarrow MB(S) \cup S$

   While $CH(g_s|D_s) < \varepsilon$ Do //The substructure of g that needs to be
      revised

      Find the CPDAG g_s^* of g_s by Algorithm 3.1

      Find the consistent extension g_s' of g_s^* by Algorithm 3.2
         //Comparing and deciding the direction of every reversible
         edge in g_s^*

      While $CH(g_s'|D_s) < \varepsilon$ Do //g needs to be revised

         Reverse, add or delete edges in g_s' from X_i by hill-climbing
         search

      End While

Algorithm 3.3 (Continued)

$\quad\quad g_s \leftarrow g_s'$

$\quad\quad S \leftarrow S',\ S' \leftarrow \text{MB}(S) \cup S$

$\quad\quad g_s \leftarrow$ the substructure of g on the nodes in S

$\quad\quad D_s \leftarrow$ the set of observed data on S

$\quad$ End While

$\quad$ Replace the substructure of g by g_s

$\quad\quad O \leftarrow O - \{X_i\}$

End While

Calculate CPTs for all nodes in g from D_n

Generally, the advantages of this algorithm can be summarized as follows:

(1) Considering the node with the currently largest influence degree in each iteration of the revision, we could ignore all the other nodes if the new data have been coincident with the local structure centered on this node. This is quite similar to the node selection strategy in the well-accepted hill-climbing algorithm for the scoring and search based learning of BN structures.

(2) Adopting the CH scoring function, one of the most widely used scoring metrics for learning BN structures from data, we could determine whether the current BN should be revised on probability parameters, edge directions, or independence substructures. This means that we adopt the same and equivalently effective scoring function as that adopted in the classical scoring and search based method to measure the coincidence between the current BN and the new dataset.

(3) Using Markov blanket as the radius of the substructure that needs to be revised, we can make revisions on the most relevant nodes, since X is independent of all the other nodes without including X and those in $\text{MB}(X)$.

The execution cost of Algorithm 3.3 mainly depends on the size of the original BN's structure, including the number of nodes and that of the nodes in their Markov blankets. Although the incremental revision of the substructures involves large amounts of tests on nodes and subgraphs, the Markov-blanket-based strategies can guarantee the effectiveness of this algorithm theoretically. Actually from the inherence and realistic situations of incremental learning, new data will only influence a few nodes in the original BN, and thus the above strategies are practical. The correctness of the influence degree and the effectiveness and efficiency of Algorithm 3.3 will be further tested by experiments in Section 3.5.

3.5 Experimental Results

We implemented relevant algorithms and made performance studies to test the effectiveness of our method. In Subsection 3.5.1, we tested the correctness of the influence degree. In Subsections 3.5.2 and 3.5.3, we tested the effectiveness and efficiency of Algorithm 3.3, respectively.

The experiments were conducted on the machine with a 2.2 GHz Intel Dual-Core CPU, 2 GB main memory, running Windows 7 operation system, and the codes were written in Java. Our experiments were based on the standard Chest-clinic network (also called Asia network) [11], a belief network for a fictitious medical domain about whether a patient has *tuberculosis, lung cancer*, or *bronchitis*, related to their *X-ray, dyspnea, visit-to-Asia*, and *smoking status*. Each node has only two possible values (i.e., True or False) described by 1 or 0, respectively. To test the efficiency and scalability of our method, we further adopted the realistic Adult dataset from UCI repository [4]. To learn the BN, we directly adopted the Chest-clinic sample data from Netica [11] and imported the Adult sample data, respectively.

3.5.1 *Correctness of influence degree*

From the whole Chest-clinic dataset with 6000 rows, we learned the BN by PowerConstructor while ignoring the CPTs when illustrating the learned BN. The network is denoted as G and shown in Fig. 3.5. Then, we divided the whole dataset into two parts with 5000 rows (denoted as D_o) and 1000 rows (denoted as D_n), respectively. We learned a BN from D_o, denoted as G_o and shown in Fig. 3.6. In this experiment, G

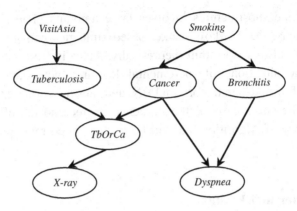

Fig. 3.5. Standard BN, *G*, learned from the whole benchmark dataset.

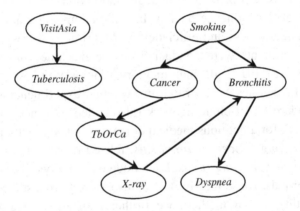

Fig. 3.6. Original BN, *G_o*, learned from the 5000 row dataset.

was looked upon as the standard network that should have been learned incrementally from G_o and D_n.

Meanwhile, we obtained the influence degree from D_n given G_o. To test the correctness of the influence degree as the basis of our incremental learning approach, we considered whether the influence degrees are consistent with the variations from G_o to G. By the results from No. 1 to No. 5 in Table 3.3, we first gave the influence degrees (denoted as ID) and the results whether the revision has been done (denoted as RES) for each node in the previous five iterations of G_o's revisions. By the last, with No. 6 in Table 3.3, we also gave the average influence

Table 3.3. Influence degree and the G_o's revision.

No	VisitAsia		Tuberculosis		Smoking		Cancer		TbOrCa		X-ray		Bronchitis		Dyspnea	
	ID	RES	ID	RES	ID	RES	ID	RES	ID	RES	ID	RES	ID	RES	ID	RES
1	0.417	no	0.549	no	1.083	no	10.644	yes	11.070	no	0.756	no	48.328	yes	81.421	yes
2	0.589	no	8.675	no	0.746	no	3.287	no	29.984	yes	11.473	no	3.276	no	2.283	no
3	0.372	no	0.763	no	23.447	yes	1.976	no	0.868	no	1.682	no	38.453	yes	9.284	no
4	1.317	no	2.538	no	0.133	no	26.534	yes	13.270	no	0.748	no	3.612	no	1.362	no
5	0.000	no	0.063	no	0.1	no	5.226	yes	5.05	yes	2.513	no	7.539	no	6.858	yes
	Avg-ID	Final-RES	Avg-ID	Final-RES	Avg-ID	Final-RES	Avg-ID	Final-RES	Avg-ID	Final-RES	Avg-ID	Final-RES	Avg-ID	Final-RES	Avg-ID	Final-RES
6	0.593	no	12.525	no	25.51	no	47.667	yes	60.242	yes	17.172	yes	101.208	yes	101.208	yes

degrees (denoted as Avg-ID) and the results whether the node has been revised finally by comparing Fig. 3.6 with Fig. 3.5 directly (denoted as Final-RES). For node X, 'yes' means that the edges connected to X are revised, and 'no' otherwise.

It can be seen from Table 3.3 that the larger the influence degree in each iteration during the incremental learning, the more probably the node was revised. Among the 40 pairs of ID and RES in the five iterations, only the results of 'Cancer' and 'TbOrCa' in the 1st iteration are not consistent with the above observation. Thus, from the perspective of the consistency of variation tendencies, the correctness ratio is $1 - 1/40 = 97.5\%$. By the average influence degree and final result of G_o's revision, we know that only the result of 'X-ray' is not consistent with the above observation. Thus, from the perspective of node revision, the average correctness ratio is $1 - 1/8 = 87.5\%$, which guarantees that the measure of influence degree is correct to some extent.

3.5.2 *Effectiveness of revised BNs*

Based on the incremental learning method given in Algorithm 3.3 by taking as input the original BN G_o and new data D_n, we obtained the revised BN, denoted as G_n and shown in Fig. 3.7. We also ignored the CPTs for simplicity. By comparing G_n and G in Figs. 3.7 and 3.5, we note that these two BNs' structures are basically consistent.

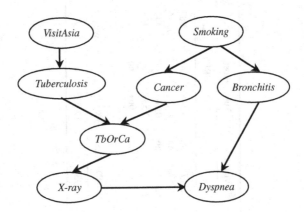

Fig. 3.7. The revised BN G_n obtained based on Algorithm 3.3.

Table 3.4. Errors of G_n's inferences.

No	Inference	R (%)	R_n (%)	Error (%)
1	$P(Cancer = 1 \mid Smoking = 1)$	9.86	9.85	0.01
2	$P(TbOrCa = 1 \mid Smoking = 1)$	10.4	10.4	0
3	$P(X\text{-}ray = 0 \mid Smoking = 1)$	15.5	15.8	0.3
4	$P(Bronchitis = 1 \mid Smoking = 1)$	58.7	59.5	0.8
5	$P(Dyspnea = 1 \mid Smoking = 1)$	52.9	53.4	0.5
6	$P(Smoking = 1 \mid Cancer = 1)$	82.8	83.1	0.3
7	$P(X\text{-}ray = 0 \mid Cancer = 1)$	98.4	95.5	2.9
8	$P(Bronchitis = 1 \mid Cancer = 1)$	53.7	54.1	0.4
9	$P(Dyspnea = 1 \mid Cancer = 1)$	82.5	65.6	16.9
10	$P(Smoking = 1 \mid Bronchitis = 1)$	65.2	66.7	1.5
11	$P(Cancer = 1 \mid Bronchitis = 1)$	7.11	7.18	0.07
12	$P(TbOrCa = 1 \mid Bronchitis = 1)$	7.66	7.78	0.12
13	$P(X\text{-}ray = 0 \mid Bronchitis = 1)$	13.3	13.1	0.2
14	$P(Dyspnea = 1 \mid Bronchitis = 1)$	78.3	79.5	1.2

It is well known that BN-related applications can be used to make analysis, prediction, or decision based on the results of probabilistic inferences. Therefore, oriented to BN's real applications, we further tested G_n's effectiveness by comparing the inference results on G_n and those on G for the same evidence and the same observation(s). We defined the error of G_n's inferences by the absolute value of the difference between the inference result on G_n and that on G. Table 3.4 shows some representative inference tasks, their inference results on G and G_n (denoted as R and R_n, respectively), and the corresponding error, respectively.

It can be seen that the errors of the inferences on G_n are less than 3%, except that of the 9th inference task. We can further obtain that the maximal, minimal, and average errors are 16.9%, 0%, and 1.8%, respectively. This verifies that high precisions of the inferences can be achieved with the revised BN. Thus, we can conclude that the revised BN obtained by Algorithm 3.3 can be effectively used in relevant applications.

3.5.3 *Efficiency of incremental learning*

Moreover, we also tested the efficiency and scalability of Algorithm 3.3 on the BNs with various numbers of nodes and those from various sizes

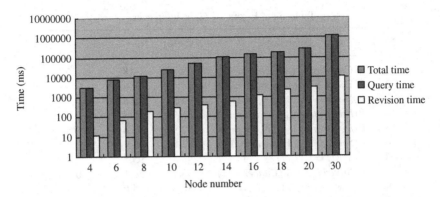

Fig. 3.8. Execution times under various numbers of nodes on manual data.

of the new data as two factors that may determine the efficiency of Algorithm 3.3.

First, to test the efficiency of Algorithm 3.3 with the increase of nodes in the original BN, we manually generated the test data by projection or unions of the Chest-clinic sample data. We tested the execution time of Algorithm 3.3 under 4, 6, ..., 30 nodes on the fixed new dataset with 2000 rows. We recorded the total time for running Algorithm 3.3, the execution time for querying the database to evaluate the CH scoring functions (called 'query time'), and the execution time for revising the original BN structure (called 'revision time'), respectively, shown and compared in Fig. 3.8. To decrease the dramatic difference of the above three kinds of execution times, we adopted the logarithmic scale.

It can be seen from Fig. 3.8 that the total time, query time, and revision time are increased with the increase of BN nodes. The query time for retrieving the new data dominates the total time and is increased sharply. For all cases, the revision time is increased linearly and only takes a small proportion of the total time. This also means that the execution time of Algorithm 3.3 is mainly determined by that for querying the sample data stored in the database, while the incremental revision itself can be fulfilled efficiently. Even for the BN with 30 nodes, the revision just takes 11320 ms, while the total execution takes 1241008 ms.

Then, to test the efficiency of Algorithm 3.3 with the increase of sample data, we obtained various sized new datasets from the Chest-clinic

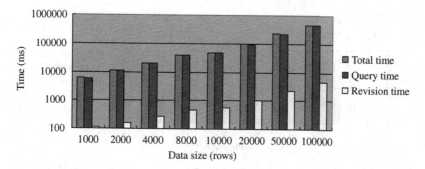

Fig. 3.9. Execution times under various sizes of new data on manual data.

sample data. We tested the execution time of Algorithm 3.3 from the datasets with $1000, 2000, \ldots, 100000$ rows on the fixed BN with eight nodes. We also recorded the total time, query time, and revision time, shown and compared in Fig. 3.9, where we also adopted the logarithmic scale. It can be seen that the total time, query time, and revision time are also increased with the increase of the sample data. The query time for retrieving the new data also dominates the total time and the revision time also takes only a small proportion of the total time. This also means that the execution time of Algorithm 3.3 is mainly determined by that for querying the database, while the incremental revision itself can be fulfilled efficiently. Even for the new dataset with 100000 rows, the revision just takes 4589 ms, while the total execution takes 459118 ms.

Further, to test the scalability of Algorithm 3.3, we further used the Adult dataset available at the UCI repository [4], including 14 variables and 32232 instances. The instances, as rows, with missing data are removed and continuous variables are discretized over the mean into binary variables. We tested the execution time of Algorithm 3.3 under $2, 4, \ldots, 14$ nodes on the fixed new dataset with 10000 rows. We also tested the execution time of Algorithm 3.3 under the datasets with $4000, 8000, \ldots, 32000$ rows on the fixed BN with 14 nodes. The total time, query time, and revision time of the above two tests are shown and compared in Figs. 3.10 and 3.11, respectively.

Therefore, we can conclude that most of the execution cost of Algorithm 3.3 comes from querying the new dataset, while the improvement can be made easily by incorporating some existing optimization strategies

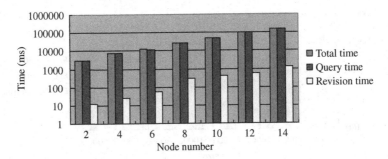

Fig. 3.10. Execution times under various numbers of nodes on UCI data.

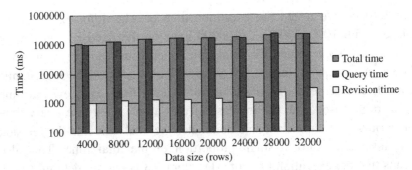

Fig. 3.11. Execution times under various sizes of new data on UCI data.

for general query processing. So, the above two aspects of experimental results on manual and real datasets show the efficiency and scalability of Algorithm 3.3 for BN's incremental learning.

Moreover, by comparing the results in Figs. 3.8 and 3.9 globally, we note that the increase of the execution time with the increase of BN nodes is much faster than that with the increase of data sizes (i.e., rows). This means that the execution time is much more sensitive to the BN's scale than with the data size by an order of magnitude. However, the characteristics of real applications that just concern a small part of the original one makes any incremental learning problem reasonable and practical. That is, only a small subset of the BN nodes should have been revised inherently, which eliminates the influence of the increased nodes on the sharply increased execution time to a great extent.

3.6 Summary

In this chapter, we present an approach for incremental learning of BN-based uncertain knowledge, useful to revise a substructure of BN when receiving new data. From the practical scenarios of social media analysis, a knowledge model is established initially and revised gradually with respect to gradually arriving data or gradually improved cognition. Without loss of generality, the approach for incremental learning of a BN is actually the approach for learning uncertain knowledge in data. As the basis of probabilistic approaches for social media analysis, our method provides the basis for modeling and inferring uncertain knowledge implied in dynamically changing social media data. Using the up to date knowledge model, similarities and associations could be represented and inferred.

References

1. Alcobé, J. An incremental algorithm for tree-shaped Bayesian network learning. *Proc. ECAI*, 2002, pp. 350–354.
2. Andersson, S., Madigan, D., and Perlman, M. A characterization of Markov equivalence classes for acyclic digraphs. *Annuals of Statistics*, 1997, **25**: 505–541.
3. Angelov, P. *Autonomous Learning Systems: From Data Streams to Knowledge in Real-Time*. John Wiley & Sons, New York, 2012.
4. Asuncion, A. and Newman, D. UCI machine learning repository, http://www.ics.uci.edu/~mlearn/MLRepository.html, 2007.
5. Bosman, H., Iacca, G., Wortche, H. J., and Liotta, A. Online fusion of incremental learning for wireless sensor networks. *Proc. DaMNet*, ICDM, 2014, pp. 525–532.
6. Bouhamed, H., Masmoudi, A., Lecroq, T., and Rebai, A. A new learning structure of Bayesian Networks from data. *Proc. MLDM*, 2012, pp. 183–197.
7. Brenner, E. and Sontag, D. SparsityBoost: A new scoring function for learning bayesian network structure. *Proc. UAI*, 2013, pp. 112–121.
8. Buntime, W. Theory refinement on Bayesian networks. *Proc. UAI*, 1991, pp. 52–60.
9. Compos, C. and Ji, Q. Efficient structure learning of Bayesian Networks using constraints. *Journal of Machine Learning Research*, 2011, **12**: 663–689.

10. Cheng, J., Bell, D., and Liu, W. Learning Bayesian networks from data: An efficient approach based on information theory. *Proc. CIKM*, 1997, pp. 325–331.
11. Netica. https://www.norsys.com/index.html, Norsys Software Corp, 2018.
12. Chickering, D. A transformational characterization of Bayesian network structures. *Proc. UAI*, 1995, pp. 87–98.
13. Chickering, D. Learning equivalence classes of Bayesian network structures. *Journal of Machine Learning Research*, 2002, **2**: 445–498.
14. Cooper, G. and Herskovits, E. A Bayesian method for the induction of probabilistic networks from data. *Machine Learning*, 1992, **9**(4): 309–347.
15. Fisher, D. Knowledge acquisition via incremental conceptual clustering. *Machine Learning*, 1987, **2**: 139–172.
16. Flores, M., Gámez, J., and Olesen, K. Incremental compilation of Bayesian networks based on maximal prime subgraphs. *International Journal of Uncertainty, Fuzziness and Knowledge-Based Systems*, 2011, 155–191.
17. Fridman, N. and Goldszmidt, M. Sequential update of Bayesian network structure. *Proc. UAI*, 1997, pp. 165–174.
18. Huang, H., Song, H., Tian, F., Lu, Y., and Wang, Q. A comparatively research in incremental learning of Bayesian networks. *Proc. WCICA*, 2004, Vol. 5, pp. 4260–4264.
19. Krauthausen, P. and Hanebeck, U. Parameter learning for hybrid Bayesian networks with Gaussian mixture and Dirac mixture conditional densities. *Proc. ACC*, 2010, pp. 480–485.
20. Lam, W. and Bacchus, F. Using new data to refine a Bayesian network. *Proc. UAI*, 1994, pp. 383–390.
21. Lemos, A., Caminhas, W., and Gomide, F. Multivariable Gaussian evolving fuzzy modeling system. *IEEE Transactions on Fuzzy Systems*, 2011, **19**(1): 91–104.
22. Lughofer, E., Cernude, C., Kindermann, S., and Pratama, M. Generalized smart evolving fuzzy systems. *Evolving Systems*, 2015, **6**(4): 269–292.
23. Liu, W., Yue, K., Yue, M., Yin, Z., and Zhang, B. A bayesian network based approach for incremental learning of uncertain knowledge. *International Journal of Uncertainty, Fuzziness, and Knowledge-based Systems*, 2018, **26**(1): 87–108.
24. Madsen, A., Jensen, F., Salmeron, A., Langseth, H., and Nielsen, T. A parallel algorithm for Bayesian network structure learning from large data sets. *Knowledge-Based Systems*, 2017, **117**: 44–55.
25. Meek, C. Causal inference and causal explanation with background knowledge. *Proc. UAI*, 1995, pp. 403–410.

26. Nielsen, S. and Nielsen, T. Adapting Bayes network structures to non-stationary domains. *International Journal of Approximate Reasoning*, 2008, **49**(2): 379–397.

27. Pearl, J. *Probabilistic Reasoning in Intelligent Systems: Networks of Plausible Inference.* Morgan Kaufmann, 1988.

28. Pratama, M., Anavatti, S., and Lughofer, E. An incremental classifier from data streams. *Artificial Intelligence: Methods and Applications.* Springer International Publishing, 2014: 15–28.

29. Provost, F. and Kolluri, V. A survey of methods for scaling up inductive algorithms. *Data Mining and Knowledge Discovery*, 1999, **3**(2): 131–169.

30. Ratnapinda, P. and Druzdzel, M. Learning discrete Bayesian network parameters from continuous data streams: What is the best strategy? *Journal of Applied Logic*, 2015, **13**(4): 628–642.

31. Režnáková, M., Tencer, L., and Cheriet, M. Incremental similarity for real-time on-line incremental learning systems. *Pattern Recognition Letters*, 2016, **74**: 61–67.

32. Russel, S. and Norvig, P. *Artificial Intelligence: A Modern Approach.* Prentice-Hall, 2003.

33. Samet, S., Min, A., and Granger, E. Incremental learning of privacy-preserving Bayesian networks. *Applied Soft Computing*, 2013, **13**(8): 3657–3667.

34. Shi, D., Nguyen, M., Zhou, S., and Yin, G. Fuzzy CMAC with incremental Bayesian Ying Yang learning and dynamic rule construction. *IEEE Transactions on Systems, Man and Cybernetics, Part B: Cybernetics*, 2006, **40**(2): 548–552.

35. Shi, D. and Tan, S. Incremental learning Bayesian network structures efficiently. *Proc. ICARCV*, 2010, pp. 1719–1724.

36. Thibault, G., Aussem, A., and Bonnevay, S. Incremental bayesian network learning for scalable feature selection. *Proc. ASONAM*, 2009, pp. 188–193.

37. Tian, F., Zhang, H., Lu, Y., and Shi, C. Incremental learning of Bayesian networks with hidden variables. *Proc. ICDM*, 2001, pp. 651–652.

38. Verma, T. and Pearl, J. Equivalence and synthesis of causal models. *Proc. UAI*, 1990, pp. 220–227.

39. Wang, W., Wang, H., Yang, B., Liu, L., Liu, P., and Zeng, G. A Bayesian network-based knowledge engineering framework for IT service management. *IEEE Transactions on Services Computing*, 2013, **6**(1): 76–88.

40. Yang, J., Leung, H., Yiu, S., Cai, Y., and Chin, F. Learning sparse Gaussian Bayesian network structure by variable grouping. *Proc. ICDM*, 2014, pp. 1073–1078.

41. Yasin, A. and Leray, P. iMMPC: A local search approach for incremental Bayesian network structure learning. *Proc. IDA*, 2011, pp. 401–412.

42. Yue, K., Fang, Q., Wang, X., Li, J., and Liu, W. A parallel and incremental approach for data-intensive learning of Bayesian networks. *IEEE Transactions on Cybernetics*, 2015, **45**(12): 2890–2904.

43. Zhu, Y., Liu, D., Jia, H., and Trinugroho, D. Incremental learning of bayesian networks based on the chaotic dual-population evaluation strategies and its application to nanoelectronics. *Journal of Nanoelectronics and Optoelectronics*, 2012, **7**(2): 113–118.

Chapter 4

Discovering User Similarities in Social Behavioral Interactions Based on Bayesian Network

Whether users in a social network are similar or not depends on the local topological structure of the social network as well as users' behaviors reflected by social interactions or user-generated contents. As the basis of latent social links, user similarities are uncertain by a quantitative degree. In this chapter, we adopt Bayesian network (BN) as the underlying framework and propose a data-intensive probabilistic approach for discovering user similarities. For the massive social behavioral interactions, we give the MapReduce-based algorithm for measuring direct similarities between users. We then construct a BN to describe these similarities by a graphical model with probabilistic properties called user Bayesian network and abbreviated as UBN. To measure indirect similarities between users, we give the method for measuring the closeness of user connections in terms of the UBN's graphical structure, and the MapReduce-based algorithm for measuring the dependence degrees by probabilistic inferences of UBN. Finally, we give experimental results and show the efficiency and effectiveness of our method.

4.1 Motivation and Basic Idea

With the rapid development of data acquisition techniques, Web 2.0 applications, and social networks, increasing numbers of user-generated data have been collected. These data include social behavioral interactions (e.g., "follow" or "comment" behaviors with respect to user blogs or ratings), and thus reflect user preference, mutual relationship, and evolution [4, 12]. Analyzing, understanding, and utilizing social media are paid great attention in the paradigms of massive data analysis, knowledge discovery, e-commerce, business intelligence, etc. In recent years, many researchers have conducted various studies on social media analysis, such

71

as community detection, collaborative filtering-based recommendation, user targeting, and click-through-rate (CTR) prediction in computational advertising [4, 12, 15]. Finding similar users is one of the key issues in these studies and relevant realistic applications, since it can help find relevant social users, understand user relationship evolution, select paths to spread specific news/political views, target factors for given scenarios, keep track of people's life, make advertising more profitable, etc. [34]. For example, user similarities can be well used in product recommendation and ad CTR prediction, since similar users tend to share their opinions together or have analogous purchasing preferences. Meanwhile, user similarities can also be used to explore one user's evaluation of another and discover user's topic/role in social networks, since the similarities provide a plausible mechanism for a complex phenomenon observed in studies of user evaluation, such as social ties, overlap relationships, distance metric, and so on [2]. Generally speaking, user similarity establishes the basis for various perspectives of social media analysis.

It is straightforward that user similarities could be obtained by analyzing their behavioral interactions, other than directly from users' demographic properties (e.g., name, age, sex, income, etc.), since the similarities reflect users' behavior when engaged in social activities. For example, the similarities among coauthors of academic papers are implied in DBLP records [8]. Multiple users may relate to various products in the Epinions social network [29], and may be connected to the same video in the Youtube social network [5]. Potential friendship among users can be investigated from users' link with friends and their check-ins in mobile social networks [36]. Thus, it is necessary to discover user similarity from social behavioral interactions oriented to various social media analysis or social network-based applications [11].

However, from the characteristics of social user relationships and inherence of user similarities implied in social media, there exist the following challenges:

- The similarity between two users, say A and B, may depend on the behavioral interactions of several users other than just these two, which means that the similarities among social users are not "linear" and the "if-then" representation is not always appropriate. To this end, we consider describing user similarities globally by a graph model in this chapter.

- The similarity between two users depends on the mutual interactions rather than those just from A to B or those just from B to A in general situations. For example, if A is a fan of B (e.g., a famous star) and A follows B frequently but not vice versa, then we can regard that A is similar to B but B may be not similar to A, that is, A is more probably influenced by B. This means that the similarity between two users are orientation (a.k.a. direction) aware, which makes us adopt the directed graphical model, where nodes and edges stand for users and direct similarity relationships, respectively.
- It is quite intuitive that whether two users are similar or not is generally uncertain but not either exactly similar or dissimilar, which is more obvious when confronted with massive social behavioral interactions. This means that user similarities should be represented not only by the assertion that A is similar to B but also the uncertain dependence degree to much A is similar to B in the universe of all concerned users. More importantly, it is desirable and challenging to discover the indirect similarities between two users without connections by direct edges in the graph model, which makes the inferences of similarities indispensable.

By incorporating BN's mechanisms of uncertainty representation and inferences into the above problem of user similarity discovery, we adopt BN as the framework for modeling social user and discovering user similarities [40]. That is, we are to find users to which the given user is similar and measure the corresponding similarity degree based on the Bayesian network. For this purpose, we discuss the following two problems:

(1) How to construct a BN to represent direct similarities between users, called user Bayesian network and abbreviated as UBN, from massive social behavioral interactions?
(2) How to derive indirect similarities between any pairs of users with the UBN?

For the problem (1), we focus on DAG construction in terms of the characteristics of social behavioral interactions, as the critical step of UBN construction and consistent with the roadmap for general BN's learning [14, 39]. By means of the co-occurrence statistics of user pairs from behavioral interactions, we propose the method to measure the orientation-aware direct similarity between a pair of users. Then, we give the algorithm to determine the existence and orientation of the edge between these two users. In particular, aiming at the massive social behavioral interactions, we consider developing data-intensive algorithms to guarantee the scalability and effectiveness.

MapReduce is a programming model for processing and generating large datasets [9]. It offers a parallel programming model for independent operations upon massive data, where "map" functions are executed in parallel to create a dataset of ⟨*key, value*⟩ pairs, and "reduce" functions are executed in parallel to aggregate the values of all pairs with the same keys. Thus, we give the MapReduce-based algorithms to fulfill the parallelizable steps in required statistic computations to construct the UBN's DAG and CPTs. Generally, massive social behavioral interactions always concern a good many users that lead to a large-scale UBN with a good many nodes, so we further give the idea for storing the constructed UBN in a distributed file system as the basis for efficient induction of indirect similarities.

For the problem (2), to derive the indirectly similar users to a certain user, we consider the structural characteristics of UBN subgraph centered on this user, as well as the corresponding quantitative dependence degrees with uncertainties. To achieve the ultimate similarity degree, we combine the two indirect similarity degrees obtained from the above two perspectives, respectively.

First, from the perspective of UBN's graphical structures, we give the method to describe the closeness of connections between user A and other ones that are possibly similar to A. As is pointed out [26], Markov blanket (MB) of a certain node A, denoted as MB(A), in a BN consists of the direct parents, direct children, and the other parents of the direct children. MB(A) describes the "relatives" nodes of A, and it has been proved semantically that the nodes in MB(A) are conditionally independent of other nodes with respect to A. Thus, by means of the concept of MB, we define the mutual similar subgraph, abbreviated as MSG, between a pair of nodes in the UBN, and outline the idea for measuring the indirect similarity degree between them.

Second, from the perspective of dependence degrees with uncertainties, we transform the discovery of indirect similarities into probabilistic inferences, since the induction of dependence degrees can be well expressed as conditional or posterior probability computations. Then, based on the idea of BN's exact probabilistic inferences and the concept of MB, we give the MapReduce-based algorithm for UBN inferences to achieve the uncertainty of dependence relationships between users as the similarity degree. By this way, the induction of the indirect similarity degree between users is implemented by data-intensive aggregations that can be executed in parallel upon the UBN stored in a distributed file system.

To test the feasibility of our method, we make experiments by adopting DBLP and Sina Weibo data upon the Hadoop-based platform. Experimental results show the efficiency and effectiveness of our method.

The remainder of this chapter is organized as follows: In Section 4.2, we introduce related work. In Section 4.3, we give the method for measuring user similarities and MapReduce-based algorithm for constructing the UBN from massive social behavioral interactions. In Section 4.4, we give the UBN-based method for deriving indirect similarities from the perspective of structural characteristics and that of probabilistic inferences. In Section 4.5, we show experimental results and performance studies. In Section 4.6, we summarize our work in this chapter.

4.2 Related Work

Social network and social media analysis, such as social network evolution [4, 12] and product recommendation [15], have been paid much attention in recent years. Finding user similarities or similar users was regarded as one of the underlying issues in these studies [34]. Anderson *et al.* [2] discussed the role of user similarities for analyzing social media and various representative social networks [5, 8, 29].

Deshpande and Karypis [10] gave the classical $L1$-Norm and Cosine similarity metrics for recommendation systems. Social links and corresponding similarities in social networks were discussed from various perspectives [2, 16, 32]. Anderson *et al.* [2] measured the similarity between two users based on that of interests by a distance metric and that of social ties by using a measure of overlap in the evaluated people. Kleinberg [16] defined the graph model-based user similarity. Schall [32] proposed the method for link prediction by mining the subgraph patterns in directed social networks such as GitHub, GooglePlus, and Twitter. As for specific domains, Ying *et al.* [38] gave the similarity measure in the paradigm of location-based services. McCallum *et al.* [20] proposed the similarity measure based on the Author–Recipient–Topic model. Bhattacharyya *et al.* [3] defined the similarity metric between a pair of users via the frequency and relative location of user keywords by combining both network and profile similarities. In these methods, user similarities were obtained from users' descriptive properties or social links, but cannot be guaranteed to be correct since users' descriptive information cannot be always reliable. Actually, users with similar descriptive information in social networks may not be really similar in social activities.

As for the discovery of user similarities, Crandall *et al.* [6] regarded that users were similar due to their association to the same communities. Nakatsuji *et al.* [22] defined the metric of user similarity based on users' assessments and the classes of products. Liu *et al.* [17] decided the user similarity by local context and global preference of user behaviors from quantitative ratings. Akcora *et al.* [1] proposed a metric of user similarity for online social networks by combining network and profile similarities. Nisgav and Patt-Shamir [24] considered users similar if their answers to some queries were mostly identical. Xu *et al.* [36] investigated the potential friendship among users from users' link with friends and their check-ins at various positions in mobile social networks, and thus achieved good performance with aggregated features of user similarities. In these methods, user similarities were measured from the results of user behavior execution, by which the users with behavioral similarities can be found.

By these methods, the similarity between two users can be measured locally, but the similarity between these two users may be actually influenced by several other users. Consequently, it is hard to achieve the similarities between any pair of users efficiently. Thus, we are to represent the similarities globally by a graph model, and then induce the similarities between any pair of users to answer the *ad hoc* similarity queries by a universal way. In particular, social behavioral interactions (e.g., "follow" or "comment" behaviors with respect to user blogs or ratings) directly associated among users, as a special kind of behavioral records, can reflect user similarities more straightforwardly. Moreover, the above methods are effective when the scale of such behavioral records of link relationships, assessment, or ratings is small, but cannot work when confronted with massive behavioral records. Thus, we are to explore the data-intensive method for user modeling and similarity discovery from massive social behavioral interactions. On the other hand, the similarity degrees with uncertainties should also be induced by a universal way simultaneously with the similarities themselves, which is also our focus in this chapter.

PGMs were used as the underlying model in social network analysis. Zhang *et al.* [41] proposed a PGM to collectively measure the entity reputations in social networks. Liu *et al.* [18] proposed a generative probabilistic model, named preference-topic model, to combine the tasks of user preference discovery and document topic mining together. Particularly, Piwowarski *et al.* [27] modeled user interactions by the BN with latent variables that explain the subjects of user actions from Web search activities. Nillius *et al.* [23] defined a similarity measure between isolated tracks based on BN and associated the identities of isolated tracks by graph constraints and similarity measurements. Yang *et al.* [37] measured the rating similarity between friends in an online social network by a set of rating conditional probabilities. But, the underlying PGM model was basically constructed from the queries, profiles, or domain characteristics, different from the model that we will construct from behavioral interactions.

Learning BN from data is always the subject of great attention in the paradigms of artificial intelligence and machine learning. Heckerman *et al.* [14] proposed the classic scoring and search based learning approach, which we extended to fit the situations with massive, distributed, and dynamically changing data [39]. In this chapter, our method for UBN construction is the trade-off between the methods in Ref. [23, 27, 37] and those in Ref. [14, 39]. Thus, the subjectivity of the former kind of methods can be avoided to a great extent by statistic computations, and the efficiency can be improved to a great extent compared to the latter kind of methods due to the incorporation of intuitive and inherent characteristics of behavioral interactions.

Probabilistic inferences are the preliminary computation task in BN-based applications, but the exact probabilistic inferences will be fulfilled in exponential time [7]. To this end, Yang *et al.* [37] gave the distributed algorithm for multiple-hop recommendation by BN inferences, and Ma *et al.* [19] proposed the parallel method for evidence propagation in junction trees and the BN's exact inferences on multicore using MapReduce. These methods focus on the parallel execution of steps in BN inferences regardless of the scale of the BN itself. In this chapter, we are to store the constructed large-scale UBN in the distributed file system and thus the similarity discovery can be implemented by data aggregation operations.

MapReduce [9] has been used in big data analysis [28] and similarity search. For example, Metwally *et al.* [21] discovered similar pairs of entities based on MapReduce. Schelter *et al.* [33] gave the scalable similarity based neighborhood method with MapReduce. Analogously, we are to give the MapReduce based algorithms for constructing UBNs and the probabilistic inferences for computing the indirect similarity degrees.

4.3 Bayesian Network Based Measurement of User Similarities

4.3.1 *Definitions and problem statement*

For convenience of computation but without loss of generality, we let $U = \{A_1, A_2, \ldots, A_n\}$ denote the ordered set of users, where A_i $(1 \leq i \leq n)$ is the identifier of the i-th user. Note that the order of users will not make the discovered similarities different, which will be proved theoretically in Section 4.4.

As given by neuroscientists [11], the relationship of one user to others defines opportunities of high-dimensional and temporal behaving. With respect to a specific record of interaction in an event or transaction, user behavior is reflected by the participation of relevant users in this interaction. For example, the behavior of authors in a paper could be reflected by the fact whether there is coauthor action and the behavior of Weibo users can be reflected by the fact whether there is forward/comment/like action. Thus, we let $T = \{\overrightarrow{T_1}, \overrightarrow{T_2}, \ldots, \overrightarrow{T_m}\}$ denote the set of behavioral interactions of the users in U in a period of time, where $\overrightarrow{T_j}$ is the vector of user identifiers concerned with or participating in the j-th interaction and $\overrightarrow{T_j}$ is supposed to include two user identifiers at least $1 \leq j \leq m$.

Example 4.1. Suppose the behavioral interactions upon $U = \{A_1, A_2, A_3, A_4\}$ are as follows: $T = \{\overrightarrow{T_1} = (A_1 A_2), \overrightarrow{T_2} = (A_1 A_2 A_4), \overrightarrow{T_3} = (A_1 A_2 A_3), \overrightarrow{T_4} = (A_1 A_2 A_3 A_4), \overrightarrow{T_5} = (A_1 A_3), \overrightarrow{T_6} = (A_3 A_4), \overrightarrow{T_7} = (A_2 A_4)$, where $\overrightarrow{T_1} = (A_1 A_2)$ means that A_1 and A_2 are concerned in one interaction.

To construct the UBN is to construct the BN taking the users in U as nodes and the behavioral interactions as data samples. First, we give the definition of BN [26, 31] as follows.

Definition 4.1. A BN is a DAG in which the following holds:

(1) A set of random variables makes up the nodes of the network.
(2) A set of directed links connects pairs of nodes. An arrow from node A to node B means that A has a direct influence on B. Each node is independent of its non-descendants given its parents.
(3) Each node has a CPT that quantifies the effects that the parents have on the node. The parents of node A are all those that have arrows pointing to it.

A BN represents the joint probability distribution (JPD) in products, and every entry in the JPD can be computed from the information in the BN by the chain rule $P(A_1 A_2, \ldots, A_n) = \prod_{i=1}^{n} P(A_i \mid Pa(A_i))$.

Based on the definition of a general BN, we then give the definition of UBN to represent the direct similarity relationships among users and corresponding uncertainties.

Definition 4.2. A user Bayesian network, abbreviated as UBN, is a pair $G = (G_U, S)$, where

(1) $G_U = (U, E)$ is the DAG of UBN, and U is the set of nodes (i.e., users) in G_U. Each node in U corresponds to a user A_i, valued 1 or 0, where 1 indicates that A_i is concerned in T, and 0 otherwise. E is the set of directed edges connecting pairs of nodes, which reflect the direct similarity relationship between them.
(2) $S = \{P(A_i \,|\, Pa(A_i))\}$ is the set of conditional probabilities and consists of the CPT of node A_i in G_U, where $Pa(A_i)$ is the set of parent nodes of A_i.

To construct the UBN in Definition 4.2, we will construct the graphical structure by deciding the orientation of each edge and computing the CPT of each node, which will be discussed, respectively in successive parts of this section.

4.3.2 *Constructing user Bayesian network based on MapReduce*

It is intuitive that the users with frequent interactions tend to build up the behavioral similarity relationship, which means that we can achieve the user similarity between two users based on their co-occurrences. Without loss of generality, we focus on the DAG construction as the critical step of UBN construction. Directed edges are used to describe direct similarities between users, which makes us consider determining the existence of an edge between two nodes and further the edge's orientation.

First, we give the measurement of association degree between a pair of users, say A_i and A_j ($1 \le i$, $j \le n$, $i \ne j$) to reflect the frequency of these two users' behavioral interactions. By the ratio of the number of interactions containing the specific two users simultaneously to that of the interactions containing at least one of them, we define the association degree between A_i and A_j, denoted as $AS(A_i, A_j)$:

$$AS(A_i, A_j) = \frac{N(A_i A_j)}{N(A_i) + N(A_j) - N(A_i A_j)} \qquad (4.1)$$

where $N(A_i)$, $N(A_i A_j)$ and $N(A_i) + N(A_j) - N(A_i A_j)$ denote the number of interactions containing "A_i", "A_i and A_j", and "A_i or A_j", respectively.

The larger the ratio, the more probability that there is an edge between these two users. Let ε be a threshold for the association degree, $0 < \varepsilon \leq 1$, and if $AS(A_i, A_j) \geq \varepsilon$, then we consider that there exists an edge between A_i and A_j. As mentioned in Section 4.1, the similarity between A and B is orientation aware, so we now further consider the orientation of the edge between A_i and A_j to determine whether A_j is similar to A_i or A_i is similar to A_j. To this end, we define the dependence degree of A_j on A_i by the conditional probability of A_j given A_i.

$$P(A_j \mid A_i) = \frac{N(A_i A_j)}{N(A_i)} \qquad (4.2)$$

The dependence degree of A_i on A_j, $P(A_i \mid A_j)$, could be defined analogously. Actually, $P(A_j \mid A_i)$ denotes the probability that the occurrence of A_i leads to that of A_j. If $P(A_j \mid A_i) \geq P(A_i \mid A_j)$, then we say A_j is similar to A_i since the dependency of A_j on A_i is larger than that of A_i on A_j. Accordingly, the orientation between A_i and A_j should be from A_i to A_j, which makes the directed edge $A_i \rightarrow A_j$, where $P(A_j \mid A_i)$ is called the direct similarity degree of A_j to A_i. By the order of users in U, we can obtain the directed edges in G_U while guaranteeing there is no cycle generated.

As the basis of Eqs. (4.1) and (4.2), the computation of $N(A_i)$ and $N(A_i A_j)$ concern statistics upon the massive behavioral interactions and the exhaustion of statistics with respect to every pair of users, where the efficiency of UBN construction is generally a great concern. On the other hand, the computation of various $N(A_i)(1 \leq i \leq n)$ or $N(A_i A_j)(1 \leq i, \ j \leq n, \ i \neq j)$ could be fulfilled independently. Thus, we design a data-intensive parallel algorithm based on MapReduce, where map functions are used to map each interaction in T into $\langle key, value \rangle$ pairs with respect to the key of A_i and $A_i A_j$, respectively, and reduce functions

---

Algorithm 4.1 Computing $N(A_i)$ and $N(A_i A_j)$

Map(*key, value*)

 String *key*: File name of $T = \{\overrightarrow{T_1}, \overrightarrow{T_2}, \ldots, \overrightarrow{T_m}\}$
 String *value*: Behavioral interaction records in T
 For each record $\overrightarrow{T_l}$ $(1 \leq l \leq m)$ in T Do
  Emit $\langle A_i, 1 \rangle$
  Emit $\langle A_i A_j, 1 \rangle$
  //For all possible pairs of users A_i and A_j $(i \neq j)$ in $\overrightarrow{T_l}$
  by the order of users in U
 End For

Reduce(*key, values*)

 String *key*: A_i or $A_i A_j$
 Iterator *values*: current list
 result←0
 For each value v in values Do
  result←*result* + *ParseInt*(*v*)
 End For
 Emit$\langle key,\ AsString(result)\rangle$

---

to achieve the $N(A_i)$ and $N(A_i A_j)$, respectively. The above ideas are given in Algorithm 4.1 taking as input the distributed storage file of T.

By one pass execution of Algorithm 4.1, various $N(A_i)$ and $N(A_i A_j)$ can be obtained in parallel, and the association degrees defined in Eq. (4.1) and dependency degrees defined in Eq. (4.2) can be obtained efficiently without sensitivity to the scale of the behavioral interactions. Upon the constructed DAG, we can compute the CPT for each node, where each entry is represented as $P(A_i \mid Pa(A_i))$. Based on the idea of likelihood estimation where parameters are estimated by counting frequency from dataset [18], we simply compute $P(A_i \mid Pa(A_i))$ by the ratio of the number of interactions including A_i and $Pa(A_i)$ to that including $Pa(A_i)$, that is

$$P(A_i \mid Pa(A_i)) = \frac{N(A_i Pa(A_i))}{N(Pa(A_i))} \tag{4.3}$$

Clearly, $N(A_i \mid Pa(A_i))$ and $N(Pa(A_i))$ can be computed by the MapReduce-based idea analogously to Algorithm 4.1.

Example 4.2. Revisiting the users and their behavioral interactions given in Example 4.1, we show steps for constructing the UBN.

(1) By the map functions in Algorithm 4.1, we can obtain $\langle A_1, 1 \rangle$, $\langle A_2, 1 \rangle$, and $\langle A_1 A_2, 1 \rangle$ from $\overrightarrow{T_1}$; $\langle A_1, 1 \rangle$, $\langle A_2, 1 \rangle$, $\langle A_4, 1 \rangle$, $\langle A_1 A_2, 1 \rangle$, $\langle A_1 A_4, 1 \rangle$, and $\langle A_2 A_4, 1 \rangle$ from $\overrightarrow{T_2}$. Similarly, we can obtain the $\langle key, value \rangle$ pairs from other interactions in T.

(2) By the reduce functions, we can obtain $\langle A_1, 5 \rangle$, $\langle A_2, 5 \rangle$, $\langle A_1 A_2, 4 \rangle$, etc.

(3) Based on Eq. (4.1), we can obtain $\mathrm{AS}(A_1, A_2) = \frac{4}{5+5-4} = 0.67$. Analogously, we can obtain the association degrees of other pairs of users. If we suppose $\varepsilon = 0.3$, then we know there are four edges in the UBN, (A_1, A_2), (A_1, A_3), (A_2, A_4), and (A_3, A_4). Based on Eq. (4.2), we have $P(A_2 \mid A_1) = P(A_1 \mid A_2) \geq 0.3$, so we have $A_1 \rightarrow A_2$. Analogously, we can obtain other directed edges. Based on Eq. (4.3), we can obtain the CPT for each node in the UBN. Finally, the UBN can be constructed as Fig. 4.1. For convenience of representation, we use $A_i = 1$ to denote that A_i is concerned in an interaction and $A_i = 0$ otherwise.

Then, we further give the idea for storing the constructed UBN in a distributed file system to support the efficient induction of indirect similarities between users. By adopting the idea proposed in [39], we store the DAG and corresponding CPTs into a file, denoted as T_{UBN}, consisting of logical rows represented as $\langle key, value \rangle$ pairs in terms of the MapReduce-based data-intensive computation, Hadoop-like platforms and the specialties of a BN. To reflect the dependence relationships between child and parent nodes, key and value is $(A_i, Pa(A_i))$ and $P(A_i, Pa(A_i))$, respectively, where

- $Pa(A_i)$ denotes the set of parent node(s) of A_i,
- $P(A_i, Pa(A_i))$ denotes the conditional probability of A_i given $Pa(A_i)$.

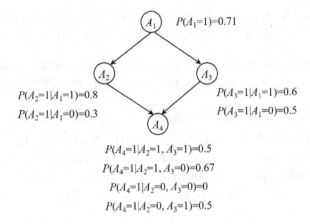

$P(A_1=1)=0.71$

$P(A_2=1|A_1=1)=0.8$

$P(A_2=1|A_1=0)=0.3$

$P(A_3=1|A_1=1)=0.6$

$P(A_3=1|A_1=0)=0.5$

$P(A_4=1|A_2=1, A_3=1)=0.5$

$P(A_4=1|A_2=1, A_3=0)=0.67$

$P(A_4=1|A_2=0, A_3=0)=0$

$P(A_4=1|A_2=0, A_3=1)=0.5$

Fig. 4.1. UBN constructed from social behavioral interactions.

Table 4.1. Fragment of T_{UBN} corresponding to Fig. 4.1.

$Key = (A_i, Pa(A_i))$	$Value = P(A_i \mid Pa(A_i))$
$A_1 = 1$	0.71
$A_1 = 0$	0.29
$A_2, A_1 = 1, 1$	0.8
$A_2, A_1 = 0, 1$	0.2
$A_2, A_1 = 1, 0$	0.3
$A_2, A_1 = 0, 0$	0.7
$A_4, (A_2A_3) = 1, (11)$	0.5
$A_4, (A_2A_3) = 0, (11)$	0.5
$A_4, (A_2A_3) = 1, (10)$	0.67
$A_4, (A_2A_3) = 0, (10)$	0.33
...	...

Example 4.3. Table 4.1 shows the fragment of T_{UBN} of the UBN in Fig. 4.1.

4.4 Deriving Indirect Similarity by Probabilistic Inferences

In this section, we first give the method to describe the closeness between a user and possible similar ones from the perspective of UBN's structural characteristics in Section 4.4.1. We then give the MapReduce-based algorithm for UBN inferences to achieve the dependence degrees with uncertainties between indirectly similar users in Section 4.4.2.

4.4.1 *Graphical structure-based indirect similarities*

Akcora *et al.* [1] gave the method for measuring user similarities within two-hop distance from the perspective of the graphical structure. Inspired by this idea and the specialties of UBN as a PGM, we consider the range of possible similar users based on the concept of MB [26, 31]. For user A, we are to determine the user(s) in MB(A) to which A is similar indirectly. Thus, the range of A's similar users is defined by MB(A) like the two-hop distance, while the former provides both structural and probabilistic semantics.

Let $X \in$ MB(A) be a possible user similar to A. We first measure the closeness of the connections between A and X (i.e., the density of the common subgraph affiliated with these two nodes in the UBN $G = (G_U = (U, E)S))$ as the indirect similarity degree from the perspective of UBN's graphical structural characteristics.

Definition 4.3. The mutually similar subgraph of A and X, abbreviated as MSG(A, X), is $G_M(A, X) = (U_M(A, X), E_M(A, X))$, where $U_M(A, X) =$ MB(A) $\cap$ MB(X), and $E_M(A, X) = \{(x, y) \mid x, y \in U_M, (x, y) \in E\}$.

Analogously, we use $G_S = ($MB(A) $\cup \{A\}, E_S(A))$ to denote the subgraph including the nodes in MB(A) $\cup \{A\}$, where $E_S(A)$ is the set of edges concerning the nodes in MB(A) $\cup \{A\}$. Then, the closeness of the connections between A and X is defined by the ratio of the size of MSG(A, X) to that of G_S as follows:

$$\text{Sim}_S(AX) = \frac{\log |E_M(A, X)|}{\log |E_S(A)|}, \quad 0 \leq \text{Sim}_S(A, X) \leq 1 \tag{4.4}$$

where the size of a subgraph is defined as the number of edges, denoted as $|E_M(A, X)|$ and $|E_S(A)|$ for MSG(A, X) and $G_S(A)$, respectively, and the logarithm scale is adopted to suit the situations when there is large difference between $|E_M(A, X)|$ and $|E_S(A)|$.

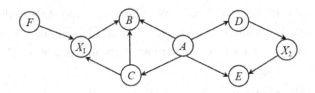

Fig. 4.2. An example of UBN.

Intuitively, Eq. (4.4) reflects that the denser the subgraph affiliated with A and X, the closer the relationship of X to A, and thus X is more likely to be similar to A. In the following, we give an example to illustrate the above idea.

Example 4.4. We consider a UBN ignoring CPTs shown in Fig. 4.2. First, we can obtain $MB(A) = \{B, C, D, E, X_1, X_2\}$, $MB(X_1) = \{A, B, C, F\}$, and $MB(X_2) = \{A, D, E\}$.

(1) By Definition 4.3, we can obtain $U_M(A, X_1) = \{A, B, C\}$, $E_M(A, X_1) = \{(A, B), (C, B), (A, C)\}$, and $E_S(A) = \{(A, B), (C, B), (A, C), (X_1, B), (C, X_1), (A, D), (A, E), (D, X_2), (X_2, E)\}$. Then, we have $\text{Sim}_S(A, X_1) = \frac{\log |E_M(A, X_1)|}{\log |E_S(A)|} = \frac{\log 3}{\log 9} = 0.5$.

(2) Analogously, we can obtain $E_M(A, X_2) = \{(A, D), (A, E)\}$ and $\text{Sim}_S(A, X_1) = \frac{\log 2}{\log 9} = 0.32$.

Thus, X_1 is more similar to A than X_2, which is consistent with people's intuition that the subgraph affiliated to A and X_1 is denser than that to A and X_2.

To obtain $E_M(A, X)$ and $E_S(A)$, we retrieve the key in T_{UBN}. If $X \in Pa(A)$, then A is the parent node of X, and thus both the value of $|E_M(A, X)|$ and that of $|E_S(A)|$ will increase by one. If $X = A$, then each node in $Pa(A)$ is the parent node of A, and thus $|E_M(A, X)|$ and $|E_S(A)|$ will be increased by one. Upon the distributed storage of the UBN, the above computations can be fulfilled by map functions, and the number of edges relevant to X can be aggregated by reduce functions.

4.4.2 *Probabilistic inference-based indirect similarities*

From the perspective of UBN's probabilistic inferences, we regard the uncertainty of the dependence relationship between indirectly similar users as the similarity degree. To derive this uncertainty quantitatively, we use $P(A = 1 \mid X = 1)$ to represent the dependency degree of X on A, and consider the probabilistic inferences upon the UBN. For convenience of expression, we call A as target user. According to the principle of BN's probabilistic inferences, the dependency degree of X on A is denoted as follows:

$$
\begin{aligned}
\text{Sim}_Q(A, X) &= P(A = 1 \mid X = 1) \\
&= \frac{P(A = 1, X = 1)}{P(X = 1)}, \quad 0 \le \text{Sim}_Q(A, X) \le 1
\end{aligned}
\tag{4.5}
$$

This means that the computation of $\text{Sim}_Q(A, X)$ can be transformed as those of two marginal probabilities, $P(A = 1, X = 1)$ and $P(X = 1)$, where $P(A = 1, X = 1)$ can be computed by the sum of the JPDs of all possible values of the combination of latent variables in U except A and X. According to the conditional independence relationships described in the UBN, each JPD can be transformed as the multiplication of a series of conditional probability distributions, which can be obtained by retrieving T_{UBN}. Analogously, $P(X = 1)$ can be obtained. All the required possible values whose marginal probabilities will be computed and stored in a distributed file system are denoted as T_{JPD}. For simplification of probability computation, we use MB(A) to decrease the concerned latent variables while preserving the conditional independence semantics. For example, to compute $P(A_1 = 1 \mid A_2 = 1)$ upon the UBN in Fig. 4.1, we just consider the latent variable A_3 since MB(A_1) = $\{A_2, A_3\}$, and thus $(A_1 = 1, A_2 = 1, A_3 = 1)$ and $(A_1 = 1, A_2 = 1, A_3 = 0)$ are included in T_{JPD}.

To make the exact probabilistic inferences although the execution time is exponential [7], we look upon the UBN as stored data and the operations for UBN inferences as data processing. We give the method in Algorithm 4.2 based on MapReduce for UBN's probabilistic inferences to derive the uncertainty of the dependence relationship between a pair

---

Algorithm 4.2 Probabilistic inferences of UBNs

Map(*key, value*)

    String *key*: File name of T_{UBN}

    String value: Records (i.e., entries) of CPTs in T_{UBN}

    For each record *r* in T_{UBN} Do

        If *r.key* (i.e., $A_i Pa(A_i)$) is in $T_{\text{JPD}}.row$ Then

        //Each *row* in T_{JPD} corresponds to a possible value of the
combination of concerned variables with respect to the MB of the
target user node

            Emit $\langle row, P(A_i Pa(A_i)) \rangle$ //Stored in T_{JPD}

        End If

    End For

Reduce1(*key, values*)

    String *key*: row in T_{JPD}

    Iterator *values*: current list

    result←1

    For each value *v* in *values* Do

        result←*result*×*ParseDouble*(*v*)

    End For

    Emit $\langle row, \ result \rangle$

Reduce2(*key, values*)

    String *key*: row in T_{JPD}

    Iterator *values*: current list

    result←0

    For each value *v* in *values* Do

        result←*result*+*ParseDouble*(*v*)

    End For

    Emit $\langle row, \ result \rangle$

---

of users. In the algorithm, `map` functions are used to find the entries in T_{UBN} concerned in the current probabilistic inference task; `reduce1` functions are used to obtain the JPD for each possible value of the combination of concerned variables, and `reduce2` functions are used to obtain the required marginal probabilities by adding the concerned JPDs.

Example 4.5. Upon the UBN in Fig. 4.1 and T_{UBN} in Table 4.1, we consider the computation of the indirect similarity degree of A_2 to A_1 from the perspective of probabilistic inferences, $Sim_Q(A_1, A_2)$, where A_1 is the target user.

(1) According to Eq. (4.5), we know $Sim_Q(A_1, A_2) = P(A_1 = 1 | A_2 = 1) = \frac{P(A_1=1, A_2=1)}{P(A_2=1)}$. Meanwhile, $(A_1 = 1, \ A_2 = 1, \ A_3 = 1)$ and $(A_1 = 1, \ A_2 = 1, \ A_3 = 0)$ are included in T_{JPD}, since $MB(A_1) = \{A_2, A_3\}$.

(2) Taking $P(A_1 = 1, A_2 = 1)$ as an example, we compare the records in T_{UBN} with those in T_{JPD}, respectively. As for $A_1 = 1$, there are two rows in T_{JPD} including $A_1 = 1$. Thus, we can obtain $\langle (A_1 = 1, A_2 = 1, A_3 = 1), 0.71 \rangle$ and $\langle (A_1 = 1, \ A_2 = 1, \ A_3 = 0), 0.71 \rangle$ by the map functions in Algorithm 4.2. Analogously, we can obtain $\langle (A_1 = 1, A_2 = 1, \ A_3 = 1), 0.8 \rangle$ and $\langle (A_1 = 1, \ A_2 = 1, \ A_3 = 0), 0.8 \rangle$ for $(A_1 = 1, \ A_2 = 1)$, as well as $\langle (A_1 = 1, \ A_2 = 1, \ A_3 = 1), 0.6 \rangle$ and $\langle (A_1 = 1, \ A_2 = 1, \ A_3 = 0), 0.5 \rangle$ for $(A_3 = 1, A_1 = 1)$.

(3) By the `reduce1` functions in Algorithm 4.2, we can obtain $P(A_1 = 1, A_2 = 1, A_3 = 1) = 0.71 \times 0.8 \times 0.6 = 0.341$, $P(A_1 = 1, A_2 = 1, A_3 = 0) = 0.71 \times 0.8 \times 0.5 = 0.284$.

(4) By the `reduce2` functions in Algorithm 4.2, we can obtain $P(A_1 = 1, A_2 = 1, A_3 = 1) = P(A_1 = 1, A_2 = 1, A_3 = 1) + P(A_1 = 1, A_2 = 1, A_3 = 0) = 0.625$. Analogously, we can obtain $P(A_2 = 1)$ and $P(A_1 = 1 | A_2 = 1)$.

4.4.3 Combining structure-based and inference-based indirect similarities

To achieve the ultimate indirect similarity degree of user X to A, we simply combine the indirect similarity degrees based on UBN's graphical structure and those based on UBN's probabilistic inference as follows:

$$Sim(A, X) = \alpha \cdot Sim_S(A, X) + \beta \cdot Sim_Q(A, X), \quad 0 \le \alpha, \beta \le 1$$

(4.6)

where α is the weight of the structure-based indirect similarity and β is that of the probabilistic inference-based indirect similarity.

In the following, we mainly discuss the theoretical properties of $\text{Sim}(A, X)$ in Eq. (4.6) to guarantee its effectiveness and applicability as a similarity measure between users. It can be seen that $\text{Sim}_S(B, A)$ may not equal $\text{Sim}_S(B, A)$, and $\text{Sim}_Q(A, B)$ may not equal $\text{Sim}_Q(B, A)$ as well. This is consistent with the discussion in Section 4.1 that the similarity between users is orientation aware. More importantly, the similarity measure in Eq. (4.6) can provide a comparable basis for finding similar users, since the similarity degree is order-preserving and the specific sequence of similar users can be obtained regardless of the order of users in U. The above conclusion is given in Theorem 4.1 as follows.

Theorem 4.1. *For any three users (say A, B, C) in U, we suppose $B, C \in \text{MB}(A)$. If $\text{Sim}(A, B) > \text{Sim}(A, C)$ under $U_1 = \{A, B, C\}$, then $\text{Sim}(A, B) > \text{Sim}(A, C)$ still holds under $U_2 = \{A, C, B\}$.*

Proof. According to Eq. (4.6), we have

$$\text{Sim}(A, B) = \alpha \cdot \text{Sim}_S(A, B) + \beta \cdot \text{Sim}_Q(A, B)$$

$$\text{Sim}(A, C) = \alpha \cdot \text{Sim}_S(A, C) + \beta \cdot \text{Sim}_Q(A, C)$$

According to Eqs. (4.4) and (4.5), we have

$$\text{Sim}(A, B) = \alpha \cdot \frac{\log |E_M(A, B)|}{\log |E_S(A)|} + \beta \cdot P(A = 1 \mid B = 1)$$

$$\text{Sim}(A, C) = \alpha \cdot \frac{\log |E_M(A, C)|}{\log |E_S(A)|} + \beta \cdot P(A = 1 \mid C = 1)$$

B lies before C in U_1, and thus B is a parent or ancestor node of C in the UBN, which means that there exists the substructure $B \rightarrow C$ or $B \rightarrow \cdots \rightarrow C$. If B is a parent of C, then $C \in \text{MB}(B)$ and $B \in \text{MB}(C)$. Analogously, C lies before B in U_2, and thus C is a parent or ancestor node of B in the UBN, which means that there exists the substructure $C \rightarrow B$ or $C \rightarrow \cdots \rightarrow B$. If C is a parent of B, then $B \in \text{MB}(C)$ and $C \in \text{MB}(B)$. This means that $\text{MB}(B)$ and $\text{MB}(C)$ are identical either under U_1 or U_2, and thus $|E_M(A, B)|$ is identical to $|E_M(A, C)|$. Thus, to prove that $\text{Sim}(A, B) > \text{Sim}(A, C)$ holds under U_1, and then it also holds under U_2, is to prove that $P(A = 1 \mid B = 1) > (A = 1 \mid C = 1)$

holds under U_1, and then it also holds under U_2. For simplification of discussion and without loss of generality, we consider B as a parent of C under U_1 and C as a parent of B under U_2.

By Eq. (4.5) and under U_1, we have

$$P(A = 1 \mid B = 1)$$
$$= P(A = 1)P(B = 1 \mid A = 1)P(C = 0 \mid A = 1, B = 1)$$
$$+ P(A = 1)P(B = 1 \mid A = 1)P(C = 1 \mid A = 1, B = 1)$$
$$P(A = 1 \mid C = 1)$$
$$= P(A = 1)P(B = 0 \mid A = 1)P(C = 1 \mid A = 1, B = 0)$$
$$+ P(A = 1)P(B = 1 \mid A = 1)P(C = 1 \mid A = 1, B = 1)$$

Since $P(A = 1 \mid B = 1) > P(A = 1 \mid C = 1)$, we have

$$P(A = 1)P(B = 1 \mid A = 1)P(C = 0 \mid A = 1, B = 1)$$
$$> P(A = 1)P(B = 0 \mid A = 1)P(C = 1 \mid A = 1, B = 1)$$

That is,

$$\frac{P(C = 0, A = 1, B = 1)}{P(A = 1)} > \frac{P(C = 1, A = 1, B = 1)}{P(A = 1)}$$

Thus, we have

$$P(C = 0, B = 1 \mid A = 1) > P(C = 1, B = 0 \mid A = 1) \qquad (4.7)$$

By Eq. (4.5) and under U_2, we know

$$P(A = 1 \mid B = 1)$$
$$= P(A = 1)P(B = 1 \mid A = 1, C = 1)P(C = 1 \mid A = 1)$$
$$+ P(A = 1)P(B = 1 \mid A = 1, C = 0)P(C = 0 \mid A = 1)$$
$$P(A = 1 \mid C = 1)$$
$$= P(A = 1)P(B = 1 \mid A = 1, C = 1)P(C = 1 \mid A = 1)$$
$$+ P(A = 1)P(B = 0 \mid A = 1, C = 0)P(C = 1 \mid A = 1)$$

We know

$$P(B = 1 \mid A = 1, C = 0)P(C = 0 \mid A = 1)$$
$$= \frac{P(B = 1, A = 1, C = 0)}{P(A = 1, C = 0)} \frac{P(C = 0, A = 1)}{P(A = 1)}$$
$$= P(B = 1, C = 0 \mid A = 1)$$

Analogously, we know $P(B = 1 \mid A = 1, C = 1)P(C = 1 \mid A = 1) = P(B = 0, C = 1 \mid A = 1)$. By Eq. (4.7), $P(A = 1 \mid B = 1) > P(A = 1 \mid C = 1)$ also holds under U_2.

Thus, we can conclude that $\text{Sim}(A, B) > \text{Sim}(A, C)$ holds under U_2.   □

4.5 Experimental Results

4.5.1 *Experiment setup*

The experiment platform was established upon Hadoop [35] including six machines with Pentium(R) Dual-Core CPU E5700@3.00GHz@3.01GHz and 2GB main memory. The HDFS cluster includes one NameNode and six DataNodes, on each of which the version of Hadoop, Linux, and Java is 0.20.2, Ubuntu 10.04, and JDK 1.6, respectively. All the codes were written in JAVA.

We generated our test data from the DBLP datasets [6] that provide bibliographic information related to computer science journals and proceedings in the areas like database, network, and machine learning. In our experiment, we adopted the records of coauthor relationships as social behavioral interactions and carried out the experiments on the extracted DBLP dataset containing 1552402 authors of 1.3GB size to test the efficiency and effectiveness of UBN construction and inferences, as well as the effectiveness of the UBN-based user similarities. Meanwhile, we also generated our test data from real social media of Sina Weibo, and adopted the records of forward/comment/like relationships of 10000 Weibo users as behavioral interactions. Further, we tested the effectiveness of the UBN-based user similarities upon the Sina Weibo dataset.

In our experiments, the number of map tasks is identical to that of CPUs on each machine by default, and the number of reduce tasks is set to one. The execution time of map and reduce tasks, as well as the algorithm's total execution time is obtained directly from the records of JobTrackers.

In Section 4.5.2, we first tested the execution time, speedup, and parallel efficiency of the MapReduce-based algorithms for UBN construction and UBN inferences, respectively, upon the DBLP test data. In Section 4.5.3, we compared the results of user similarities discovered by our proposed UBN's inference algorithm, the general BN's inference algorithm [7, 25, 26], and the straightforward statistics upon the social behavioral interactions of the DBLP dataset. In Section 4.5.4, we finally tested the effectiveness of the discovered similarities by comparing the results obtained by our method and those by the known $L1$-Norm and Cosine metrics [10] upon the DBLP and Sina Weibo datasets.

4.5.2 *Efficiency of UBN construction and inferences*

4.5.2.1 *Efficiency of UBN construction*

The total execution time of map tasks, reduce tasks, and HDFS start-up is called *total time* and abbreviated as TT. The execution time of map tasks and reduce tasks (except that of the HDFS start-up) is called *algorithm time* and abbreviated as AT. From Algorithm 4.1 given in Section 4.3.2, we know that the efficiency of UBN's DAG construction is dependent on the size of behavioral interactions, the number of UBN nodes (i.e., users), and the number of DataNodes in the HDFS.

First, we tested TT of Algorithm 4.1 for constructing the UBN's DAG with the increase of behavioral interactions under various numbers of DataNodes, shown in Fig. 4.3. It can be seen that TT of UBN's DAG construction is increased with the increase of behavioral interactions under various numbers of DataNodes. The more the DataNodes, the more slowly TT is increased when the size of the behavioral interactions is larger than 152.6 MB. TT is increased sharply by the algorithm's sequential execution with just one DataNode when the size of behavioral interactions is larger than 830.5 MB. This means that the scalability of our method for UBN's DAG construction can be achieved by adding DataNodes appropriately for massively increased behavioral interactions.

Then, we compared TT and AT of Algorithm 4.1 with the increase of nodes in the UBN under six DataNodes, shown in Fig. 4.4. Meanwhile,

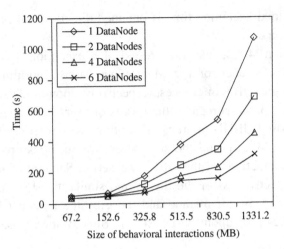

Fig. 4.3. TT of Algorithm 4.1 with the increase of social behavioral interactions under various numbers of DataNodes.

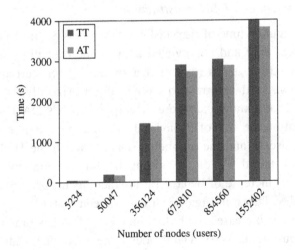

Fig. 4.4. TT and AT of Algorithm 4.1 with the increase of UBN nodes (users).

we compared TT and AT of Algorithm 4.1 under various numbers of DataNodes for the UBN with 1552402 nodes, shown in Fig. 4.5. It can be seen that the proportion of the start-up time is slightly increased for extra communications with the increase of nodes in UBN, and the more the nodes, the less the proportion, which also holds with the

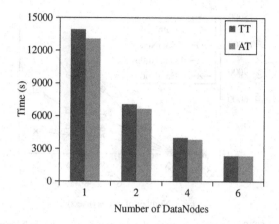

Fig. 4.5. TT and AT of Algorithm 4.1 with various numbers of DataNodes.

increase of DataNodes. This means that the efficiency of Algorithm 4.1 is mainly dependent on the execution time of the *map* and *reduce* functions themselves. As well, both TT and AT are increased slowly even when the nodes are more than 356124, which further verifies the scalability of Algorithm 4.1.

We also tested TT of UBN's CPT computation with the increase of social behavioral interactions under various numbers of DataNodes, shown in Fig. 4.6. Compared to the results in Fig. 4.4, we can conclude that UBN's CPT computation can be fulfilled slightly faster than DAG construction for specific UBNs, which is consistent with the characteristics of general BNs. TT of CPT computation is increased slowly with the increase of the number of nodes under the HDFS with more than one DataNode. Thus, both the DAG construction and CPT computation are scalable with respect to the size of social behavioral interactions and the number of the concerned users.

Speedup is defined as the ratio of the time of parallel execution and that of sequential execution. It is used to measure the times by which the parallel algorithm improves the corresponding sequential algorithm. Under various numbers of DataNodes in the HDFS, we tested the speedup of Algorithm 4.1 for constructing UBN's DAG with the increase of social behavioral interactions, shown in Fig. 4.7. It can be seen that the larger the size of the behavioral interactions under the specific

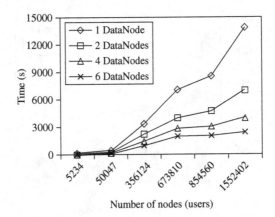

Fig. 4.6. TT of CPT computation with the increase of social behavioral interactions under various numbers of DataNodes.

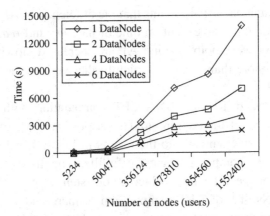

Fig. 4.7. Speedup of Algorithm 4.1 with the increase of social behavioral interactions under various numbers of DataNodes.

numbered DataNodes, the larger the speedup, and meanwhile, the more the DataNodes in the HDFS for specific sized behavioral interactions, the larger the speedup.

Parallel efficiency is defined as the ratio of the speedup and the number of processors in the system (referred to as DataNodes in our experiments). Under various numbers of DataNodes, we tested the parallel efficiency of Algorithm 4.1 with the increase of social behavioral interactions, shown in Fig. 4.8. It can be seen that the parallel efficiency

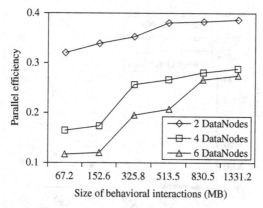

Fig. 4.8. Parallel efficiency of Algorithm 4.1 with the increase of social behavioral interactions under various numbers of DataNodes.

is increased with the increase of behavioral interactions under specific numbered DataNodes, but the increase is gradually slower and slower when the size of the behavioral interactions is larger and larger. The parallel efficiency under 2, 4, and 6 DataNodes tends to be fixed when the size of behavioral interactions is larger than 67.2 MB, 325.8 MB, and 830.5 MB, respectively. On the other hand, the parallel efficiency is decreased with the increase of DataNodes with respect to the specific sized behavioral interactions, since the more the DataNodes, the higher the costs including physical resources and communications of the HDFS. This means that the HDFS for UBN construction should be established by considering the size of behavioral interactions and the trade-off between speedup and relevant costs.

4.5.2.2 *Efficiency of UBN inferences*

On the one hand, according to the comparisons between TT and AT of UBN construction, the efficiency of Algorithm 4.2 is also mainly dependent on the execution of the map and reduce functions (i.e., AT). On the other hand, it is known that the efficiency of BN inferences mainly depend on the number of nodes in the BN. Thus, to test the efficiency of Algorithm 4.2 for MapReduce-based UBN inferences, we recorded AT of the algorithm under various numbers of DataNodes with the increase of nodes in UBN, shown in Fig. 4.9. It is straightforward that

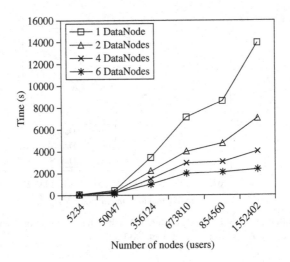

Fig. 4.9. AT of Algorithm 4.2 with the increase of UBN nodes (users).

AT is increased slowly with the increase of UBN nodes under various numbers of DataNodes, and the more the DataNodes, the more slowly the increase of AT. It can also be seen that the execution time of UBN inferences is less than that of UBN's DAG construction but close to that of UBN's CPT computation with the same numbers of UBN nodes and DataNodes, which is consistent with the characteristics of general BN's learning and inferences.

Then, under various numbers of DataNodes in the HDFS, we tested the speedup and parallel efficiency of Algorithm 4.2 with the increase of UBN nodes, shown in Figs. 4.10 and 4.11, respectively. It can be seen that the tendency of the increase of speedup and parallel efficiency of Algorithm 4.2 are similar to those of Algorithm 4.1 with the increase of nodes in UBN. Under the situation with the same number of DataNodes, the more the nodes, the closer the speedup to the ideal situation. When the number of nodes is increased from 5234 to 1552401, the speedup of Algorithm 4.2 is increased from 1.441 to 5.521, close to 6 as the ideal value under six DataNodes. Meanwhile, with the same number of UBN nodes, the more the DataNodes, the larger the speedup, and the speedup is increased from 1.961 to 5.521 when the DataNodes are increased from two to six with 1552402 UBN nodes. As well, we note

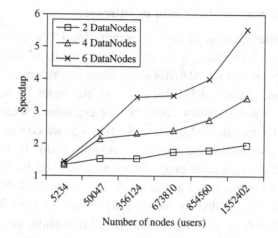

Fig. 4.10. Speedup of Algorithm 4.2 with the increase of UBN nodes (users).

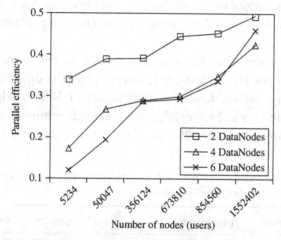

Fig. 4.11. Parallel efficiency of Algorithm 4.2 with the increase of UBN nodes (users).

that both the speedup and parallel efficiency of Algorithm 4.2 are higher than those of Algorithm 4.1 with the same numbers of UBN nodes and DataNodes, which means that the MapReduce algorithm can be well suitable for the probabilistic inferences of large-scale UBNs. Thus, we conclude that Algorithm 4.2 can be efficiently used for discovering the similarities (executed several times) between users upon the constructed UBN (executed just once).

4.5.3 *Effectiveness of UBN and its inferences*

To test the effectiveness of the algorithms for UBN construction and its probabilistic inferences, we compared the results of user similarities discovered by our proposed UBN's inference algorithm and the general BN's inference algorithm [7, 25, 26] with the same UBN, as well as the straightforward statistics upon the corresponding social behavioral interactions. By the method given in Section 4.3, we constructed a UBN with 100 nodes (users), and then we randomly chose 10 pairs of users to compute the conditional probabilities as described by Eq. (4.5). We obtained the inference result as the similarity degree of each pair of users by Algorithm 4.2 and that by Netica [25] (a well-adopted BN inference tool), denoted as I_{UBN} and I_{BN}, respectively. Meanwhile, we computed the probability from the behavioral interactions by straightforward statistics, denoted as I_{STA}. We used $Error_{UBN-BN}$ and $Error_{UBN-STA}$ to denote the difference (i.e., absolute of the minus value) between I_{UBN} and I_{BN} and that between I_{UBN} and I_{STA}, respectively. The comparisons are shown in Table 4.2.

It can be seen that the maximal, minimal, and average value of $Error_{UBN-BN}$ are 1%, 0, and 0.5%, respectively. The difference between I_{UBN} and I_{BN} derives from the introduction of MB in Algorithm 4.2 for UBN inferences. Meanwhile, the maximal, minimal, and average value of $Error_{UBN-STA}$ are 2%, 0, and 1.2%, respectively. $Error_{UBN-BN}$

Table 4.2. User similarities obtained by Algorithm 4.2, general BN's inference algorithm, and straightforward statistics.

No. of user pairs	I_{UBN}	I_{BN}	I_{TA}	$Error_{UBN-BN}$	$Error_{UBN-STA}$
#1	0.64	0.64	0.66	0	0.02
#2	0.38	0.38	0.391	0.004	0.011
#3	0.55	0.548	0.53	0.002	0.02
#4	0.91	0.909	0.913	0.001	0.003
#5	0.88	0.861	0.88	0.019	0
#6	0.73	0.728	0.72	0.002	0.01
#7	0.92	0.93	0.895	0.01	0.025
#8	0.81	0.817	0.819	0.007	0.009
#9	0.66	0.66	0.648	0	0.012
#10	0.85	0.855	0.86	0.005	0.01

is less than $Error_{UBN-STA}$, since the UBN is constructed according to the given order of users. The above results show that the inference results obtained by Algorithm 4.2 are both basically equal to those obtained by the general BN's inference algorithm and quite close to those obtained by straightforward statistics from behavioral interactions. Thus, the algorithms for UBN construction and inferences proposed in this chapter can be effectively used to represent and infer the dependence relationships as well as the corresponding uncertainties implied in social behavioral interactions.

4.5.4 *Effectiveness of UBN-based user similarity*

To test the effectiveness of the discovered user similarities, we compared the results obtained by our method and those by the known $L1$-Norm and Cosine metrics [10], respectively, defined as follows:

$$L1(A, X) = \frac{|S_a \cap S_b|}{|S_a| \cdot |S_b|}, \ \cos(A, X) = \frac{|S_a \cap S_b|}{\sqrt{|S_a| \cdot |S_b|}}$$

where S_A and S_X is the set of users directly connected to A and X, respectively, in the UBN.

Upon the UBN constructed from the DBLP test data, we randomly chose a target user and 10 possible similar users, denoted as A and $X_1, X_2, \ldots, X_{10}$, respectively, and then computed the similarity degrees of these 10 users to the target user. For each pair of users, we obtained the similarity degrees by Eq. (4.6), those by the above L1-Norm and Cosine metrics, respectively, shown in Table 4.3. It is clear that the comparable tendency of similarity degrees of the 10 pairs of users by the three metrics is consistent, which means that our UBN-based method is effective from the perspective of discovering similar users. Furthermore, it can be seen that both $Sim(A, X_7)$ and $Sim(A, X_8)$ are equal to 0.039 by $L1$-Norm and 0.234 by Cosine, but $Sim(A, X_7)$ and $Sim(A, X_8)$ are comparable with different similarity degrees (0.128 and 0.114, respectively) by our method. From this point of view, our method can provide a finer granularity than the $L1$-Norm and Cosine metrics, since the results can also be comparably differentiated by our method even for the equal results by the $L1$-Norm and Cosine metrics.

Table 4.3. Similarity degrees by UBN-based, $L1$-Norm, and Cosine metrics upon DBLP test data.

	UBN-based	$L1$-Norm	Cosine
$Sim(A, X_1)$	0.686	0.074	0.805
$Sim(A, X_2)$	0.541	0.063	0.626
$Sim(A, X_3)$	0.501	0.062	0.592
$Sim(A, X4)$	0.474	0.039	0.28
$Sim(A, X_5)$	0.334	0.041	0.263
$Sim(A, X_6)$	0.257	0.039	0.276
$Sim(A, X_7)$	0.128	0.039	0.243
$Sim(A, X_8)$	0.114	0.039	0.243
$Sim(A, X_9)$	0.113	0.031	0.223
$Sim(A, X_{10})$	0.101	0.029	0.171

Table 4.4. Similarity degrees by UBN-based, $L1$-Norm, and Cosine metrics upon Sina Weibo test data.

	UBN-based	$L1$-Norm	Cosine
$Sim(A, X_1)$	0.534	0.055	0.716
$Sim(A, X_2)$	0.502	0.052	0.704
$Sim(A, X_3)$	0.403	0.041	0.625
$Sim(A, X_4)$	0.338	0.041	0.603
$Sim(A, X_5)$	0.305	0.036	0.598
$Sim(A, X_6)$	0.213	0.034	0.483
$Sim(A, X_7)$	0.211	0.034	0.482
$Sim(A, X_8)$	0.105	0.021	0.357
$Sim(A, X_9)$	0.102	0.019	0.357
$Sim(A, X_{10})$	0.009	0.018	0.231

Further, we constructed the UBN from the 80% Sina Weibo test data by the algorithm proposed in Section 4.3. Analogously, we randomly chose a target user and 10 possible similar users, and the similarity degrees obtained by Eq. (4.6), those by $L1$-Norm and Cosine are shown in Table 4.4. The above conclusion on generated social media also holds for discovering similar users from real social media. This means that our method can be used to discover and rank similar users effectively.

Then, we chose the users (i.e., nodes in the UBN) whose behavioral interactions exist in the left 20% Sina Weibo test data, and obtained the

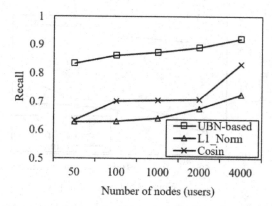

Fig. 4.12. Recall by UBN-based, L1-Norm, and Cosine metrics under various numbers of UBN nodes (users).

similar users for each one by straightforward search if there is direct forward/comment/like relationship, denoted as CS and called 1-order similarity. At the same time, we obtained the similar users for each one by UBN, L1-Norm, and Cosine, respectively, upon which we tested the recall (the ratio of discovered similar users to those in CS), respectively, under various numbers of UBN nodes, shown in Fig. 4.12. It can be seen that the recall of our UBN-based method is higher than that by L1-Norm and Cosine metrics, and the more the UBN nodes the higher the recall.

In the following, we tested the effectiveness of our method for discovering indirectly similar users by considering recall with respect to the 1-order, 2-order, and 3-order similarities. The 2-order CS of user A consists of the directly similar users of A (denoted as S_A) and those directly similar to the users in S_A, and the 3-order CS can be obtained analogously. We tested the recall of 2-order similarities by UBN, L1-Norm, and Cosine, respectively, under various numbers of UBN nodes, shown in Fig. 4.13. As well, we tested the recall of 1-order, 2-order, and 3-order similarities by our UBN-based method under various numbers of UBN nodes, shown in Fig. 4.14. It can be seen that the 2-order recall of our UBN-based method is much higher than that by L1-Norm and Cosine metrics. The higher the order, the larger the difference between the recall of our method and those of the other two metrics. Meanwhile, the higher the order, the larger the recall of our

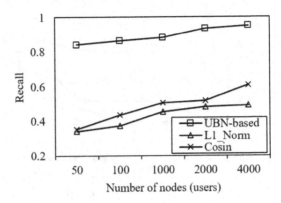

Fig. 4.13. 2-order recall by UBN-based, $L1$-Norm, and Cosine metrics under various numbers of UBN nodes (users).

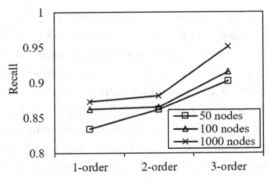

Fig. 4.14. 1-order, 2-order, and 3-order recall by UBN-based metric under various numbers of UBN nodes (users).

UBN-based method, and this tendency is more and more clear with the increase of UBN nodes. This means that our UBN-based method can make the indirectly similar users be discovered effectively, especially for large-scale UBNs.

4.6 Summary

To discover user similarities implied in massive social behavioral interactions, this chapter proposed the BN-based method for describing the dependencies among social users and that for measuring the similarity degrees from the perspectives of UBN's graphical structure and probabilistic inferences. By our method, the global similarities between users can be represented by a graph model to improve the linear or if-then formatted representation, where the similarities between users are obtained from all relevant social behavioral interactions. Then, the orientation-aware user similarities with uncertainties can be discovered by a finer granularity than the classic methods.

References

1. Akcora, C., Carminati, B., and Ferrari, E. User similarities on social networks. *Journal of Social Network Analysis and Mining*, 2013, **3**(3): 475–495.
2. Anderson, A., Huttenlocher, D., Kleinberg, J., and Leskovec, J. Effects of user similarity in social media. *Proc. WSDM*, 2012, pp. 703–712.
3. Bhattacharyya, P., Gerg, A., and Wu, S. Analysis of user keyword similarity in online social networks. *Social Network Analysis and Mining*, 2011, **1**(3): 143–158.
4. Bringmann, B., Berlingerio, M., Bonchi, F., and Gionis, A. Learning and predicting the evolution of social networks. *Journal of Intelligent Systems*, 2010, **25**(4): 26–35.
5. Burgess, J. and Green, J. *YouTube: Online Video and Participatory Culture.* Polity Press, 2013.
6. Crandall, D., Cosley, D., Huttenlocher, D., Kleinberg, J., and Suri, S. Feedback effects between similarity and social influence in online communities. *Proc. SIGKDD*, 2008, pp. 160–168.
7. Cooper, G. The computational complexity of probabilistic inference using Bayesian belief networks. *Artificial Intelligence*, 1990, **42**(2–3): 393–405.
8. DBLP Datasets. http://dblp.uni-trier.de/xml/, 2015.
9. Dean, J. and Ghemawat, S. MapReduce: A flexible data processing tool. *Communications of the ACM*, 2010, **53**(1): 72–77.
10. Deshpande, M. and Karypis, G. Item-based top-*n* recommendation algorithms. *ACM Transactions on Information Systems*, 2004, **22**(1): 143–177.
11. Gomez-Marin, A., Paton, J., Kampff, A., Costa, R., and Mainen, Z. Big behavioral data: Psychology, ethology and the foundations of neuroscience. *Nature Neuroscience*, 2014, **17**: 1455–1462.
12. Gong, N., Xu, W., Huang, L., Mittal, P., Stefanov, E., Sekar, V., and Song, D. Evolution of social-attribute networks: Measurements, modeling, and implications using google+. *Proc. IM*, 2012, pp. 131–144.

13. He, L., Liu, B., Hu, D., Wen, Y., Wan, M., and Long, J. Motor imagery EEG signals analysis on Bayesian network with Gaussian distribution. *Neurocomputing*, 2016, **188**: 217–224.

14. Heckerman, D., Geiger, D., and Chickering, D. Learning Bayesian networks: The combination of knowledge and statistic data. *Machine Learning*, 1995, **20**: 197–243.

15. Jiang, M., Gui, P., Wang, F., Zhu, W., and Yang, S. Scalable recommendation with social contextual information. *IEEE Transactions on Knowledge and Data Engineering*, 2014, **26**(11): 2789–2802.

16. Kleinberg, J. *Small-World Phenomena and the Dynamics of Information. Advances in Neural Information Processing Systems*, MIT Press, Cambridge, 2001, pp. 431–438.

17. Liu, A., Hu, Z., Mian, A., Tian, H., and Zhu, X. A new user similarity model to improve the accuracy of collaborative filtering. *Knowledge-Based Systems*, 2014, **56**: 156–166.

18. Liu, L., Zhu, F., Zhang, L., and Yang, S. A probabilistic graphical model for topic and preference discovery on social media. *Neurocomputing*, 2012, **95**: 78–88.

19. Ma, N., Xia, Y., and Prasanna, V. Parallel exact inference on multicore using mapreduce. *Proc. SBAC-PAD*, 2012, pp. 187–194.

20. McCallum, A., Corrada-Emmanuel, A., and Wang, X. Topic and role discovery in social networks. *Proc. IJCAI*, 2005, pp. 786–791.

21. Metwally, A. and Faloutsos, C. V-smart-join: A scalable MapReduce framework for all-pair similarity joins of multisets and vectors. *PVLDB*, 2012, **5**(8): 704–715.

22. Nakatsuji, M., Fujiwara, Y., Uchiyama, T., and Fujimura, K. User similarity from linked Texonomies: Subjective assessments of items. *Proc. IJCAI*, 2011, pp. 2305–2311.

23. Nillius, P., Sullivan, J., and Carlsson, S. Multi-target tracking-linking identities using Bayesian network inference. *Proc. CVPR*, 2006, pp. 2187–2194.

24. Nisgav, A. and Patt-Shamir, B. Finding similar users in social networks. *Proc. SPAA*, 2009, pp. 169–177.

25. Norsys Software Corp. Netica Bayesian network development software, http://www.norsys.com, 2015.

26. Pearl, J. *Probabilistic Reasoning in Intelligent Systems: Networks of Plausible Inference*. Morgan Kaufmann, 1988.

27. Piwowarski, B., Dupret, G., and Jones, R. Mining user web search activities with layeres Bayesian Networks or how to capture a click in its context. *Proc. WSDM*, 2009, pp. 162–171.

28. Qian, J., Lv, P., Yue, X., Liu, C., and Jing, Z. Hierarchical attribute reduction algorithms for big data using MapReduce. *Knowledge-Based Systems*, 2015, **73**: 18–31.

29. Rafter, M. 10 Companies to watch: Epinions.com. *The Industry Standard Magazine*, 2000.

30. Ren, Z., Yang, Y., Bao, F., Deng, Y., and Dai, H. Directed adaptive graphical lasso for causality inferences. *Neurocomputing*, 2016, **173**: 1989–1994.

31. Russell, S., Norvig, P., Canny, J., Malik, J., and Edwards, D. *Artificial Intelligence: A Modern Approach* (3rd edn), Englewood Cliffs: Prentice Hall, 1995.

32. Schall, D. Link prediction in directed social networks. *Social Network Analysis and Mining*, 2014, **4**(1), DOI: 10.1007/s13278-014-0157-9.

33. Schelter, S., Boden, C., and Markl, V. Scalable similarity-based neighborhood methods with MapReduce. *Proc. RecSys*, 2012, pp. 163–170.

34. Velardi, P., Navigli, R., Cucchiarelli, A., and D'Antonio, F. A new content-based model for social network analysis. *Proc. SC*, 2008, pp. 18–25.

35. White, T. *Hadoop: The Definitive Guide*, O'Reilly Media, Inc., 2009.

36. Xu, K., Zou, K., Huang, Y., Yu, X., and Zhang, X. Mining community and inferring friendship in mobile social networks. *Neurocomputing*, 2016, **174**: 650–616.

37. Yang, X., Guo, Y., and Liu, Y. Bayesian-inference based recommendation in online social networks. *IEEE Transactions on Parallel and Distributed Systems*, 2013, **24**(4): 642–651.

38. Ying, J., Lu, E., Lee, W., Weng, T., and Tsang, V. Mining user similarity from semantic trajectories. *Proc. SIGSPATIAL*, 2010, pp. 19–26.

39. Yue, K., Fang, Q., Wang, X., Li, J., and Liu, W. A parallel and incremental approach for data-intensive learning of Bayesian networks. *IEEE Transactions on Cybernetics*, 2015, **45**(12): 2890–2904.

40. Yue, K., Wu, H., Fu, X., Xu, J., Yin, Z., and Liu, W. A data-intensive approach for discovering user similarities in social behavioral interactions based on the bayesian network. *Neurocomputing*, 2017, **219**: 364–375.

41. Zhang, K., Downey, D., Chen, Z., Xie, Y., Cheng, Y., Agrawal, A., Liao, W., and Choudhary, A. A probabilistic graphical model for brand reputation assessment in social networks. *Proc. ASONAM*, 2013, pp. 223–230.

Chapter 5

Associative Categorization of Frequent Patterns in Social Media Based on Markov Network

Discovering the hierarchical structures of different classes of object behaviors can satisfy the requirements of various degrees of abstraction in association analysis, behavior modeling, data preprocessing, pattern recognition, and decision-making, etc. In this chapter, we call this process as associative categorization, which is different from classic clustering, associative classification, and associative clustering. Focusing on representing the associations of behaviors and corresponding uncertainties, we give the method for constructing a Markov network (MN) from the results of frequent pattern mining, called item-associative Markov network (IAMN), where nodes and edges represent the frequent patterns and their associations, respectively. We further discuss the properties of a probabilistic graphical model to guarantee the IAMN's correctness theoretically. Then, we adopt the concept of chordal graph to reflect the closeness of nodes in the IAMN. Adopting the algorithm for constructing join trees from an MN, we give the algorithm for IAMN-based associative categorization by hierarchical bottom-up aggregations. Experimental results show the effectiveness, efficiency, and correctness of our method.

5.1 Motivation and Basic Idea

With the rapid development and wide application of Web 2.0, e-commence, and social network, more and more data are generated by the behaviors of Internet users instead of classical database transactions. To depict the inherence of a certain user, the data generated by his behaviors play an important role or an even more important one than those describing his own properties, since user behaviors reflect the associations between one user and the others. Generally speaking, realistic objects are described by their behaviors probably associated in real-world applications, although they may be mutually independent to some certain extent if we just consider their own attributes.

Discovering different classes (also called groups) of object behaviors is useful for association analysis, behavior modeling, data preprocessing, pattern recognition, and decision-making, etc. [20]. Moreover, discovering the hierarchical structures of different granularities of behavior classes can satisfy the requirements of various degrees of abstraction. For example, the relevant classes of participants can be discovered by means of grouping their behaviors in coauthored publications or co-operated projects. Initially, suppose we obtain the classes of papers corresponding to the behaviors (e.g., keywords) in these papers: *association rule* (c_1), *graph mining* (c_2), *classification* (c_3), and *probabilistic graph model* (c_4). Then, by the hierarchical manner, we can obtain the following classes with larger granularities: *association rule mining* (c_1') composed of c_1 and c_2, *uncertain knowledge* (c_2') composed of c_2 and c_4, and *associative classification* (c_3') composed of c_1 and c_3. Similarly, we can obtain the higher-level classes by gradual bottom-up aggregation. In this chapter, we call the above process of discovering different classes based on the associations of object behaviors as associative categorization, by which the hierarchical classes can be generated pertinent to the practical requirements of various abstraction degrees.

First, from the perspective of representing behavior associations, it is well known that frequent patterns (i.e., items) and the consequent association rules, originated by Agrawal *et al.* [1], are effectively used to search for their interesting association relationships from the given database transactions. Many researchers focused on mining frequent patterns and association rules due to their practical characteristics and straightforward expressions for behavior associations [10, 11]. Association rules can be discovered from frequent patterns in the academic paradigm of data mining research [11]. However, complex associations among behaviors (i.e., frequent items) cannot be represented globally by means of $X \rightarrow Y$ manner, where X and Y are frequent itemsets. As well, the uncertainties of the association rules, measured by *confidence* and *support*, cannot be inferred, which is actually critical in decision-making on indirect behaviors. In particular, hierarchical mining and analysis of frequent patterns were also paid much attention [4, 6, 15, 28]. For example, Chaoji *et al.* [4] introduced pattern property hierarchy to define and mine different pattern types in the template library. Sudhamathy and Venkateswaran [28] gave the hierarchical frequent pattern mining approach suitable for analyzing Web log data and to predict useful information from the analyzed data. In these methods, the hierarchies or hierarchical properties of frequent patterns were defined or obtained on the basis of the link structure of expert knowledge and used to task partitioning or pattern visualization. This is different from the behavior categorization by generating classes level-by-level with gradually higher abstraction degrees.

Second, from the perspective of categorization, it is different from the classic clustering, associative classification, and associative clustering in data mining and machine learning paradigms. Clustering is the process of grouping data into classes or clusters so that objects within a cluster have high similarity in comparison to one another, but are very dissimilar to those in other clusters [11]. Various clustering methods have been proposed from various perspectives [8, 13, 23] based on the attributes of objects. However, the association among object behaviors has not been incorporated, although the ultimate classes actually depend on associations greatly.

Associative classification is a supervised classification approach by integrating association rule mining and classification. It is one of the current topics of great interest in data mining paradigm due to the high accuracy of classification. The selection of items and pruning, as well as the adaptive associative classification, were widely studied [2, 29, 30] and applied into realistic systems [21]. However, the associative categorization cannot be fulfilled by associative classification, due to the lack of the global representation of behavior associations and their uncertainties implied in association rules. As well, huge number of classification rules and the sensitivity to the minimal support have great influence on classification. Meanwhile, associative clustering considers the mutual dependencies among clusters of co-occurrence samples [16, 27].

Therefore, we can conclude that the classic clustering, associative classification, and associative clustering methods cannot be well suitable for the associative categorization problems that we will discuss in this chapter [19].

From the object-behavior point of view, it is natural to describe the relationships among behaviors by an undirected graph G, where the nodes represent behaviors and edges represent the connections among these behaviors. A subgraph of G, in which the interconnection among nodes is closed, can be looked upon as a larger node or higher-level abstraction of the component nodes in G. By regarding these subgraphs as classes of object behaviors, we can accordingly obtain a new undirected graph of nodes of larger granularities.

In particular, probabilistic graphical model (PGM), such as Markov network (MN) and Bayesian network (BN) [24, 31], is the well-adopted framework for representing probabilistic dependencies among random variables by a graphical model. PGM has been incorporated into frequent pattern mining [7, 9, 12]. For example, George *et al.* [9] used BN to encode the knowledge of how patterns change, and Hu *et al.* [12] used BN for frequent pattern interestingness computation and the corresponding pruning. Actually, both association rules and PGMs are effectively used to represent behavior associations or data dependencies, while PGMs focus on the causal inferences [3]. In recent years, PGMs and association rules have been integrated for data mining and knowledge discovery [10]. For example, Jaroszewicz *et al.* [14] adopted BN as the background knowledge and discovered unexpected patterns. Malhas *et al.* [22] gave the method for mining BN for interesting patterns expressed as association rules. Yu *et al.* [32] gave the product recommendation and associative classification, respectively, by incorporating BN and associations rules. These methods provide inspirations for our work to describe the behavior associations of frequent patterns by a global and quantitative manner. But none of them discussed the semantic equivalence between the representation of association rules and that of PGMs, which is really the basis for causal inferences of direct or latent dependencies of frequent patterns, as well as the ultimate associative categorization.

MN focuses on mutual dependence and BN focuses on causal relationships. With respect to associative categorization, we focus on MN-based mutual dependences of frequent patterns instead of the BN-based influences from a certain causal pattern to resulting ones. This means that

MN, as a knowledge base quantifying the probabilistic among random variables, is exactly effective enough to describe the associations among object behaviors as well as the corresponding uncertainties. To fulfill the MN-based associative categorization, we will have to address the following two problems:

(1) How to construct the MN to describe the behavior associations?
(2) How to derive the hierarchical classes starting from the initial MN?

For the first problem, we can learn an MN from the given database transactions directly by the existing dependency analysis and scoring-and-search methods [24, 31], but the computational complexities of these learning algorithms are very high for large datasets. On the other hand, frequent pattern mining has been pervasively studied and the theoretical achievements have been applied in real applications. Therefore, we consider making full use of the discovered frequent itemsets, instead of the original transactions, to derive the implied MN by incorporating the mechanisms of MN-based uncertainty representation into frequent patterns. Then, the complexity of MN construction will be reduced and the behavior associations of frequent patterns could be inferred for further use of analysis, prediction, decision-making, etc.

That frequent itemsets imply the information about probabilistic conditional independence is the important concept in association rule mining, which is the basis for constructing an MN from frequent patterns. We note that there may exist probabilistic conditional independences among frequent items in the same frequent itemset, whereas there may exist probabilistic dependences among frequent items in different itemsets. To build the linkage between the MN and the frequent itemsets, we first acquire the knowledge of probabilistic conditional independences from the frequent itemsets, and then propose the algorithm for constructing the MN as the graphical representation of these conditional independences. To guarantee the correctness of the constructed MN, we further give the theorems to show that the MN's topology reflects the probabilistic conditional independences implied in frequent itemsets theoretically.

For the second problem, an MN, as an undirected graph, can be transformed into a tree (called join tree) if the MN satisfies the specific condition (called chordal) [30], by which the hierarchical classes of nodes can be obtained. For this purpose, we first show the chordal characterizations of the MN based on which we discussed the hierarchical categorization approach.

Generally, the main contributions of this chapter can be summarized as follows:

- We state the associative categorization problem and define the item-associative Markov network (IAMN) to model the probabilistic conditional independences implied in frequent itemsets.
- We build the linkage between the MN and the frequent pattern, and give the algorithm for constructing an IAMN from frequent itemsets, so that the existing achievements of frequent pattern mining could be well incorporated into MN and uncertain knowledge representation could be incorporated into frequent patterns.
- We discuss the chordal characterizations of the IAMN, and then give the algorithm for hierarchical associative categorization.
- We conduct experiments to test the performance of the methods given in this chapter. Experimental results show the effectiveness, efficiency, and correctness of our methods.

The remainder of this chapter is organized as follows. In Section 5.2, we give the method to construct the item-associative MN from frequent itemsets. In Section 5.3, we give the method for hierarchical associative categorization based on the item-associative MN. In Section 5.4, we present experimental results and performance studies. In Section 5.5, we present the empirical study on hierarchical categorization of microblog users. In Section 5.6, we summarize our work in this chapter.

5.2 Constructing Item-Association Markov Network from Behavioral Interactions in Social Media

We assume that readers are familiar with the basic concepts and algorithms about frequent pattern mining [10, 11]. Now we briefly introduce these concepts.

Let the task-relevant data be a set of database transactions where each transaction t_i is a set of items and let $I = \{i_1, \ldots, i_n\}$ be the universal itemset. A set $X \subseteq I$ of items is frequent if $P(X) \geq \lambda$, where $P(X)$ is the *support* of an itemset X and defined as the proportion of transactions in the dataset that contain X, and λ is the threshold of *support*. We know that if X is a frequent itemset, then all the non-empty subsets of X must also be frequent. A frequent itemset X is maximal if there is no itemset $Y \supset X$ in I, such that Y is a frequent itemset.

As one type of PGMs, MN is a dependency model incorporating the graphical structure and the probabilistic independencies represented among various sets of nodes [24]. This means that to represent the dependencies quantitatively in the graphical dependency model, the probabilistic conditional independencies are tested and reflected. By the algorithms for mining frequent itemsets [1], we can obtain different frequent itemsets, which reflect the dependence relations between object behaviors. These dependence relations imply the information about probabilistic conditional independence among frequent items, exactly as the theoretical bridge between itemsets and MN. In the following, as the basis of IAMN construction, we first find the conditional independence relations from the result of frequent pattern mining.

Let $\mathcal{U}$ be a set of random variables, and let $\mathcal{X}$, $\mathcal{Y}$, and $\mathcal{Z}$ be three disjoint subsets of U. $\langle \mathcal{X} \mid \mathcal{Z} \mid \mathcal{Y} \rangle$ stands for the phrase "$\mathcal{X}$ is independent of $\mathcal{Y}$ given $\mathcal{Z}$", that is, $P(\mathcal{X}\mathcal{Y}\mathcal{Z}) = P(\mathcal{X}\mathcal{Z})P(\mathcal{Y}\mathcal{Z})/P(\mathcal{Z})$. From the perspective of a probability model [24], a set $\mathcal{M}$ of triplets $(\mathcal{X}, \mathcal{Y}, \mathcal{Z})$ in $\mathcal{U}$ is called a dependency model if the assertion $\langle \mathcal{X} \mid \mathcal{Z} \mid \mathcal{Y} \rangle$ is true, denoted as $\langle \mathcal{X} \mid \mathcal{Z} \mid \mathcal{Y} \rangle_{\mathcal{M}}$.

Analogously considering the frequent items, let $U = \{a_1, \ldots, a_n\}$ be the set of 1-frequent items in the transaction set D, and let X, Y, and Z be three disjoint subsets of U. M is a probability model of triples (X, Y, Z) in U satisfying the conditional independence assertion. An IAMN $G = \langle V, E \rangle$ is an undirected graphical representation of M, where V is the set of nodes and E is the set of edges. This means that a direct correspondence between the 1-frequent items in U and the nodes in the undirected graph G can be built, such that the topology of G can reflect the properties of M.

As already indicated, the notion of conditional independence is strikingly similar to that of separation in graphs, which is the bridge between a probability model and a graphical model. For an undirected graph, we consider the concept of u-separation [24], defined as follows.

Definition 5.1. Let $\mathcal{G} = \langle \mathcal{V}, \mathcal{E} \rangle$ be an undirected graph and $\mathcal{X}$, $\mathcal{Y}$, and $\mathcal{Z}$ be three disjoint subsets of nodes. $\mathcal{Z}$ u-separates $\mathcal{X}$ and $\mathcal{Y}$ in $\mathcal{G}$, written $\langle \mathcal{X} \mid \mathcal{Z} \mid \mathcal{Y} \rangle_\mathcal{G}$, if and only if all paths from a node in $\mathcal{X}$ to a node in $\mathcal{Y}$ contain a node in $\mathcal{Z}$. A path that contains a node in $\mathcal{Z}$ is called blocked (by $\mathcal{Z}$), otherwise it is called active.

Separation means that all paths are blocked. Alternatively, we may say that $\mathcal{Z}$ u-separates $\mathcal{X}$ and $\mathcal{Y}$ in $\mathcal{G}$ if and only if after removing the nodes in $\mathcal{Z}$ and their associated edges from $\mathcal{G}$, there is no path from a node in $\mathcal{X}$ to a node in $\mathcal{Y}$. That is, in the graph without the nodes in $\mathcal{Z}$, the nodes in $\mathcal{X}$ are not connected to those in $\mathcal{Y}$. This interception $\langle \mathcal{X} \mid \mathcal{Z} \mid \mathcal{Y} \rangle_\mathcal{G}$ corresponds to the conditional independence between $\mathcal{X}$ and $\mathcal{Y}$ given $\mathcal{Z}$ (i.e., $\langle \mathcal{X} \mid \mathcal{Z} \mid \mathcal{Y} \rangle_\mathcal{M}$). Based on the concept of u-separation in an undirected graph, the definition of MN is as follows.

Definition 5.2. An undirected graph $\mathcal{G}$ is an Independency map (I-map) (or called I-map) of dependency model $\mathcal{M}$ if $\langle \mathcal{X} \mid \mathcal{Z} \mid \mathcal{Y} \rangle_\mathcal{G} \Rightarrow \langle \mathcal{X} \mid \mathcal{Z} \mid \mathcal{Y} \rangle_\mathcal{M}$. An undirected graph $\mathcal{G}$ is a minimal I-map of $\mathcal{M}$ if deleting any edge of $\mathcal{G}$ would make $\mathcal{G}$ cease to be an I-map. We call such an undirected graph an MN of $\mathcal{M}$.

Based on the concepts of frequent itemsets and MN, we first give an example of MN taking the frequent items as nodes, and then give the definition of IAMN.

Example 5.1. Suppose $\{A, B, C, D\}$ is a frequent itemset, in which C is independent of D given B, and A is independent of D given B. Figure 5.1 shows an MN taking A, B, C, and D as nodes and reflecting the conditional independencies.

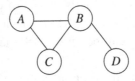

Fig. 5.1.   MN of the given frequent itemset.

Definition 5.3. An MN with 1-frequent item nodes in U is called an Item-association Markov network (IAMN).

Pearl [24] gave the necessary condition that an undirected graph is an MN. This also gives us the idea for constructing the MN upon given random variables by focusing on conditional independence (CI) tests.

Theorem 5.1. *Every dependency model M satisfying symmetry, decomposition, and intersection has a unique minimal I-map $\mathcal{G} = \langle \mathcal{V}, \mathcal{E} \rangle$ produced by connecting only those pairs (x, y) for which $\langle x \mid \mathcal{U} - x - y \mid y \rangle_\mathcal{M}$ is false, (i.e., $(x, y) \notin \mathcal{E}$, if $\langle x \mid \mathcal{U} - x - y \mid y \rangle_\mathcal{M}$ is true), where symmetry, decomposition, and intersection can be represented as follows:*

- *Symmetry $\langle \mathcal{X} \mid \mathcal{Z} \mid \mathcal{Y} \rangle_\mathcal{M} \Leftrightarrow \langle \mathcal{Y} \mid \mathcal{Z} \mid \mathcal{X} \rangle_\mathcal{M}$;*
- *Decomposition $\langle \mathcal{X} \mid \mathcal{Z} \mid \mathcal{Y} \cup \mathcal{W} \rangle_\mathcal{M} \Rightarrow \langle \mathcal{X} \mid \mathcal{Z} \mid \mathcal{Y} \rangle_\mathcal{M} \wedge \langle \mathcal{X} \mid \mathcal{Z} \mid \mathcal{W} \rangle_\mathcal{M}$;*
- *Intersection $\langle \mathcal{X} \mid \mathcal{Z} \cup \mathcal{W} \mid \mathcal{Y} \rangle_\mathcal{M} \wedge \langle \mathcal{X} \mid \mathcal{Z} \cup \mathcal{Y} \mid \mathcal{W} \rangle_\mathcal{M} \Rightarrow \langle \mathcal{X} \mid \mathcal{Z} \mid \mathcal{Y} \cup \mathcal{W} \rangle_\mathcal{M}$.*

Note that if the denominator of each conditional independence expression is strictly positive, then the above-mentioned three conditional expressions hold.

To construct the IAMN based on Theorem 5.1, we first acquire the conditional independence relations implied in the 1-frequent itemset U. For this purpose, we give the concept of probability cut value at first.

Definition 5.4. We call $P_\lambda(X)$ as the probability cut value of itemset X, where

$$P_\lambda(X) = \begin{cases} 0 & P(X) < \lambda \\ 1 & P(X) \geq \lambda \end{cases} \tag{5.1}$$

where λ is the minimal-support threshold to determine whether X is frequent or not.

It is worth noting that the probability of the itemset with the small support is assigned to 0, that is only frequent itemsets are concerned when computing $P(X)$ in Definition 5.4, similar to that all non-frequent items are neglected in association rule mining. Furthermore, by this definition, we can discuss the probability computations and the corresponding properties (e.g., conditional independence) which cannot be well described just from $P(X)$. Thus, the probability distribution of

$P_\lambda(X)$ is the approximation of the real distribution due to the introduction of λ, which determines the approximation degree. All the computations of $P(X)$ can be obtained from the Apriori algorithm [1, 11] for mining frequent patterns.

To represent the mutual relationships among the multiple frequent itemsets as an IAMN, we consider the properties of the conditional independence relations between frequent itemsets over U. If two items are in two itemsets with intersections, then we join them by an edge due to the conditional dependence relationship stated in Lemma 5.1. If two items are in two itemsets without intersections, we keep them unconnected due to the conditional independence relationship stated in Lemma 5.2. For any two independent items that are not included in any maximal itemset, we keep them unconnected as stated in Lemma 5.3.

Lemma 5.1. *Let X and Y be two maximal frequent itemsets and $X \cap Y = Z$. If there are $\alpha \in X$ and $\beta \in Y$ such that (α, β) is non-frequent, then $\langle \alpha \mid Z \mid \beta \rangle_M$ is false (denoted as $\overline{\langle \alpha \mid Z \mid \beta \rangle_M}$), where α and β are 1-frequent items and (α, β) means $\{\alpha\} \cup \{\beta\}$ for simplification.*

Proof. Since (α, β) is non-frequent, (α, Z, β) is non-frequent. Thus, $P_\lambda(\alpha, Z, \beta) = 0$ according to Eq. (2.1). Since $(\alpha \cup Z) \subseteq X$ and $(\beta \cup Z) \subseteq Y$, we know that $P_\lambda(\alpha, Z) \neq 0$, $p_\lambda(\beta, Z) \neq 0$, and $p_\lambda(Z) \neq 0$. Then, $P_\lambda(\alpha, \beta, Z) \neq P_\lambda(\alpha, Z) \cdot P_\lambda(\beta, Z)/P_\lambda(Z)$, so $\langle \alpha \mid Z \mid \beta \rangle_M$ is false. $\qquad\square$

Lemma 5.2. *Let X and Y be two maximal frequent itemsets and $X \cap Y = \emptyset$. If (α, β) is non-frequent for all $\alpha \in X$ and $\beta \in Y$, then $\langle \alpha \mid U - \alpha - \beta \mid \beta \rangle_M$ is true.*

Proof. First, we test $\langle \alpha \mid \gamma \mid \beta \rangle_M$, where $\gamma \in X$. Since (X, β) is non-frequent, $P_\lambda(\alpha, \gamma, \beta) = 0$. We note that $P_\lambda(\gamma, \beta) = 0$ and $P_\lambda(\gamma) \neq 0$. Then, $P_\lambda(\gamma, \beta) \cdot P_\lambda(\gamma, \alpha)/P_\lambda(\gamma) = 0$, and thus $\langle \alpha \mid \gamma \mid \beta \rangle_M$ is true. By the same way, we know that for $\gamma \in Y$, $\langle \alpha \mid \gamma \mid \beta \rangle_M$ is true as well.

Next, we test $\langle \alpha \mid \gamma \mid \beta \rangle_M$, where $\gamma \notin X$ and $\gamma \notin Y$. Since (α, β) is non-frequent, $P_\lambda(\alpha, \gamma, \beta) = 0$. For any $\gamma(\gamma \notin X, Y)$, since (α, β) is non-frequent, we know that if $P_\lambda(\alpha, \gamma) \neq 0$, then $P_\lambda(\beta, \gamma) = 0$. We know that $P_\lambda(\gamma) \neq 0$, since $\gamma \in U$. Thus, $P_\lambda(\alpha, \gamma) \cdot P_\lambda(\beta, \gamma)/P_\lambda(\gamma) = 0$, and $\langle \alpha \mid U - \alpha - \beta \mid \beta \rangle_M$ is true. $\qquad\square$

Lemma 5.3. *Let* X *be a maximal frequent itemset,* $\alpha, \beta \in X$ *and* $\langle \alpha \mid X - \alpha - \beta \mid \beta \rangle_M$ *holds. If there is no maximal frequent itemset* $Y(Y \neq X)$ *in* U, *such that* $\alpha, \beta \in Y$, *then* $\langle \alpha \mid U - \alpha - \beta \mid \beta \rangle_M$ *is true.*

Proof. Let $\gamma (\gamma \notin X)$ be any one frequent item in U. Since (α, β, γ) is non-frequent, we know that (α, γ) is non-frequent or (β, γ) is non-frequent. Thus, $P_\lambda(\alpha, \beta, \gamma) = 0$ and $P_\lambda(\alpha, \gamma) = 0$ (or $P_\lambda(\beta, \gamma) = 0$). Since $P_\lambda(\gamma) \neq 0$, we have $P_\lambda(\alpha, \beta, \gamma) = P_\lambda(\alpha, \gamma) \cdot P_\lambda(\beta, \gamma)/P_\lambda(\gamma) = 0$. Since γ is an arbitrary frequent item in $U - X$, we conclude that $\langle \alpha \mid U - \alpha - \beta \mid \beta \rangle_M$ is true.

Based on Lemmas 5.1–5.3, we present Algorithm 5.1 for constructing an IAMN from U. □

Now, we give the following example to illustrate the execution of Algorithm 5.1.

Example 5.2. Let $U = \{A, B, C, D, E, F\}$ be the set of 1-frequent items and $\{A, B, C\}$, $\{C, D\}$, $\{D, E, F\}$ be three maximal frequent itemsets over U.

By Step 2 of Algorithm 5.1, we obtain three undirected complete subgraphs in Fig. 5.2. According to Lemma 5.1 and by Step 3 of Algorithm 5.1, we add the undirected edges (A, D), (B, D), (C, E), (C, F) to G by dotted lines shown in Fig. 5.3.

According to Lemma 5.2, we know that there are no edges between the following pairs of nodes: (A, E), (A, F), (B, E), (B, F). Suppose the conditional independence tests show that $\langle E \mid D \mid F \rangle_M$ and $\langle E \mid C \mid F \rangle_M$ hold. Then, according to Lemma 5.3, the edge (E, F) will be removed from G by Step 4 of Algorithm 5.1. Then, the result MN is shown in Fig. 5.4.

The correctness of Algorithm 5.1 is guaranteed by Theorem 5.2 based on Lemmas 5.1–5.3.

Theorem 5.2. *The result of Algorithm 5.1 is a minimal I-map of the dependence model M over U.*

Proof. First, we know $p_\lambda(a_{ij}) = 1$ by Definition 5.4, where $a_{ij} \in U$ $(1 \leq i \leq m, i_1 \leq j \leq i_n)$ is a 1-frequent item. Thus, for any X and Y in N, we have $P_\lambda(X) = 1$, $P_\lambda(Y) = 1$, and $P_\lambda(X \cup Y) = 1$, that is

---

Algorithm 5.1 Constructing an IAMN from U

Input:

    U: the set of 1-frequent items

    $A_i = \{a_{i1}, \ldots, a_{in}\}(i = 1, \ldots, m)$: the maximal frequent itemset, where $a_{ij} \in U$

    $N = \{A_1, \ldots, A_m\}$

Output: The minimal I-map (i.e., MN) over U

Steps:

1. Construct the initial undirected graph $G = \langle V, E \rangle$:

    $V \leftarrow U$; $E \leftarrow \emptyset$

2. Generate an undirected complete subgraph for each maximal frequent itemset:

    For each A_i, Do

        Join each pair of distinct nodes in A_i to generate the complete subgraph $G(A_i)$

    End For

3. For each pair (A_i, A_j) and $A_i \cap A_j \neq \emptyset$ Do // According to Lemma 5.1

    Join each pair (a_{il}, a_{jk}) to obtain G, where $a_{il} \in A_i - A_j$, $a_{jk} \in A_j - A_i$

    End For

4. For each $G(A_i)$ Do // $G(A_i)$ represents the subgraph of G on A_i

    For each edge $(a_{il}, a_{ik}) \in G(A_i)$ Do // According to Lemma 5.2

        If $\overline{\langle a_{il} \mid A_i - a_{il} - a_{ik} \mid a_{ik} \rangle}_M$ Then continue

        For each A_j $(A_j \neq A_i)$ Do // According to Lemma 5.3

            If $a_{il}, a_{ik} \in A_j$ and $\overline{\langle a_{il} \mid A_j - a_{il} - a_{ik} \mid a_{ik} \rangle}_M$ Then continue

        End For

        $G(A_i) \leftarrow G(A_i) - (a_{il}, a_{ik})$

    End for

    End for

5. Return G

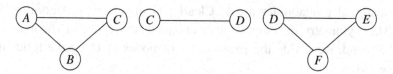

Fig. 5.2. Three undirected complete subgraphs.

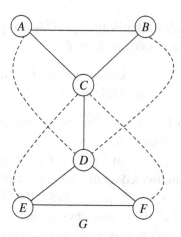

Fig. 5.3. Undirected graph generated by Step 3 of Algorithm 5.1.

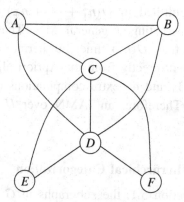

Fig. 5.4. Result MN over *U*.

all marginal probabilities are 1. Clearly, G obtained by Algorithm 5.1 satisfies symmetry, decomposition, and intersection stated in Theorem 5.1.

Second, we divide the pairs (α, β) of nodes in U by the following three cases:

(1) $\alpha \in A_i, \beta \in A_j, A_i \cap A_j = \varnothing$; (2) $\alpha \in A_i, \beta \in A_j, A_i \cap A_j \neq \varnothing$; (3) $\alpha, \beta \in A_i$.

Case 1. By Lemma 5.2, we know that $\langle \alpha \mid U - \alpha - \beta \mid \beta \rangle_M$ is true. From Algorithm 5.1, we can obtain $(\alpha, \beta) \notin E$.

Case 2. By Lemma 5.1, we know that $\langle \alpha \mid U - \alpha - \beta \mid \beta \rangle_M$ is false. From Algorithm 5.1, we can obtain $(\alpha, \beta) \in E$.

Case 3. According to Lemma 5.3, by the CI test $\langle \alpha \mid A_i - \alpha - \beta \mid \beta \rangle_M$, we can determine whether $\langle \alpha \mid U - \alpha - \beta \mid \beta \rangle_M$ holds or not. If $\langle \alpha \mid U - \alpha - \beta \mid \beta \rangle_M$ holds, then $(\alpha, \beta) \notin E$, else $(\alpha, \beta) \in E$.

Thus, G is the undirected graph by only connecting the pairs as (α, β), on which $\langle \alpha \mid U - \alpha - \beta \mid \beta \rangle_M$ is false. By Theorem 5.1, we know G is a minimal I-map of the dependency model M of U.

In Algorithm 5.1, Step 2 is executed in $O(n_1 + \cdots + n_m)$ time, where n_i is the number of nodes in A_i and $n_1, \ldots, n_m \leq n$, so $O(n)$ time. Step 3 is conducted in $O(n^2)$ time at most. Step 4 runs CI tests and could be fulfilled in $O(n_1^2 + \cdots + n_m^2)$ time, which is less than $O(n^2)$ for constructing a general MN. That is, Algorithm 5.1 can be done in less than $O(n^2)$ time. Furthermore, all the probability values can be obtained directly from the Apriori algorithm for frequent pattern mining [1, 11] and no extra computations on the given sample data are necessary. Therefore, an IAMN over U can be constructed efficiently. $\square$

5.3 IAMN-Based Hierarchical Categorization

As mentioned in Section 5.1, the subgraphs in G can be merged into an aggregation if the interconnection among nodes in the subgraph is close. This bottom-up strategy starts by placing each subgraph in its own aggregation and then merges these initial aggregations into larger and larger ones, until the undirected graph G is in a single aggregation.

Thus, the categorization of the behaviors concerned in the given frequent patterns can be obtained by means of bottom-up aggregation of nodes in the IAMN. This is the basic idea of our hierarchical categorization method.

Actually, the nodes at every hierarchy could be aggregated if these nodes are associated closely. To measure the closeness among the nodes in G, we adopt the concept of "chordal" [24] in probabilistic graphical models, defined and interpreted as follows.

Definition 5.5. An undirected graph $G = \langle V, E \rangle$ is said to be chordal if every cycle of length four or more has a chord, i.e., an edge joining two nonconsecutive nodes.

Example 5.3. A simple undirected graph G in Fig. 5.5 is chordal according to Definition 5.5.

As pointed out that a chordal I-map G [24] can be used to determine whether the probability model M corresponding to G is decomposable or not.

Definition 5.6. A probability mode M is decomposable if the joint distribution of M can be written as a product of the distributions of chordal subgraphs divided by a product of the distributions of their intersection. M is said to be decomposable relative to an undirected graph G if the following two conditions are satisfied: (1) G is an I-map of M; (2) G is chordal.

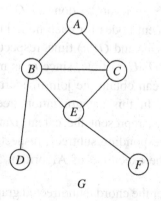

G

Fig. 5.5. A chordal undirected graph.

The relation between the chordal I-map G of M and the decomposition expression of M is as follows [24, 31]:

Let probability model M be decomposable relative to the undirected graph G. Let $(C_1, \ldots, C_m)$ be an increasing order of chordal subgraphs of G such that $(C_1 \cup C_2 \cup \cdots \cup C_{i-1}) \cap C_i \subseteq C_j (1 \leq j \leq i)$. The joint distribution of M can be expressed as follows:

$$\frac{P(C_1) \cdot P(C_2)}{P(C_1 \cap C_2)} \cdot \frac{P(C_3)}{P((C_1 \cup C_2) \cap C_3)} \cdots \frac{P(C_m)}{P((C_1 \cup \cdots \cup C_{m-1}) \cap C_m)} \tag{5.2}$$

According to the order of chordal subgraphs of G, a chordal undirected graph G can be described as a tree, called join tree, by looking at the chordal subgraphs as single nodes, respectively.

Definition 5.7. A join tree T is an I-Map of M with nodes corresponding to the cliques of G, such that for every node x in G, if we remove all cliques without including x from T, then the remaining subtree stays connected.

From Definitions 5.5 and 5.7, we know that each node in the join tree is composed of the corresponding frequent items that are closely associated. Thus, we can fulfill the associative categorization based on the algorithm for constructing the join tree from a chordal I-map of M [31], given as follows.

In this algorithm, Step 1 can be done in $O(|U|^2)$ time in the worst case by searching adjacent nodes for each node in G. Steps 2 and 4 can be fulfilled in $O(m \log_2 m)$ and $O(m)$ time, respectively. Thus, Algorithm 5.2 can be fulfilled in $O(|U|^2)$ time, since m is much smaller than $|U|$. By Algorithm 5.2, we can obtain the join-tree-structured categorizations in various hierarchies. In this categorization tree, intermediate nodes, as the roots of subtrees, represent the categorizations composed of the child nodes in the corresponding subtrees, respectively. Now we give an example to illustrate the execution of Algorithm 5.2.

Example 5.4. Consider the chordal undirected graph G in Fig. 5.5, where (C_1, C_2, C_3, C_4) is the order of chordal cliques in G, $C_1 = (A, B, C)$,

---

Algorithm 5.2 Chordal I-map_to_join tree

Input: The chordal I-map $G = \langle V, E \rangle$ of M
Output: The join tree T corresponding to G
Steps:

1. Identify all maximum complete subgraphs $\{S_1 \cdots S_m\}$ of G, each of which corresponds to a maximal frequent itemset. Let $\{C_1 \cdots C_m\}$ be the chordal cliques corresponding to $\{S_1 \cdots S_m\}$
2. Sort $\{C_1, \ldots, C_m\}$ by increasing order to obtain $\{C'_1 \cdots C'_m\}$ satisfying $(C_1 \cup C_2 \cup \cdots \cup C_{i-1}) \cap C_i \subseteq C_j (1 \leq j \leq i)$
3. $T \leftarrow C'_1$
4. For $j \leftarrow 2$ to m Do

    Form the join tree by connecting C'_j to a predecessor $C'_k(C'_k \in \{C'_1, \ldots, C'_{j-1}\})$ that shares the highest number of nodes with C'_j

    End for
5. Return T

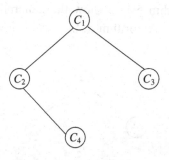

Fig. 5.6. Join tree T corresponding to G.

$C_2 = \{B, C, E\}, C_3 = \{B, D\}$, and $C_4 = \{E, F\}$. By Algorithm 5.2, we can obtain the join tree T corresponding to G as shown in Fig. 5.6.

As expected, we are to derive the classes with larger and larger granularities by gradual bottom-up node aggregation, corresponding to higher and higher abstraction degrees in real applications. Whether this can be implemented depends on the inherent properties of the join tree. Fortunately, Pearl [24] pointed out that if a probability model M is decomposable relative to an undirected graph G, then the join tree T of the chordal cliques of G is an I-Map of M.

Obviously, a join tree is chordal, since it has no cycle. Thus, as long as we run Algorithm 5.2 repeatedly, different hierarchical categorizations can be obtained. First, we transform the chordal undirected graph G_0 into its join tree T_1, and then merge the endpoints of the edges in T_1 into a larger node to create a new join tree T_2. The process of the hierarchical categorization is illustrated as $G_0 \rightarrow T_1 \rightarrow T_2 \rightarrow \cdots \rightarrow T_n$.

Example 5.5. Let us consider the join tree T in Example 5.4. We know that (C_1', C_2', C_3') is the increasing order of chordal cliques in T (denoted as T_1 for discussion convenience), where $C_1' = (C_1, C_2)$, $C_2' = (C_2, C_4)$, and $C_3' = (C_1, C_3)$. By Algorithm 5.2, we can obtain the new join tree T_2 as shown in Fig. 5.7. Similarly, we can merge the nodes in T_2 to obtain T_3. The process of the hierarchical categorization is shown in Fig. 5.8.

Now we discuss the chordal property of the undirected graph G resulting from Algorithm 5.1 to show the generality of the hierarchical categorization given in Algorithm 5.2.

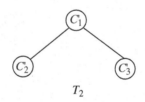

Fig. 5.7. New join tree T_2.

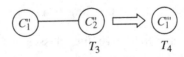

Fig. 5.8. Process of the hierarchical categorization.

Theorem 5.3. *Let G be the undirected graph resulting from Algorithm 5.1. If subgraph $G(A_i)$ of G over each maximal frequent itemset is chordal, then G is chordal.*

Proof. We show the conclusion to be true by the following induction:

Basis: $i = 1$. Since there is only one maximal frequent itemset A_1 (i.e., $U = A_1$), the claim is true.

Induction: Suppose the claim is true for the proofs of $i (i < n)$ maximal frequent itemsets.

Suppose $i = n$. We consider $G(A_n)$ and $G(A_k)$ $(k = 1, \ldots, n-1)$, where $A_n \cap A_k \neq \emptyset$. Let $G(A_n A_k)$ denote the subgraph of G over $A_n \cup A_k$, and $G^*(A_n)$, $G^*(A_k)$, and $G^*(A_n A_k)$ denote the complete graph over A_n, A_k, and $A_n \cup A_k$, respectively.

By Algorithm 5.1, we know that if there is an edge $e \in E^*(A_n A_k)$ but $e \notin E(A_n A_k)$, then $e \in (E^*(A_k) - E(A_k))$ or $e \in (E^*(A_n) - E(A_n))$, where $E^*(A_k)$ and $E(A_k)$ are the set of edges of $G^*(A_k)$ and $G(A_k)$, respectively.

If $G(A_n A_k)$ is non-chordal, then $G(A_n)$ or $G(A_k)$ is non-chordal, since $G^*(A_n A_k)$ is chordal. Therefore, the claim is true. $\square$

By Algorithm 5.1, taking as input the results of frequent pattern mining, we could construct the IAMN efficiently by constructing and linking the subgraphs for each maximal frequent itemset, respectively. Theorem 5.3 indicates that the subgraphs over the maximal frequent itemsets are chordal, which guarantees the correctness of the generated join trees. Therefore, the IAMN is always chordal, and our proposed method for hierarchical categorizations can work in general situations.

5.4 Experimental Results

5.4.1 Experiment setup

To verify the feasibility of the methods proposed in this chapter, we implemented the algorithms for IAMN construction and the corresponding associative categorization. Then, we tested the efficiency of IAMN construction and the correctness of the constructed IAMN as the focus of this empirical study as well as the underlying technique of this chapter. Moreover, we tested the efficiency of IAMN-based hierarchical categorization and evaluated the categorization results.

The experiments were conducted on the machine running Windows XP Professional, Intel Pentium Dual-Core Processor 2.53GHz CPU, 2GB memory. The codes were written in Java by Eclipse9 with JDK 1.7. The test data were obtained from ScienceDirect publications [25]. We abstracted keywords from 1209 papers in the following subjects: *physical sciences and engineering, life science, health science* and *social science and humanities*. From these subjects, we choose 441, 313, 255, and 200 papers randomly, respectively, adopted as transactions including keywords. On average, there are six keywords in each paper. The keywords were regarded as "behaviors" of the dataset, which we stored on disk as txt files. For each subject, we consider three hierarchies of classes, such as *artificial intelligence* (the lowest hierarchy), *computer science*, and *physical sciences and engineering* (the highest hierarchy). The classes including a keyword in various hierarchies are recorded.

5.4.2 *Efficiency of IAMN construction*

We implemented the method for IAMN construction taking as input the abstracted keywords, where frequent patterns of keywords were obtained by the Apriori algorithm [1, 11]. The most frequent keywords were selected as the nodes of the IAMN. The execution time of IAMN construction was dependent on the number of nodes in the network (denoted as *number*) and the threshold to determine whether a keyword is frequent (denoted as *range*). First, we generated various sized samples including various numbers of keywords to be nodes, so long as they satisfied the threshold. We recorded the total execution time of IAMN construction with the increase of keywords under *range* $= 5$ when *number* $= 10$ and *number* $= 15$, respectively, shown in Fig. 5.9. The frequent itemsets have not been generated when keywords are less than 600 ($\times 6$). It can be seen that the execution time of IAMN construction is basically linear to the number of keywords under various numbers of nodes in the network, and the total time for IAMN construction is not sensitive to the number of nodes in the IAMN.

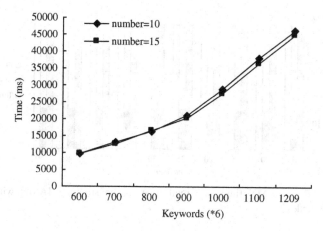

Fig. 5.9. Total time for constructing IAMN.

Then, we further tested the influence of *number* on the execution time of IAMN construction. Under *range* = 5 and various values of *number* (i.e., node numbers), we recorded the execution times of Apriori-based frequent pattern generation (denoted as FP time) and those of Algorithm 5.1-based MN construction (denoted as MN time), respectively, as well as the total time, shown in Fig. 5.10. To reduce the dramatic difference among FP time, total time, and MN time, the logarithm scale (base 10) was adopted. It can be seen that the execution time of IAMN construction was dominantly spent on generating the maximal frequent itemsets, and both the FP time and MN time are almost not increased with the increase of the nodes in the IAMN. This means that the method for IAMN construction is scalable with respect to *number*, that is, the IAMN can be constructed efficiently without sensibility to the number of frequent behaviors in the transaction database.

Meanwhile, we tested the influence of *range* on the execution time of IAMN construction. Under *number* = 10 and various values of *range* (i.e., criteria of frequent patterns), we recorded the FP time, MN time, and total time, respectively, shown in Fig. 5.11. The logarithm scale of "Time" was adopted as well. It can be seen that the execution time of IAMN construction was dominantly spent on generating the maximal frequent itemsets, and both the FP time and MN time are almost not

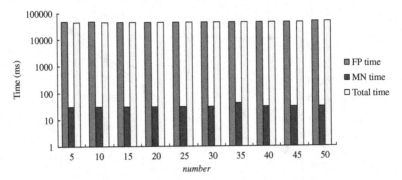

Fig. 5.10. FP time, MN time, and total time for constructing IAMN with various numbers of nodes.

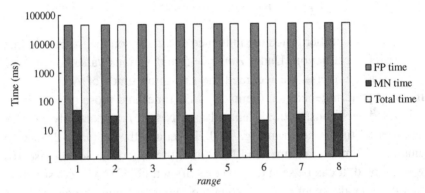

Fig. 5.11. FP time, MN time, and total time for constructing IAMN with various values of *range*.

increased with the increase of the *range* values. This means that the method for IAMN construction is scalable with respect to range, that is, the IAMN can be constructed without sensibility to the threshold to determine whether a behavior is frequent. Meanwhile, we know from the experiments that only one frequent itemset can be generated when range was 6, 7, and 8, and no frequent itemset can be generated when range is larger than 14. Thus, an appropriate *range* value could be determined according to specific situations.

Actually, other than *number* and *range*, there are still other relevant parameters when constructing the IAMN, such as the threshold of conditional independence for CI tests in Algorithm 5.1. From empirical

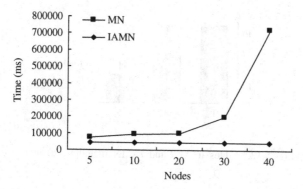

Fig. 5.12. Execution time of IAMN construction and MN learning with the increase of nodes.

tests in the experiment, we know that these parameters have little influence on the execution time of IAMN construction as well as the topology of the resulting IAMN.

Furthermore, we compared the execution time of our method for constructing the IAMN and that of the standard method for learning the corresponding MN from data [5], both of which take the abstracted keywords as input. Under *range* = 1 on IAMN construction, the comparison of IAMN and general MN construction with various numbers of nodes is shown in Fig. 5.12. It is clear that the IAMN can be constructed more efficiently than MN. The method for IAMN construction is scalable to the number of nodes while the execution time of the general method for learning MN from data is increased sharply with the increase of nodes in the network.

5.4.3 *Effectiveness of IAMN*

To test the correctness of the IAMN, we compared the chordal IAMN by our method and the BN structure learned by the general learning method [5], since the BN's structure without orientations is a chordal MN [24]. For simplicity, we use IAMN and MN to denote the chordal IAMN and BN structure without orientations, respectively. To compare the edges in these two networks, we used "Total" to denote the number of edges in the MN, and used "Equivalent" to denote those in both IAMN and MN simultaneously. First, we recorded the comparison for

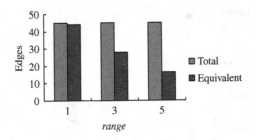

Fig. 5.13. Edges in MN and IAMN including 20 nodes.

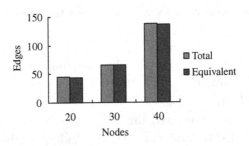

Fig. 5.14. Edges in MN and IAMN when *range* = 1.

various *range* values when the two networks include 20 nodes, as shown in Fig. 5.13. It can be seen that the smaller the value of *range*, the larger the value of "Equivalent", and specifically the two networks are basically equivalent when *range* = 1. This means that the IAMN is correct with respect to the MN learned from the abstracted keywords (i.e., *range* = 1).

Second, we recorded the comparison for various numbers of nodes in two networks under *range* = 1, shown in Fig. 5.14. It can be seen that the edges in the IAMN are basically equivalent to those in the MN for various numbers of nodes, which also verifies that Algorithm 5.1 for IAMN construction is correct.

5.4.4 *Effectiveness of associative categorization*

We further tested the performance of the IAMN-based hierarchical categorization, including the execution time of categorization process and the evaluation of the categorization results.

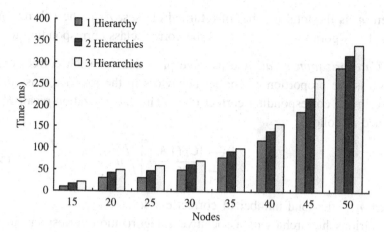

Fig. 5.15. Execution time of hierarchical associative categorization upon IAMN.

First, by focusing on the hierarchical node aggregation upon the IAMN, we recorded the execution time when running Algorithm 5.2 once, twice, and three times to generate 1, 2, and 3 hierarchies of categories, respectively, with the increase of nodes in the IAMN, as shown in Fig. 5.15. It can be seen that the categorization can be fulfilled efficiently while the execution time is not sensitive to the increase of nodes for different hierarchies of categories. Meanwhile, for the same IAMN, the higher the hierarchies (i.e., the more the times of Algorithm 5.2's execution), the less the proportion of the execution time of the ultimate node aggregation will be. This is reasonable since the nodes in the chordal graph of higher hierarchies will be less than that of lower ones.

Second, we evaluated the categorization results by the following two metrics:

(1) *Categorization precision*: the average recall for each correct class, which is the proportion of the correct behaviors (i.e., keywords in papers) in the returned class to all those returned. The categorization precision P_c is defined as follows:

$$P_c = \left[\sum_{i=1}^{m} \frac{|A_i \cap C_i|}{|A_i|} \right] \bigg/ m \tag{5.3}$$

where m is the total number of returned classes, A_i is the i-th returned class by Algorithm 3.1, and C_i is the correct class corresponding to A_i.

(2) *Categorization recall*: the average precision for each correct class, which is the proportion of correct behaviors in the returned class to all those in the corresponding correct class. The categorization recall R_c is defined as follows:

$$R_c = \left[\sum_{i=1}^{n} \frac{|C_i \cap A_i|}{|C_i|} \right] \Big/ n \qquad (5.4)$$

where n is the total number of correct classes.

Various hierarchies of associative categorization correspond to the hierarchical subjects in ScienceDirect, respectively. We considered the categorization results in 1, 2, and 3 hierarchies from the lowest to the highest hierarchies. For example, "artificial intelligence", "computer science", and "physical sciences and engineering" correspond to the categories in 1, 2, and 3 hierarchies. To decide whether a behavior (i.e., keyword) is categorized correctly or not, the subject that most of the keywords in the category belong to was simply regarded as the subject of this category (i.e., class). We then recorded the values of P_c and R_c of the categorization results in 1, 2, and 3 hierarchies with the increase of nodes in the IAMN, shown in Figs. 5.16 and 5.17, respectively.

It can be seen that high categorization precisions were achieved in most cases, and relatively a little lower, but still fairly good. Categorization

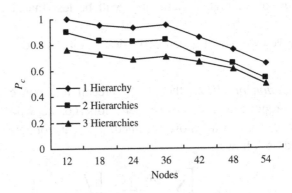

Fig. 5.16. Precision of categorization.

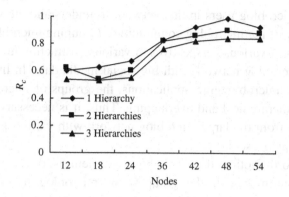

Fig. 5.17. Recall of categorization.

recalls were achieved as well. The higher the hierarchies, the lower the values of P_c and R_c will be, but the decrease of R_c is smaller than that of P_c with the increase of nodes in the IAMN. This means that the correct categorization results of frequent patterns can be obtained, and those behaviors in the correct classes can also be found basically. As well, between P_c and R_c, P_c is the dominant advantage of our method with respect to the realistic behavior categorization.

Meanwhile, we note that P_c was decreased and R_c was increased with the increase of nodes in the IAMN for all the results with 1, 2, and 3 hierarchies. This is reasonable since some frequent patterns have not been included in the IAMN when the number of nodes is small. But when more and more frequent patterns are included, some returned classes are sure to include some incorrectly categorized patterns, which makes P_c decreased and R_c increased. However, the best result in this experiment was obtained upon the IAMN with 36 nodes. This means that good categorization results are dependent on the appropriate number of nodes in the IAMN, which could be determined in real applications.

5.5 Empirical Study on Hierarchical Categorization of Microblog Users

5.5.1 *Basic idea*

Users with communications of microblog messages can be described as a network in a specific domain. It is useful to achieve the similar groups of microblog users in this network to understand the structure or functionality of the microblog communities. Grouping microblog users is necessary from various perspectives in various abstraction hierarchies on the large microblog network with big social media data. In line with the inherence of microblogging applications, the groups of microblog users are usually hierarchical and overlapping. Thus, it is necessary to achieve such groups from the large microblog network with various granularities and overlapping users.

It is worth noting that the above problem is different from the classic clustering. First, the grouping of microblog users is mainly determined by the behavioral interactions between users instead of their own attributes. As well, the topological properties of the network will affect the dynamics in a very fundamental way. Meanwhile, the above problem is similar but not the same as the community detection in complex or social network paradigm [26], since the former focuses more on the groups of users than the internal structural properties of the group components that the latter focuses on. Therefore, it is desirable to explore a method for grouping microblog users with hierarchical and overlapping properties while starting from their graphical topology and their interactive relationships. We call such grouping process as categorization.

From the perspective of complex networks, Shen *et al.* [26] proposed an agglomerative hierarchical clustering algorithm EAGLE by focusing on the hierarchical and overlapping properties. EAGLE established a basis for our study on microblog user categorization, but the inherent characteristics of microblogging should be incorporated, such as the actually large scale of the microblog network and the different strengths of the interactions between users.

As per the empirical study of the associative categorization method given in Sections 5.3 and 5.4, we develop our algorithms for microblog users' categorization based on the MapReduce programming model to make relevant computations possibly oriented to realistic large microblog networks [33].

We store the original microblog network (regarded as massive data source for categorization) by a distributed manner, where the edge directions reflect the "follow" relationships in realistic microblog services.

Then, we develop a MapReduce-based model to evaluate the similarity metric between users by considering both the number and the strength of their associations. Consequently, we can transform the original directed network into an undirected graph to describe the mutual relationships between pairs of users. In the following, we propose the MapReduce algorithm for bottom-up node aggregation by adopting the concepts of chordal and join tree in the graph theory mentioned in Section 5.3, where "chordal" describes the closeness among nodes in a graph, and the chordal subgraphs constitute join trees. Furthermore, a join tree is also chordal, which makes the nodes in a join tree be able to be looked upon as those in the initial chordal subgraph for repeated aggregation. Thus, we obtain the join trees on the derived undirected graph model level-by-level in bottom-up manner, corresponding to higher and higher abstraction hierarchies of microblog user categories.

5.5.2 *Graph model of microblog users*

Microblog has two special tweet types for communication among users called replies and retweets. In the network of microblog users, edges correspond to direct interactions of replies or retweets among users. A "reply" is a tweet sent in response to an earlier tweet and includes the earlier tweet ID. All of the users following either the replying or the replied-to user can read this tweet. When a tweet is "retweeted" (abbreviated as RT) by a user, it is broadcast to the user's followers. For an official RT with twitter's retweet command, the tweet is simply reposted without changing the original message.

Suppose that user i calls user j w_{ij} times and user j calls user i w_{ji} times in a microblog network. It is intuitive that the more reciprocal and frequent the interactions between a pair of users, the closer their relationship will be. Therefore, the relationship strength can be simply defined as

$$F_{ij} = \text{Rec}_{ij} * \text{Fre}_{ij}$$

where F_{ij}, Rec_{ij}, Fre_{ij} represent the relationship, reciprocity, and frequency strength between i and j, respectively. Note that F_{ij} is

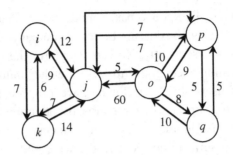

Fig. 5.18. An original microblog network.

computed by adopting the weights in the directed microblog network directly.

Without loss of generality, we can look upon the microblog users and the communicative interactions ("reply" and "retweets") between them as a set of vertexes and a set of weighted directed edges, respectively, so the original microblog network can be represented as a directed weighted graph as shown in Fig. 5.18.

By an analogy between microblog users and frequent items, microblog users could be regarded as the 1-frequent items in corresponding behavioral interactions. Then, an IAMN of microblog users could be constructed using Algorithm 5.1 by incorporating the weights of relationships. On the other hand, it is also necessary to make the direction-aware weighted associations between microblog users universally interpretable in terms of the inherence of IAMN.

Actually in the microblog applications, the information on some nodes is always transmitted enormously by other nodes, but these nodes themselves transmit little on the others. This appears frequently between the nodes corresponding to stars and their fans. Although the sum of interaction is very high, stars and their fans are generally not very close to each other. For example, given two different pairs of weights (w_{ij}) from i to j and that (w_{ji}) from j to i, (1, 10) and (1, 1000), the relationship strength of the first should be closer than the second. To make a distinction of the mutual relationship between i and j determined by the number and strength simultaneously, the increase of Fre_{ij} should tend to flatten with the increase of total interactions. So, the frequency strength can be computed by $\text{Fre}^*_{ij} = \sqrt{w_{ij}w_{ji}}$ and we have

$$F_{ij} = \text{Rec}_{ij} * \text{Fre}^*_{ij} = \frac{\min(w_{ij}, w_{ji})}{\max(w_{ij}, w_{ji})}\sqrt{w_{ij}w_{ji}}$$

By using Eq. (5.6), we can fulfill this transformation from the original directed graph model (denoted as G_0) into an undirected one for categorization, since the mutual relationship can be described by the results quantitatively.

Definition 5.8. A graph of mutual relationships of microblog users, called MG, is an undirected graph $G = (V, E)$, where V is a node set of users and E is a set of undirected edges. For each e in E between users i and j in $V (1 \leq i, \ j \leq n, \ I \neq j)$, only if $F_{ij} \geq \varepsilon$, where ε is a given threshold of strength between a pair of users in G.

In the following, we discuss the evaluation of Eq. (5.6) on the large microblog network G_0 with large scale of users. In the distributed storage system, each edge of the original directed microblog network G_0 will be stored in a record, respectively. Based on the MapReduce programming model, the weight of each edge in G_0 can be obtained in parallel, since the value of F_{ij} between i and j can be obtained in parallel. In the map process, the weight on each directed edge will be obtained from the distributed storage system and the weights w_{ij} and w_{ji} between the same pair of nodes will be outputted in a group as intermediate results. In the reduce process, the weights w_{ij} and w_{ji} between the same nodes in a group will be used to compute F_{ij} from the intermediate results. As the result, the MG can be stored the same way as G_0. The above ideas are given in Algorithm 5.3.

By using Algorithm 5.3 on the original microblog network in Fig. 5.18, we can obtain the MG shown in Fig. 5.19.

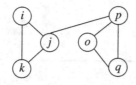

Fig. 5.19. MG of Fig. 5.18.

Algorithm 5.3 Deriving MG

Input:

$G_0 = (V_0, E_0)$, the original directed microblog network in the distributed system

ε, the threshold value of relationships between a pair of users

Output: MG $G = (V, E)$ // MG of G_0

Steps:

$V \leftarrow V_0$, $E \leftarrow \varphi$ // initialization of G

Obtain E by the following map/reduce program:

Map (String *key*, String *value*)

// *key*: key of the weight of each edge in G_0, *value*: weight on each edge

   Obtain w_{ij}

   If $i > j$ Then Generate key/value pairs $\langle ij, w_{ij} \rangle$

   Else Generate key/value pairs $\langle ji, w_{ij} \rangle$

Reduce (String *key*, Iterator *values*)

// *key*: ij, *values*: weights in the Iterator and with the same key in $\langle key, value \rangle$ pairs

   max $\leftarrow 0$, *min* $\leftarrow 0$

   For each *key*/*value* pair Do

     value $\leftarrow$ Interator.next()

     If *value*>*max* Then

       max $\leftarrow$ *value*

     Else

       min $\leftarrow$ *value*

     End If

   End For

   $F_{ij} \leftarrow$ *min*/*max**sqrt(*min**max) // by Eq. (5.6)

   If $F_{ij} \geq \varepsilon$ Then // ignore the edges with weak relationships

     Output $\langle ij, F_{ij} \rangle$

     $E \leftarrow E \cup (i, j)$

   End if

5.5.3 *Hierarchical categorization of microblog users*

To categorize the nodes in the MG obtained in Section 5.5.2, we can merge the subgraphs into an aggregation if the interconnection among the nodes in the subgraph is close. This bottom-up strategy starts by placing each subgraph in its own aggregation and then merges these initial aggregations into larger and larger ones, until the undirected graph is in a single aggregation. Thus, the categorizations of microblog users can be obtained by means of the gradual aggregation of nodes in the MG. To reflect the closeness property by means of graphical characteristics, we adopt the concept of "chordal" [24], stated in Definition 5.5. Thus, the nodes in each cycle of length three or less form a chordal subgraph by Algorithm 5.2, denoted as C_i, which contains the nodes closely associated and then generates an initial category of microblog users.

To merge the chordal subgraphs one by one, we consider the increasing order of chordal subgraphs of G, denoted as $(C_1, \ldots, C_m)$ with respect to every C_i $(1 \leq j < i)$ if the following holds for each j:

$$(C_1 \cup \cdots \cup C_{i-1}) \cap C_i \subseteq C_j \quad (1 \leq j < i)$$

$(C_1, \ldots, C_m)$ reflects the order of closeness of chordal subgraphs, that is, the closeness between C_i and C_{i-1} will be higher than that between C_{i+1} and C_{i-1}, since the sharing nodes between C_i and C_{i-1} are more than those between C_{i+1} and C_{i-1}. Consequently, from Eq. (5.7), for any two consecutive chordal subgraphs C_i and C_{i+1}, we have $C_i \cap C_{i+1} \neq \phi$, which naturally reflects the overlap of two categories of microblog users. For the MG in Fig. 5.19, (C_1, C_2, C_3) will be the order of chordal subgraphs, where $C_1 = (i, j, k)$, $C_2 = (j, p)$, $C_3 = (o, p, q)$.

According to the order of chordal subgraphs, a chordal subgraph can be described as a tree, called join tree, by adopting the corresponding concept in the graph theory [21], stated in Definition 5.7. From the definitions of chordal subgraph and join tree, we know that each node in the join tree is composed of microblog users that are closely associated. In the distributed storage system, each subgraph in the maximum complete subgraphs $(S_1, S_2, \ldots, S_m)$ of G will be stored in a record. In the map/reduce program, each subgraph will be changed to be chordal in parallel in the map process. $(C_1, C_2, \ldots, C_m)$ will be sorted by Eq. (5.6) to obtain $(C_1', C_2', \ldots, C_m')$, and the join tree will be formed by connecting C_j' to a predecessor $C_k'(C_k' \in \{C_1', \ldots, C_{j-1}'\})$ in the reduce process. Accordingly, we can fulfill the hierarchical categorization by constructing join trees from a chordalized MG, given in Algorithm 5.4.

By Algorithm 5.4, the join-tree-structured categories can be obtained in various hierarchies. Each node in the categorization tree, as the root of the subgraph, represents the category composed of child nodes in the corresponding subtree, respectively. The join tree obtained by Algorithm 5.4 is acyclic and thus also chordal. This means that we can

---

Algorithm 5.4 Chordal MG_to_join tree

Input: chordalized MG G

Output: join tree corresponding to G

Steps:

Map (String *key*, String *value*)

    // *key*: id of a subgraph in $(S_1, S_2, \ldots, S_m)$ of G,

    value: a subgraphs in $(S_1, S_2, \ldots, S_m)$ of G

    $C_i \leftarrow$ chordal subgraphs corresponding to S_i

    Generate key/value pairs $\langle G, C_i \rangle$

Reduce (String *key*, Iterator *values*)

    //*key*: G, *values*: subgraphs in the Iterator and with the same

    key in $\langle key, value \rangle$ pairs

    Sort $(C_1, C_2, \ldots, C_m)$ to obtain $(C_1', C_2', \ldots, C_m')$

    Output $(C_1', C_2', \ldots, C_m')$

    $T \leftarrow C_1'$

    For $j \leftarrow 2$ to m Do

        Form the join tree by connecting C_j' to a predecessor C_k'

        $(C_k' \in \{C_1', \ldots, C_{j-1}'\})$

        // C_k' shares the highest number of nodes with C_j'

    End For

    Return T

also merge the nodes in a join tree, as those in an initial MG, to generate the chordal subgraphs and new join trees of higher abstraction degrees.

However, it will not make sense if we know that all microblog users just belong to one category. Meanwhile, there is no fixed condition for all hierarchies to determine the appropriateness of the category granularities, and the number/size of categories are unknown in advance. In the following, we further discuss how to stop the process of node aggregation when the categories have been already good enough, which we call adaptive node aggregation. This strategy could be regarded as the optimization or improvement of the hierarchical categorization given by Algorithm 5.4.

By extending the modularity measurement of community quality, Shen *et al.* [26] proposed a quality measure of communities in a complex network concerning the hierarchical and overlapping properties. A high value of the quality metric indicates a significant community with overlappings. If we represent the MG by an adjacency matrix composed of $A_{ij} = 1$ (or 0), corresponding to an edge that exists between i and j (or not), the metric of a partition of the MG, denoted as Q, can be written as follows:

$$Q = \frac{1}{2m} \sum_{ij} \frac{1}{O_i O_j} \left(A_{ij} - \frac{k_i k_j}{2m} \right) \delta(C_i, C_j) \qquad (5.8)$$

where $m = \frac{1}{2} \sum_{ij} A_{ij}$ is the total number of edges in the MG; k_i is the degree of node i; C_i represents the category that node i belongs to, in which $\delta(C_i, C_j) = 0$ if and only if $C_i = C_j$; O_i is the number of categories, including node i.

Therefore, Q can be adopted to determine whether the aggregation should be made further if $Q \geq \delta$, where δ is a given threshold of the quality of MG's current partition. By incorporating Q into the bottom-up aggregation of nodes, either for those of initial users or those of chordal subgraphs, node aggregation can be stopped adaptively according to the characteristics of the currently achieved categories. Note that the computation of Eq. (5.8) can also be efficiently fulfilled in parallel upon the distributed storage of the large scale of MG.

5.5.4 *Performance studies*

To evaluate the feasibility of the method for microblog user categorization, we also made performance studies on the efficiency of MG construction from the original microblog network and the corresponding hierarchical categorization as well as the effectiveness of the categorization results. Our experiment platform includes four machines, where one is master node and the others are slave nodes. The CPU of each machine is Pentium(R) Dual-Core CPU E5700 @3.00GHz @3.01GHz with 2GB main memory. On each machine, the version of Hadoop, Linux, and Java is 0.20.2, Ubuntu 10.04, and JDK 1.6, respectively. We adopted the benchmark computer-generated networks (denoted as FLR) proposed by Lancichinetti *et al.* [18]. The networks have a heterogeneous distribution of node degree, edge weight, and community size, which are exactly the features of real microblog networks.

First, we tested the efficiency of our method by recording the total execution times (time of initialization of Hadoop, I/O, and algorithm execution) of MG construction from the original microblog network and the gradual aggregation until only one node remains in the join tree. This experiment was made on the cluster with 1, 2, and 3 slave nodes, respectively, with the increase of users (nodes in the network), and the results are shown in Fig. 5.20. It can be seen that the increase of the total execution time is not sensitive to the increase of microblog users for every number of slave nodes. Meanwhile, the total execution time is decreased with the increase of slave nodes. Thus, the hierarchical categorization can be fulfilled efficiently to a certain extent.

Second, we further tested the efficiency of our algorithm by comparing the total execution time (denoted as TET) and the algorithm execution time (denoted as AET) excluding that of Hadoop initialization and I/O. The comparisons were made on the cluster with 1, 2, and 3 slave nodes concerning 4000, 6000, 8000, and 10000 microblog users, respectively, shown in Figs. 5.21(a), (b), (c), and (d), respectively. It can be seen that the AETs are much smaller than TETs for various numbers of microblog users. This means that the execution time of our algorithms just takes less than 60% of the total time, while the systems initialization and I/O takes a large portion of the total time, especially for the case with a small number of users.

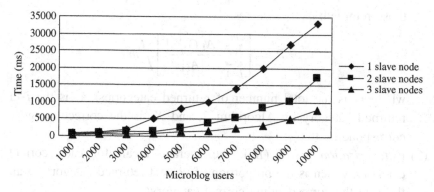

Fig. 5.20. Total execution time.

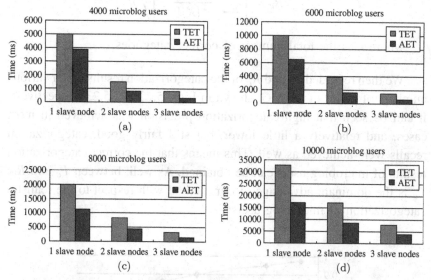

Fig. 5.21. TET vs AET: (a) TET vs AET upon 4000 microblog users; (b) TET vs AET upon 6000 microblog users; (c) TET vs AET upon 8000 microblog users; (d) TET vs AET upon 10000 microblog users.

Third, we tested the effectiveness of the hierarchical categorization. Inspired by precision and recall in IR, we evaluated the categorization results by the following two metrics:

(1) *Categorization precision* (P_c): the average precision for each correct category, which is the proportion of the correct categories to all

those returned:

$$P_c = \left[\sum_{i=1}^{m} \frac{|A_i \cap X_i|}{|A_i|} \right] \bigg/ m$$

where m is the total number of returned categories, A_i is the i-th returned category by Algorithm 2, and X_i is the correct category corresponding to A_i.

(2) *Categorization recall* (R_c): the average recall for each correct category, which is the proportion of correct returned category to all those in the corresponding correct category:

$$R_c = \left[\sum_{i=1}^{n} \frac{|X_i \cap A_i|}{|X_i|} \right] \bigg/ n$$

where n is the total number of correct categories.

We then recorded P_c and R_c of the categorization results under various numbers of nodes in the MG, shown in Figs. 5.22 and 5.23, respectively. It can be seen that high categorization precision was achieved in most cases, and relatively a little lower, but still fairly good, categorization recalls were achieved as well. This means that the correct categorization results of microblog users can be obtained. As well, between P_c and R_c, P_c is the dominant advantage of our method with respect to the realistic categorization of microblog users.

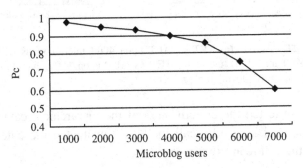

Fig. 5.22. Precision of categorization of microblog users.

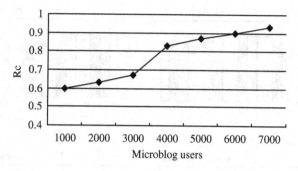

Fig. 5.23. Recall of categorization of microblog users.

Fourth, we further tested the effectiveness of our categorization method by comparing the normalized mutual information (NMI) [17] of our method and that of EAGLE. NMI is used to quantify the results of overlapping clusters or communities based on the framework of information theory. The closer the NMI value is to 1, the more similar the users in one category, and thus the better the cluster will be. Accordingly, we compared the NMI values of the categorization results obtained by our method (HCMU) and the clustering results obtained by the EAGLE algorithm [26] by adopting the same metric of the partition quality in Eq. (5.8). The comparisons were made on the FLR benchmark friend networks with 2000, 4000, 6000, 8000, and 10000 users and various threshold values of ε in Definition 5.8, respectively. The comparisons are shown in Fig. 5.24. It can be seen that the smaller the value of ε, the more effective our method will be. Actually, the larger the value of ε, the fewer the nodes in MG will be, and thus the smaller the cohesion of the users in one category will be. But, a small ε will lead to relatively high computation complexity of Algorithm 5.4 for node aggregation, which means that we could assign the appropriate value of ε based on the trade-off between effectiveness and efficiency. As well, NMI values are decreased with the increase of microblog users in the network. Actually, the more the users, the more additional edges may be added during MG chordalization, so the effect of chordalization on the categorization results should be further tested in the future.

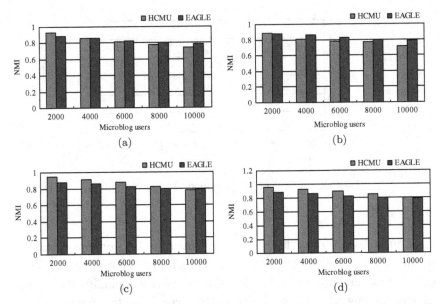

Fig. 5.24. NMI values of HCMU and EAGLE: (a) NMI comparisons when $\varepsilon = 5$; (b) NMI comparisons when $\varepsilon = 4$; (c) NMI comparisons when $\varepsilon = 3$; (d) NMI comparisons when $\varepsilon = 2$.

5.6 Summary

To discover different classes of object behaviors from social media in a hierarchical manner, we give the method for representing the association of object behaviors with uncertainties based on the MN. From the results of frequent pattern mining, the item-associative Markov network (IAMN) is constructed, and thus the linkage between frequent pattern mining and probabilistic graphical model is built. This facilitates the representation of complex associations among object behaviors and probabilistic inferences among frequent patterns. The IAMN-based associative categorization could be used to obtain the hierarchical classes with various granularities by incorporating the concept of chordal and join tree. The empirical study on categorization of microblog users by using the IAMN-based associative categorization also illustrates the feasibility of our method. Experimental results show the efficiency and correctness of our method presented in this chapter.

References

1. Agrawal, R., Imielinski, T., and Swami, A. Mining association rules between sets of items in large databases. *Proc. SIGMOD*, 1993, pp. 207–216.
2. Baralis, E. and Garza, P. I-prune: Item selection for associative classification. *International Journal of Intelligent Systems*, 2012, **27**(3): 279–299.
3. Bowes, J., Neufeld, E., Greer, J., and Cooke, J. A comparison of association rule discovery and bayesian network causal inference algorithms to discover relationships in discrete data. *Proc. Canadian AI*, 2000, pp. 326–336.
4. Chaoji, V., AI Hasan, M., Salem, S., and Zaki, M. An integrated, generic approach to pattern mining: Data mining template library. *Data Mining and Knowledge Discovery*, 2008, **17**(3): 457–495.
5. Cheng, J., Bell, D., and Liu, W. Learning Bayesian network from data: An efficient approach based on information theory. *Proc. CIKM*, 1997, pp. 325–331.
6. Cui, P., Liu, Z., Sun, L., and Yang, S. Hierarchical visual event pattern mining and its applications. *Data Mining and Knowledge Discovery*, 2011, **22**(3): 467–492.
7. Fauré, C., Delprat, S., Boulicaut, J., and Mille, A. Iterative Bayesian network implementation by using annotated association rules. *Proc. EKAW*, 2006, pp. 326–333.
8. Forestier, G., Gancarski, P., and Wemmert, C. Collaborative clustering with background knowledge. *Data and Knowledge Engineering*, 2010, **69**(2): 211–228.
9. George, D. and Hawkins, J. A hierarchical Bayesian model of invariant pattern recognition in the visual cortex. *Proc. IJCNN*, 2005, vol. 3, pp. 1812–1817.
10. Han, J. Cheng, H., Xin, D., and Yan, X. Frequent pattern mining: Current status and future directions. *Data Mining and Knowledge Discovery*, 2007, **15**(1): 55–85.
11. Han, J. and Kamber, M. *Data Mining: Concepts and Techniques (1st Edition)*. Morgan Kaufmann, California, 2000.
12. Hu, C., Wu, X., Hu, X., and Yao, H. Computing and pruning method for frequent pattern interestingness based on bayesian networks. *Journal of Software*, 2011, **22**(12): 2934–2950.
13. Jain, A. Data Clustering: 50 years beyond k-means. *Pattern Recognition Letters*, 2010, **31**(8): 651–666.
14. Jaroszewicz, S. and Scheffer, T. Fast discovery of unexpected patterns in data, relative to a Bayesian network. *Proc. SIGKDD*, 2005, pp. 118–127.

15. Ji, L., Tan, K., and Tung, A. Compressed hierarchical mining of frequent closed patterns from dense data sets. *IEEE Transactions on Knowledge and Data Engineering*, 2007, **19**(9): 1175–1187.
16. Kaski, S., Nikkila, J., Sinkkonen, J., Lahti, L., Knuuttila, J., and Roos, C. Associative clustering for exploring dependencies between functional genomics data sets. *IEEE/ACM Transactions on Computational Biology and Bioinformatics*, 2005, **2**(3): 203–216.
17. Lancichinetti, A., Fortunato, S., and Kertész, J. Detecting the overlapping and hierarchical community structure in complex networks. *New Journal of Physics*, 2009, **11**(3): 033015.
18. Lancichinetti, A., Fortunato, S., and Radicchi, F. Benchmark graphs for testing community detection algorithms. *Physical Review E*, 2008, **78**(4): 046110.
19. Liu, W., Yue, K., Liu, H., Zhang, P., Luo, Y., Liu, S., and Wang, Q. Associative categorization of frequent patterns based on the probabilistic graphical model. *Frontiers of Computer Science*, 2014, **8**(2): 265–278.
20. Liu, W., Yue, K., Wu, T., and Wei, M. An approach for multi-objective categorization based on the game theory and markov process. *Applied Soft Computing*, 2011, **11**(6): 4087–4096.
21. Lucas, J., Laurent, A., Moreno, M., and Teisseire, M. A Fuzzy associative classification approach for recommender systems. *International Journal of Uncertainty, Fuzziness and Knowledge-Based Systems*, 2012, **20**(4): 579–617.
22. Malhas, R. and Aghbari, Z. Interestingness filtering engine: Mining Bayesian networks for interesting patterns. *Expert Systems with Applications*, 2009, **36**(3): 5137–5145.
23. Nguyen, V. and Yamamot, A. Mining of closed frequent subtrees from frequently updated databases. *Intelligent Data Analysis*, 2012, **16**(6): 953–967.
24. Pearl, J. *Probabilistic Reasoning in Intelligent Systems: Network of Plausible Inference*. Morgan Kaufmann, Publishers, San Mateo, CA, 1988.
25. ScienceDirect. http://www.sciencedirect.com/, 2012.
26. Shen, H., Cheng, X., Cai, K., and Hu, M.-B. Detect overlapping and hierarchical community structure in networks. *Physica A: Statistical Mechanics and its Applications*, 2009, **388**(8): 1706–1712.
27. Sinkkonen, J., Nikkilä, J., Lahti, L., and Kaski, S. Associative clustering. *Proc. ECML*, 2004, pp. 396–406.

28. Sudhamathy, G. and Venkateswaran, C. An efficient hierarchical frequent pattern analysis approach for web usage mining. *International Journal of Computer Applications*, 2012, **43**(15): 1–7.

29. Thabtah, F. A review of associative classification mining. *The Knowledge Engineering Review*, 2007, **22**(1): 37–65.

30. Wang, X., Yue, K., Niu, W., and Shi, Z. An approach for adaptive associative classification. *Expert Systems with Applications*, 2011, **38**(9): 11873–11883.

31. Wong, S. and Butz, C. Constructing the dependency structure of a multiagent probabilistic network. *IEEE Transactions on Knowledge and Data Engineering*, 2001, **13**(3): 395–415.

32. Yu, K., Wu, X., Ding, W., Wang, H., and Yao, H. Causal associative classification. *Proc. ICDM*, 2011, pp. 914–923.

33. Yue, K., Zhou, M., Zhang, J., Zhang, P., Fang, Q., and Liu, W. Graph-based hierarchical categorization of microblog users. *Proc. BigData Congress*, 2013, pp. 156–163.

Chapter 6

Markov Network Based Latent Link Discovery and Community Detection in Social Behavioral Interactions

How to represent and discover social links from the perspective of user behaviors, in particular latent links, is critical for social media analysis. In this chapter, we discuss a probabilistic approach for latent link analysis and consequent community detection in social behavioral interactions. We adopt Markov network (MN) as the framework and propose the algorithm to discover latent links among social objects implied in their behavioral interactions without regard for the topological structures of social networks. First, we construct the item-association Markov network (IAMN) to represent users and their latent links implied in social behavioral interactions. Then, we give the algorithm to detect communities by incorporating the concepts of k-clique and k-nearest neighbor set as the typical application of the constructed IAMN. Experimental results show the effectiveness and efficiency of our proposed method.

6.1 Motivation and Basic Idea

In recent years, a variety of techniques and models of complex networks have been developed to understand or predict the behavior of networked systems, such as the Internet, social networks, biological networks, etc. [21]. Social network and social media analysis is an important topic with the rapid development of Web 2.0 and computational social science [12, 15]. Social connections, also known as social links, are the basis for generating social networks and fundamental in different perspectives of analysis, such as social behavior computation [3], personalized recommendation [30], community detection, and so on [16]. These connections are established by various social organizations, such

153

as families, friendship circles, virtual groups, online communities, and so on.

However, from the perspective of user behaviors, some associations among users in social networks are latent (i.e., implied in social behaviors and inferred from the existing links), such as the indirect friendships among microblog users or paper authors. Latent social links are useful for many practical applications of analysis or decision-making, such as drug gangs capturing by using the latent social connections implied in drug dealers' activities of contacts and transactions. Therefore, how to discover and represent the social links, in particular latent links, is generally the critical step for social network analysis to comprehensively reflect the associations among individuals. As the typical application of social media analysis, community detection [22, 31] focuses on discovering the global structure of heterogeneities in social networks to unveil insights into their functional organizations and behavior relationships. This means that if latent links could be described effectively, community detection could be also fulfilled precisely and effectively from a new perspective of social behavioral data analysis. In this chapter, we discuss the method for latent link analysis for community detection in social networks.

It is obvious that latent links are implied in behavior interactions of users and correspondingly reflect their behavioral pattern or preference. We suppose that each record of the behavior observation involving several persons is an observed event that could be looked upon as a transaction like that in the paradigm of frequent pattern mining [8, 9]. From the perspective of behavior association representation, frequent itemsets and consequent association rules are well adopted as the effective methods to discover interesting association relationships. The frequent itemsets discovered from behavior observations reflect statistic results of user behavioral pattern and preference. Consequently, association rules can be discovered as the model for describing associations among object behaviors [9]. However, complex associations among behaviors (i.e., frequent items) cannot be represented globally by means of the form like $X \to Y$, where X and Y are frequent itemsets. As well, the uncertainties of the association rules, generally existing in large-scale social media and measured by confidence and support, cannot be inferred, which is useful for decision-making in realistic situations.

As the typical application of social network analysis, community detection that focuses on potential structural properties of the group components and grouping of users could be fulfilled from the topological structures of social networks. Instead, from the perspective of social behavioral interaction analysis, community detection could be fulfilled by using the behavioral links between users, which is exactly the sense of "community" highlighted in this chapter. To this end, community detection in the context of social behavior associations is different from the classic clustering in data mining paradigm [13], and the classic associative classification established upon association rules [2], as well as the community detection in the context of topological structures of social networks. Therefore, it is desirable to develop the effective model for representing latent links with uncertainties, as well as the method for community detection.

It is well known that graph model has been well adopted for representing complex mutual relationships among objects. Meanwhile, statistic analysis is one of the widely adopted approaches for describing the relationships among objects. Probabilistic graphical models, such as Markov network (MN), Bayesian network (BN), and Latent Dirichlet Allocation (LDA) [25], have been well adopted as the framework for representing and inferring uncertainties due to their advantages brought about by integrating graph model and probability theory. In order to describe the associations (both observed and latent links) with uncertainties, we will adopt probabilistic graphical model as the theoretic basis and knowledge framework. For community detection, we are to discover the mutually associated users based on latent links, instead of causal relationships among them, that is, we need not differentiate the direction of the associations between social users from the graphical model point of view. To this end, we adopt the undirected MN to describe the latent links implied in the transactions of behavioral observations of users [20].

Intuitively, frequent itemsets constitute the dominant and critical part in the given transactions, which are analogously the objects with great interest in behavioral observations. Thus, we make use of the method of frequent itemset mining from the given transactions of behavioral observations, and then construct the MN from the discovered frequent itemsets by using the algorithm given in Chapter 5. By acquiring the knowledge of probabilistic conditional independence implied in frequent itemsets, we could construct a probabilistic undirected graph $G = \langle V, E \rangle$, called item-association Markov network (IAMN) [19], where V is the set of vertexes (or nodes) and represents the set of users, and E is the set of edges representing relationships among these users. Taking IAMN as the framework for representing associations and corresponding uncertainties, we discover latent social links as the basis of community detection.

In social networks, the distribution of edges is often inhomogeneous, with high concentrations in special groups of participant users, and low concentrations between these groups. This feature is called community structure [22, 31], which reflects social relationships of the concerned participant users. It has been pointed out that overlapped groups should be obtained for community detection, since communities are often interwoven in real-world situations [24, 26]. In this chapter, we focus on detecting overlapping community structures based on the constructed IAMN from the perspective of social behaviors instead of social network structures.

It is known that the k-clique algorithm finds all complete subgraphs with k-vertices that are not parts of larger complete subgraphs [23]. By the idea of k-clique, Palla *et al.* [24] uncovered the overlapping community structure of complex networks. By relaxing the strict prerequisites of Palla's method, we consider the practical cases that edges are used to represent social links with different strengths and extend the concept of k-clique to β-maximum-clique by the following steps. First, based on the number of occurrences of frequent itemsets, we assign a weight to every pair of vertices, called reversible confidence, where we make use of the properties of frequent itemsets obtained by the Apriori algorithm [8, 9]. Second, we define β-maximum-clique of vertex u by its nearest neighbor set, which consists of vertex v with the maximal reversible confidence between u and v. Third, we define association degree to describe the concentration of the edges in a set of vertex's nearest neighbors, and introduce threshold β to determine whether the neighbors form a community.

Consequently, we give the IAMN-based algorithm to discover the β-maximum-cliques approximately. Furthermore, we discuss the interaction relation between β-maximum-cliques. Then, we give the concept of α–β-community and give the algorithm to discover α–β-community structures, where α is the threshold of community interaction.

In summary, our contributions in this chapter are as follows:

- Taking as input social behavioral interactions, we propose the algorithm to discover latent links among social objects by using the idea of statistic analysis on behavioral data without regard for the topological structure of social networks.
- Adopting probabilistic graphical model as the framework of uncertainty representation, we adopt IAMN to represent the latent links by a general and theoretically-interpretable model rather than linear formations.
- We introduce the concepts of β-maximum-clique, α–β-community, and corresponding properties based on the basic idea of k-clique. Then, we give the algorithm to detect overlapping communities upon the discovered latent links described by the IAMN.
- We implement the algorithms presented in this chapter. Experimental results and performance studies show the effectiveness and efficiency of our method.

It is worth noting that the above work is established by statistic analysis taking as input social behavioral interactions instead of social networks. This makes our method applicable to the situation without knowing the topological structures specifically for the analysis of realistic online large-scale social networks.

The rest of this chapter is organized as follows. In Section 6.2, we introduce related work. In Section 6.3, we give the algorithm for IAMN-based community detection, followed by the brief review of IAMN construction. In Section 6.4, we show experimental results and performance studies. In Section 6.5, we summarize our method in this chapter.

6.2 Related Work

Link prediction was studied in the paradigm of social network analysis. Ibrahim and Chen [10] proposed the method for link prediction by integrating temporality, community structure, and node cardinality.

Possible links were predicted if they appear frequently in recent times, or they are connected by the nodes in one community. Different from the idea discussed in our work from the perspective of social data analysis, we discover latent links implied in social behavioral interactions from the perspective of participants' behaviors instead of social network structures. Latent interactions upon online social networks, such as profile browsing, which cannot be observed by traditional measurements, were modeled by graphs to understand user browsing behaviors [11], different from our work to discover the latent associations among social behaviors rather than those of latent interactions upon visitors for user profiles. The latent links that we discover between nodes in social networks can be interpreted theoretically by probabilistic properties of graph models, which gives basis for community detection.

PGMs have been used in social network analysis in recent years. Koelle *et al.* [14] pointed out that PGM can be used for uncertainty inferences, search and link inferences in social network analysis applications. Yang *et al.* [29] gave the Bayesian framework for community detection by integrating content and link. Wan *et al.* [27] proposed the method for community detection in mobile social networks based on conditional random field. Yue *et al.* [32] gave the data-intensive and BN-based approach for discovering similar users in social media by BN's graphical properties and probabilistic inferences. Liu *et al.* [19] gave the method for constructing IAMN from the results of frequent pattern mining, and proved the theoretic properties of IAMN as a probabilistic model. These methods provide basis for PGM-based social network analysis, but the representation and discovery of latent social links are not of concern.

The small community phenomenon is common in social networks. A large amount of research works have been devoted to detecting communities in social networks [6, 7, 17, 33]. For example, Atzmueller *et al.* [1] identified communities based on the characteristic descriptions of communities themselves. Ding *et al.* [6] gave the definition of community relevance to discover the "missing link" between communities. From the perspective of link analysis and user behaviors, Zhao *et al.* [33] gave the method for topic-oriented community detection. Li *et al.* [17]

proposed the multi-objective optimization model based on link density for community detection in complex social networks. But social network may not be modeled as signed network due to the heterogeneous and evolving nature. The method in [17] was contributed to network partition inherently, which is different from our idea of community detection by using the discovered latent links implied in social behavior interactions. In contrast, in this chapter we are to discover the latent links of individuals from their behavioral observations, and then incorporate these latent links to detect communities. This makes our method for community detection more effective than the classic ones due to the consideration of implied latent links that could be used to determine the potential structural properties of possible communities.

Many algorithms for detecting communities have been proposed and classified as overlapping clustering and partitional clustering algorithms. Graph partitioning is a common approach for community identification. To assess the goodness of a network partition, a quality function is chosen, by which a value is assigned to each partition of the network [22, 31]. Then, partitions can be ranked on the basis of the values of their quality functions, where the most popular is NG modularity proposed by Girvan and Newman.

Social networks often have overlapping structures [24, 26, 28], also as the background and prerequisite of our study in this chapter. Overlapping clustering indicates another popular class of methods to find clusters in social networks. These algorithms have been widely studied as subjects of great interest. For example, Palla *et al.* [24] introduced the clique percolation method based on local topological properties. They gave the concept of k-clique-communities, in which a k-community was defined as a set of vertices that can be reached by a series of overlapping k-cliques, and "overlap" means that the k-cliques share $k - 1$ vertices. Palla's method allowed for overlapping communities, where vertices have multiple community memberships, but the definition on overlapping cliques is too strict for real situations. Therefore, in this chapter, we relax the constraint in topological structures of communities and focus on the community detection from latent interactions represented by the edges in an IAMN, such that the detection results could be consistent with the characteristics of practical social networks as much as possible.

6.3 Community Detection from IAMN-based Latent Links

Upon behavioral interactions, we construct the IAMN to represent the dependence relationships among frequent objects in social interactions. As given in Algorithm 5.1, if two items are in two itemsets with intersections, then we join them by an edge due to the conditional dependence relationship. If two items are in two itemsets without intersections, we keep them unconnected due to the conditional independence relationship. For any two independent items that are not included in any maximal itemset, we keep them unconnected. With respect to the representation of latent links in social behavioral interactions, IAMN establishes the relationship between frequent itemsets and MN, where objects and latent links correspond to nodes and edges, respectively [19]. Specifically, we could use IAMN to represent the dependence relationships among authors included in papers. An edge in the constructed IAMN was regarded as a latent link if the two concerned nodes belong to two different papers.

Based on the IAMN that reveals both observed and latent relationships between individuals, we discuss the method for community detection in this section.

6.3.1 *Definitions*

From the practical situation of social networks, we are to relax and then extend the concept of k-clique to β-maximum-clique by augmenting weights to the edges and introducing a threshold β of association degree to each vertex set. Based on the number of occurrences of frequent itemsets, we assign a weight to every pair of vertex u and v to describe the association degree between them. Different from the confidence of an association rule, the assigned weight between u and v is not direction-aware but reversible, so we call it reversible confidence between u and v. The β-maximum-clique of a vertex u is the set of u's nearest neighbors, which consists of the vertex v with the maximal reversible confidence between u and v.

To obtain the reversible confidence of each pair of vertices, we consider the following three cases:

(1) Let u and v $(u, v \in U)$ be two 1-frequent items in a frequent itemset X. By Algorithm 6.1, we know that the set U of 1-frequent items is the set V of vertices in $G = \langle V, E \rangle$, where $e(u, v) \in E$. By the Apriori algorithm, we can obtain the number of occurrences of every subset X' in X, denoted as $N(X')$. Then, the reversible confidence $C(u, v)$ of pair (u, v) is defined as

$$C(u, v) = \frac{N(u, v)}{N(u) + N(v) - N(u, v)} \quad (u \neq v) \tag{6.1}$$

(2) Let (u, v) $(u, v \in U)$ be non-frequent and $e(u, v)$ be the edge in E. By Algorithm 6.1, we know that there exists vertex $w \in U$ such that $e_1(u, w) \in E$, $e_2(w, v) \in E$, and (u, w) and (w, v) belong to two different itemsets. The reversible confidence $C(u, v)$ is defined as

$$C(u, v) = C(u, w) * C(w, v) \tag{6.2}$$

(3) Let (u, v) $(u, v \in U)$ be non-frequent and $e(u, v)$ be the edge in E, while there are many paths between u and v. Suppose there are two vertices w and w' $(w, w' \in U, w \neq w')$, such that $e_1(u, w)$, $e_2(v, w)$, $e_3(u, w')$, $e_4(v, w') \in E$. The reversible confidence $C(u, v)$ is defined as

$$C(u, v) = [C(u, w)C(v, w) + C(u, w')C(v, w')]$$
$$- [C(u, w)C(v, w)C(u, w')C(v, w')] \tag{6.3}$$

It is worth noting that the definitions of $C(u, v)$ in Eqs. (6.1)–(6.3) can guarantee $0 \leq C(u, v) \leq 1$, which makes the reversible confidence suitable for the pairs of any two vertices in G.

Definition 6.1. The nearest neighbor set $NN(u)$ of a vertex $u (u \in V)$ is defined as $NN(u) = \{v \in V \mid \text{there does not exist } v' \text{ such that } C(u, v') > C(u, v)\}$.

Based on the concept of k-clique [23], we now give the concept of k-nearest neighbor set.

Definition 6.2. For a vertex $u \in V$, the k-nearest neighbor set of u, denoted as $KNN(u)$, constitutes the most closest k-vertices to u in V, that is, if $v \in KNN(u)$, then there are no k vertices $v' \in V$ such that $C(u, v) < C(u, v')$.

For expression simplification, we use V' to denote $KNN(u)$, where $V' \subseteq V$. To describe the weight between each pair of vertices in V', we give the concept of association degree of V' as follows.

Definition 6.3. For the k-nearest neighbor set of u, the association degree of V' is the average reversible confidence of all the pairs (v_i, v_j) $(v_i, v_j \in V', v_i \neq v_j)$, denoted as $A(V')$ and defined as

$$A(V') = \sum_{v_i, v_j \in V', v_i \neq v_j} C(v_i, v_j)/[|V'| * (|V'| - 1)/2] \qquad (6.4)$$

where $|V'| * (|V'| - 1)/2$ is the number of edges in the complete graph on V'.

Based on Definitions 6.2 and 6.3, we define the β-k-clique of vertex u as follows.

Definition 6.4. Let $G = \langle V, E \rangle$ be an IAMN, $V' \subseteq V(|V'| = k)$ and $u \in V'$. Given the parameter $\beta(0 \leq \beta \leq 1)$, a subgraph of G, denoted as $S'(V', E')$ and induced by $V' = KNN(u)$, is the β-k-clique of u, if $A(V') > \beta$ holds. If there is no β-k'-clique of u in G such that $k' > k$, we say that this β-k-clique is the β-maximum-clique of u.

6.3.2 Algorithm for community detection

As is known, the problem for finding maximum-cliques is NP-hard [23], and finding the β-maximum-clique is NP-hard accordingly. Thus, we give a simple approximate algorithm run in polynomial time for finding the β-cliques that are nearly the β-maximum-cliques specified in Definition 6.4. For every vertex v_i, we find the set N_i of all β-neighbors of v_i. Then, we find a β-maximum-clique in N_i, approximately. This means that there is no such β-clique of v_i, including those which have been discovered currently.

Algorithm 6.1 Approximate β-maximum-clique

Input:

$G = \langle V, E \rangle$, the IAMN, where $V = \{v_1, \ldots, v_n\}$

$C(v_i, v_k)$, the reversible confidence, $v_i, v_k \in V$, $i \neq k$

β, the reversible confidence threshold

Output:

$\rho^* = \{S_1, \ldots, S_n\}$, where S_i is the β-maximum-clique of vertex v_i

$K = \{k_1, \ldots, k_n\}$, where k_i is the number of vertices in S_i

Local variables:

N_i, the set of neighbors of vertex v_i

V_i, the set of vertices in S_i

$\rho = \{V_1, \ldots, V_n\}$

Steps:

1. Initialization:

$\rho \leftarrow \emptyset, \quad K \leftarrow \emptyset$

2. Find V_i of vertices in every β-maximum-clique:

For $i \leftarrow 1$ To n Do

(1) $V_i \leftarrow \{v_i\}, k_i \leftarrow 1$

(2) Find the set N_i of all neighbors of v_i

(3) While $N_i \neq \emptyset$ Do

    Select a vertex $v_k \in N_i$

    For every $v_k \in N_i$ Do

      If $A(V_i \cup \{v_k\}) > \beta$ Then

        $V_i \leftarrow V_i \cup \{v_k\}, N_i \leftarrow N_i \backslash \{v_k\}, k_i \leftarrow k_i + 1$

      Else

        $N_i \leftarrow N_i \backslash \{v_k\}$

      End If

    End For

  End While

(4) $\rho \leftarrow \rho \cup V_i, K \leftarrow K \cup \{k_i\}$

Algorithm 6.1 (Continued)

---

(5) If there exist V_i, $V_j \in \rho$ and $V_j \subset V_i$ Then

$\qquad V_j \leftarrow V_i$, $k_j \leftarrow k_i$

$\quad$ End If

End For

3. Generate the subgraph from V_i:

$\quad S_i \leftarrow$ the subgraph induced by $V_i \in \rho$

$\quad \rho^* \leftarrow \{S_1, \ldots, S_n\}$

4. Return ρ^* and K

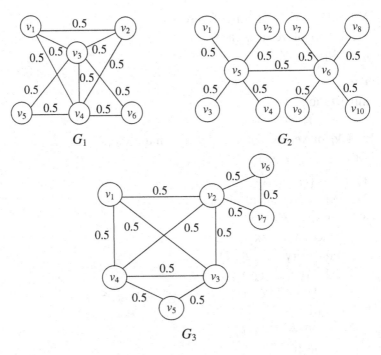

Fig. 6.1. IAMNs G_1, G_2, and G_3.

Example 6.1. Upon three representative and typical IAMNs as undirected graphs, denoted as G_1, G_2, and G_3, shown in Fig. 6.1, we illustrate the execution of Algorithm 6.1. Assume that the reversible confidence of every edge $e(v_i, v_j)$ in G is 0.5, i.e., $C(v_i, v_j) = 0.5$. For every vertex in G, we choose $\beta = 0.15$. It can be seen that the β-maximum-clique of vertex v_1 is $S_1 = (V_1 = \{v_1, v_2, v_3, v_4\}, E_1)$. Meanwhile, we can obtain other five communities: $S_2 = (V_2, E_2)$, $S_3 = (V_3, E_3)$, $S_4 = (V_4, E_4)$, $S_5 = (V_5, E_5)$, and $S_6 = (V_6, E_6)$, where $V_2 = \{v_1, v_2, v_3, v_4\}$, $V_3 = \{v_1, v_2, v_3, v_4, v_5, v_6\}$, $V_4 = \{v_1, v_2, v_3, v_4, v_5, v_6\}$, $V_5 = \{v_3, v_4, v_5\}$, and $V_6 = \{v_3, v_4, v_6\}$. Thus, $A(V_1) = A(V_2) = (0.5 + 0.5 + 0.5)/6 = 0.25$, $A(V_3) = A(V_4) = (0.5 + 0.5 + 0.5 + 0.5 + 0.5)/15 = 0.17$, $A(V_5) = A(V_6) = (0.5 + 0.5)/3 = 0.33$.

Similarly, for every vertex in G_2, we choose the same $\beta = 0.15$. We can obtain ten communities: $S_1(V_1, E_1)$, $S_2(V_2, E_2)$, $S_3(V_3, E_3)$, $S_4(V_4, E_4)$, $S_7(V_7, E_7)$, $S_8(V_8, E_8)$, $S_9(V_9, E_9)$, and $S_{10}(V_{10}, E_{10})$, where $V_1 = \{v_1, v_5\}$, $V_2 = \{v_2, v_5\}$, $V_3 = \{v_3, v_5\}$, $V_4 = \{v_4, v_5\}$, $V_7 = \{v_6, v_7\}$, $V_8 = \{v_6, v_8\}$, $V_9 = \{v_6, v_9\}$, and $V_{10} = \{v_6, v_{10}\}$, and $S_5(V_5, E_5)$, $S_6(V_6, E_6)$, where $V_5 = \{v_1, v_2, v_3, v_4, v_5, v_6\}$ and $V_5 = \{v_5, v_6, v_7, v_8, v_9, v_{10}\}$. For every vertex in G_3, we also choose $\beta = 0.15$. We then obtain seven communities: $S_1(V_1, E_1)$, $S_2(V_2, E_2)$, $S_3(V_3, E_3)$, $S_4(V_4, E_4)$, $S_5(V_5, E_5)$, $S_6(V_6, E_6)$, and $S_7(V_7, E_7)$, where $V_1 = \{v_1, v_2, v_3, v_4\}$, $V_2 = \{v_1, v_2, v_3, v_4, v_6, v_7\}$, $V_3 = V_4 = \{v_1, v_2, v_3, v_4, v_5\}$, $V_5 = \{v_3, v_4, v_5\}$, and $V_6 = V_7 = \{v_2, v_6, v_7\}$.

It can be seen that the communities in G_1, G_2, and G_3 obtained by Algorithm 6.1 are consistent with the results intuitively, which verifies that Algorithm 6.1 is correct to some extent.

As the basic operation in Algorithm 6.1, comparison for finding the β-maximum-cliques is the most time-consuming operation. By neglecting the reversible confidences between nonadjacent vertices, we know that the average number of vertex neighbors is $2m/n$, given an IAMN with n vertices and m edges. The operations of line (3) of Step 2 in Algorithm 6.1 are executed $n[(2m/n)(2m/n - 1)]/2$ times, and thus the whole algorithm can be fulfilled in $O(m^2/n)$ time.

6.3.3 *Community combination*

The β-maximum-cliques obtained by Algorithm 6.1 are looked upon as the basic structure of communities. If two β-cliques are overlapped to a great extent, then these two β-cliques could be combined as a larger community. Now, we discuss the interaction between two β-maximum-cliques

S_i and S_j, described by an interaction function $\xi(S_i, S_j)$, which intuitionally ought to satisfy the following properties:

(1) Commutativity: $\xi(S_i, S_j) = \xi(S_j, S_i)$.
(2) Maximal property: $\xi(S_i, S_i) = 1$ (i.e., $\xi(S_i, S_i)$ is maximal).
(3) Minimal property: $\xi(S_i, S_j) = 0$ (i.e., $\xi(S_i, S_j)$ is minimal), if S_i and S_j are disconnected.
(4) Overlap-incrementality: Let S_i, S_j, and S_k be three β-maximum-cliques. $\xi(S_i, S_k) \geq \xi(S_j, S_k)$ if $V_i \cap V_k \geq V_j \cap V_k$, where V_i is the set of vertices in S_i.

According to the above properties, we define an interaction function as follows.

Definition 6.5. Given an IAMN $G = \langle V, E \rangle$ with β-maximum-cliques $\{S_1, \ldots, S_m\}$, the interaction function $\xi(S_i, S_j)$ between S_i and $S_j (i, j \in \{1, \ldots, m\}, i \neq j)$ is

$$\xi(S_i, S_j) = N(E_i \cap E_j) * 2/[N(E_i) + N(E_j)]$$

where $N(E_i \cap E_j)$ is the number of common edges of S_i and S_j, and $N(E_i)$ is the number of edges in E_i.

It is easy to prove that the interaction function in Definition 6.5 satisfies the aforementioned properties (1)–(4). In the following, we define α–β-community by introducing a threshold α of community interaction.

Definition 6.6. Given the parameter $\alpha(0 \leq \alpha \leq 1)$, the union of S_i and S_j is called a α–β-community if $\xi(S_i, S_j) \geq \alpha$, where every β-maximum-clique S_i is looked upon as a basic community.

According to the idea of this definition, the α–β-communities can be formed level by level, and the procedure for combining the β-maximum-cliques will be continued until there are no α–β-communities S_k and S_l, such that $\xi(S_l, S_k) \geq \alpha$. We adopt β-maximum-cliques as the basic α–β-communities for the first level, and select the new α–β-communities from the pairwise combinations of $l - 1$ levels of communities for level l. The above ideas are summarized in Algorithm 6.2.

Algorithm 6.2 $\alpha-\beta$-community

Input:

$S = \{S_1, \ldots, S_m\}$, the set of different β-maximum-cliques

α, the interaction threshold

Output:

A, the set of $\alpha-\beta$-communities

Local variables:

l, the level number

A_l, the candidate set of $\alpha-\beta$-communities in level l

n_l, the number of $\alpha-\beta$-communities in A_l

Steps:

1. Initialization:

    (1) $l \leftarrow 1$

    (2) For $j \leftarrow 1$ To n_l Do

        $A_{1j} \leftarrow S_j$ // Basic $\alpha-\beta$-communities in level l,

          $S_1, \ldots, S_{nl}$

    End For

    $A_1 \leftarrow \{A_{11}, A_{12}, \ldots, A_{1nl}\}$

2. Generate candidate set A_l level by level:

    Repeat

    (1) $l \leftarrow l + 1$

    (2) For $i \leftarrow 1$ To n_{l-1} Do

        1) Find $(A_{l-1,i}, A_{l-1,k})$ such that $\xi(A_{l-1,i}, A_{l-1,k}) \geq \alpha$

          and $\xi(A_{l-1,i}, A_{l-1,k}) = \max\{\xi(A_{l-1,i}, A_{l-1,i+1}),$

          $\xi(A_{l-1,i}, A_{l-1,i+2}), \ldots, \xi(A_{l-1,i}, A_{l-1,n-1})\}$

        2) Replace $A_{l-1,i}$ and $A_{l-1,k}$ by $A_{l-1,i} \cup A_{l-1,k}$ in A_l

    End For

    Until $A_l = A_{l-1}$

3. $A \leftarrow A_l$

4. Return A

Suppose there are m-different β-maximum-cliques. Now, we focus on line (2) of Step 2 in Algorithm 6.2. The comparisons are executed for $(m-1) + (m-3) + \cdots + (m-5) = \lfloor m^2/4 \rfloor$ times. Thus, comparisons are run $\lfloor m^2/4 \rfloor + \lfloor m^2/4^2 \rfloor + \lfloor m^2/4^3 \rfloor + \cdots + \lfloor m^2/4^l \rfloor$ times and the time complexity of Algorithm 6.2 is $O(m^2)$.

6.4 Experimental Results

6.4.1 *Experiment setup*

To verify the feasibility of our method in this chapter, we implemented the algorithms for IAMN construction and IAMN-based community detection. First, we tested the effectiveness of the constructed IAMN, including the effectiveness of latent link discovery, correctness of IAMN as a PGM, and correctness as a knowledge framework when applied to social community detection. Then, we tested the efficiency of the proposed algorithms, respectively.

The experiments were conducted on the machine running Windows XP Professional, Intel Core2 Duo processor 2.00 GHz CPU, 2 GB memory. All codes were written in Java by Eclipse Kepler Release with JDK 1.6. The test data were obtained from DBLP computer science bibliography [5] and stored as files on disk, where the coauthors of a paper constitute a transaction to describe the authors' behavioral observation of paper cooperation and publication. According to the inherence of the concerned thresholds, the larger the minimal support, the less the IAMN nodes; the larger the value of β, the more the discovered communities; the larger the value of α, the less probable the community combination, and thus the more the ultimate communities. By multiple repetitions of tests on the DBLP dataset, we assign the threshold of the minimal support, β and α by 0.2, 0.04, and 0.015, respectively, under which the IAMN and corresponding communities can be exhibited clearly and interpreted reasonably.

6.4.2 *Effectiveness*

In this section, we tested the effectiveness of IAMN from the following three perspectives: as a model to describe the discovered latent links, as a probabilistic graphical model itself, and as a knowledge framework when applied to social community detection.

6.4.2.1 *Effectiveness of discovered latent links*

First, an edge in the complete graph constructed from the maximum frequent itemsets was regarded as a latent link if the two concerned nodes (i.e., authors) belong to two different papers. Second, an edge in the constructed IAMN was regarded as a latent link if the two concerned nodes belong to two different papers. Third, latent interactions discussed in [11] are visiting logs of user profiles instead of direct interactions like friends or comments. Analogously, we suppose that there exists a latent link of indirect coauthoring relationship between any two different authors in two different papers if there is an intersection between the two sets of authors of these two papers. Fourth, without loss of generality, there exists a correct latent link between any two different frequent authors in two different papers (i.e., frequent items with respect to the given threshold of the minimal support), if there exists intersection between the authors of these two papers.

Latent links from the above four perspectives are denoted as L_{FP}, L_{IAMN}, L_{LI}, and L_C, respectively. We define *recall* as the ratio of the number of discovered and correct latent links to that of the correct latent links, and *precision* as the ratio of the number of discovered and correct latent links to that of the discovered latent links. That is, the *recall* and *precision* for L_{FP}, L_{IAMN}, and L_{LI} are denoted as follows:

$$recall_{FP} = \frac{|L_{FP} \cap L_C|}{|L_C|}, \quad recall_{IAMN} = \frac{|L_{IAMN} \cap L_C|}{|L_C|},$$

$$recall_{LI} = \frac{|L_{LI} \cap L_C|}{|L_C|}$$

$$precision_{FP} = \frac{|L_{FP} \cap L_C|}{|L_{FP}|}, \quad precision_{IAMN} = \frac{|L_{IAMN} \cap L_C|}{|L_{IAMN}|},$$

$$precision_{LI} = \frac{|L_{LI} \cap L_C|}{|L_{LI}|}$$

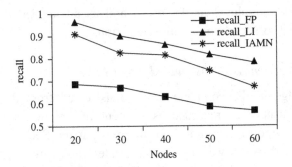

Fig. 6.2. *Recall*$_{FP}$, *Recall*$_{LI}$, and *recall*$_{IAMN}$.

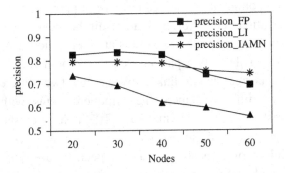

Fig. 6.3. *Precision*$_{FP}$, *precision*$_{LI}$, and *precision*$_{IAMN}$.

Figure 6.2 shows the comparisons between *recall*$_{FP}$, *recall*$_{LI}$, and *recall*$_{IAMN}$ with various numbers of nodes. It can be seen that *recall*$_{FP}$, *recall*$_{LI}$, and *recall*$_{IAMN}$ are decreased with the increase of nodes (i.e., frequent authors), but *recall*$_{IAMN}$ is always higher than *recall*$_{FP}$ and *recall*$_{LI}$ is higher than both *recall*$_{FP}$ and *recall*$_{IAMN}$ for all situations with different numbers of nodes. Meanwhile, Fig. 6.3 shows the comparisons between *precision*$_{FP}$, *precision*$_{LI}$, and *precision*$_{IAMN}$ with various numbers of nodes. It can be seen that both *precision*$_{FP}$ and *precision*$_{LI}$ are decreased with the increase of nodes, while *precision*$_{IAMN}$ is basically fixed to 0.75. This means that latent links implied in social behavioral observations can be discovered by our IAMN-based method more comprehensively than by the frequent-pattern-based method. Furthermore, the latent links discovered by our IAMN-based method are precise to a certain extent and the precision is not sensitive to the number of nodes.

6.4.2.2   *Correctness of IAMN-based community detection*

In this experiment, we adopted the coauthors of the 394 publications of three famous scientists, *Amol Deshpande, Jon M. Kleinberg,* and *Dan Suciu* before 2000. *Zachary G. Ives* was not only coauthored with *Amol Deshpande* but also with *Dan Suciu,* which reflects the overlap characteristics in author cooperation. To test the effectiveness of IAMN-based community detection, we compared the results obtained by our algorithm with those coauthoring at least two papers in the coauthor index provided by DBLP computer science bibliography. Table 6.1 shows and compares the three communities obtained by our algorithm (denoted as AC) and those in DBLP coauthor index (denoted as AD), where the coauthors in AD but not in AC are underlined.

To evaluate the result of community detection by our IAMN-based algorithm, we defined correctness and coverage similar to precision and recall. *Correctness* is defined as the ratio of coauthors in AC and also in AD, which means the proportion of coauthors correctly detected in the DBLP coauthor index. *Coverage* is defined as the ratio of coauthors in AD and also in AC, which means the proportion of coauthors in the DBLP coauthor index that can be detected. Let $|AC|$ and $|AD|$ be the number of authors in AC and AD, respectively. These two metrics are as follows:

$$correctness = |AC \cap AD|/|AC|, \quad coverage = |AC \cap AD|/|AD|$$

By simple statistics, we evaluated the three communities in Table 6.1 based on the above two metrics, as shown in Table 6.2. It can be seen that an author's community consisting of his coauthors could be discovered with the acceptable correctness and coverage. It is worth noting that AD consists of the coauthors who published at least two papers together, and thus the members in community AD are more dependent mutually than those coauthored in one or more papers given directly in the DBLP coauthor index. This means that the correctness of our results will be higher than those currently presented in Table 6.2 if we made the comparisons directly with the content in the DBLP coauthor index (published one or more papers together). Therefore, the effectiveness of IAMN-based community detection also verifies the effectiveness of

Table 6.1. Communities obtained by our algorithm and coauthors in DBLP coauthor index.

Author	AC	AD
A. Deshpande	M. Franklin; S. Chandrasekaran; J. Hellerstein; P. Gibbons; S. Nath; V. Raman; S. Madden; C. Guestrin; W. Moustafa; A. Deshpande; J. Li; K. Mukherjee; A. Malekian; S. Khuller; P. Sen; K. Tzoumas; B. Saha; K. Kumar; W. Hong; A. Condon; L. Hellerstein; M. Garofalakis; T. Rekatsinas; G. Namata	S. Chandrasekaran; M. Franklin; M. Garofalakis; L. Getoor; P. Gibbons; C. Guestrin; J. Hellerstein; L. Hellerstein; W. Hong; C. Jensen; B. Kanagal; S. Khuller; U. Khurana; K. Kumar; J. Li; S. Madden; W. Moustafa; S. Nath; V. Raman; T. Rekatsinas; B. Saha; P. Sen; S. Seshan; K. Tzoumas
J. Kleinberg	B. Karrer; L. Backstrom; J. Ugander; D. Huttenlocher; J. Kleinberg; C. Dwork; D. Crandall; D. Kempe; J. Leskovec; E. Anshelevich; M. Sudan; D. Cosley; A. Anderson; D. Chakrabarti; É. Tardos; D. Easley; L. Blume; R. Kleinberg; V. Guruswami; S. Suri; C. Danescu-Niculescu-Mizil; B. Pang; T. Wexler; F. Chierichetti; S. Oren; A. Dasgupta; R. Ravi; R. Fagin; P. Raghavan; M. Charikar; A. Frieze; S. Rajagopalan; Y. Rabani; A. Slivkins; A. Gupta; K. Dhamdhere; J. Cheng; C. Papadimitriou; G. Kossinets; L. Lee; M. Sandler; R. Kumar; D. Bindel	A. Anderson; E. Anshelevich; L. Backstrom; L. Blume; M. Charikar; J. Cheng; D. Easley; F. Chierichetti; C. Danescu-Niculescu-Mizil; A. Dasgupta; R. Fagin; C. Faloutsos; A. Gupta; D. Huttenlocher; R. Kleinberg; G. Kossinets; A. Kumar; R. Kumar; L. Lee; J. Leskovec; D. Liben-Nowell; S. Oren; C. Papadimitriou; Y. Rabani; P. Raghavan; S. Rajagopalan; T. Roughgarden; A. Sahai; M. Sandler; A. Slivkins; M. Sudan; S. Suri; É. Tardos; J. Ugander; T. Wexler

D. Suciu   A. Morishima; J. Madhavan; I. Tatarinov; A. Gupta;
G. Miklau; Y. Kadiyska; Z. Ives; X. Dong; A. Halevy;
M. Fernandez; T. Green; C. Li; C. Re; N. Dalvi;
R. Chirkova; M. Onizuka; M. Cafarella; M. Hay;
D. Li; V. Rastogi; F. Neven; N. Alon; N. Klarlund;
T. Schwentick; T. Milo; D. Suciu; S. Mathur;
M. Balazinska; R. Ramamurthy; R. Kaushik;
G. Borriello; P. Upadhyaya; B. Howe; P. Koutris;
N. Anderson; J. Letchner; P. Beame; Y. Kwon;
A. Meliou; E. Welbourne; N. Khoussainova;
W. Gatterbauer; K. Moore

N. Alon; M. Balazinska; P. Beame; G. Borriello;
J. Brinkley; M. Cafarella; N. Dalvi; O. Etzioni;
W. Gatterbauer; A. Gupta; A. Halevy; M. Hay;
B. Howe; Z. Ives; A. Jha; R. Kaushik;
N. Khoussainova; P. Koutris; Y. Kwon; J. Letchner;
A. Meliou; G. Miklau; T. Milo; K. Moore;
A. Morishima; F. Neven; V. Rastogi; C. Ré;
T. Schwentick; M. Shaw; W. Tan; I. Tatarinov;
P. Upadhyaya; V. Vianu; E. Welbourne; M. Fernandez

Table 6.2. Correctness and coverage of three communities in Table 6.1.

Author	Node number in IAMN	|AC|	|AD|	|AC ∩ AD|	Correctness (%)	Coverage (%)
A. Deshpande	35	24	24	20	83.3	83.3
J. Kleinberg	60	44	35	30	68.2	85.7
D. Suciu	67	43	36	32	74.4	88.9

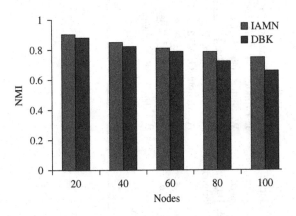

Fig. 6.4. NMI of IAMN and DBK.

IAMN to represent latent links in behavioral observations with respect to classic social network applications.

Further, we tested the effectiveness of community detection by comparing the normalized mutual information (NMI) [4] of communities obtained by our method and those by the density-based k-means algorithm [18], where we adopted the IAMN as the topological structure of the corresponding social network with various numbers of coauthored scientists. Figure 6.4 shows the comparisons between NMI by IAMN and that by the density-based k-means algorithm (abbreviated as DBK) upon the IAMN with 20, 40, 60, 80, and 100 nodes. It can be seen that the NMI by IAMN is basically consistent with that by DBK, and the decrease of NMI is not sensitive to the increase of nodes in the IAMN, which means that the detected communities are effective to a great extent.

6.4.3 *Efficiency*

Taking as input the transactions from various numbers of papers, we could construct the IAMN, where the frequent items of authors were obtained by the Apriori algorithm. The most frequent authors were selected as the IAMN nodes. As shown in Chapter 5, the efficiency of IAMN construction is not sensitive to the increase of items (i.e., nodes), while the execution time of Apriori dominates the total time in IAMN construction from the given transactions of behavioral observations. IAMN could be efficiently used to represent the latent links implied in social behavioral observations.

We implemented Algorithm 6.1 for β-clique detection upon the IAMN and Algorithm 6.2 for $\alpha-\beta$-community detection upon the discovered β-cliques. To test the efficiency of community detection, we recorded the average execution time of Algorithm 6.1 (denoted as αT) and that of Algorithm 6.2 (denoted as $\alpha\beta$T) under the IAMN with 3000, 6000, 9000, 12000, 15000, and 18000 nodes, respectively, compared and shown in Fig. 6.5. It can be seen that both the execution time for discovering β-cliques and that for discovering $\alpha-\beta$-communities is increased linearly with the increase of nodes in the IAMN, but the latter is much more than the former that takes much time on evaluating the nearest neighbor and interaction function. This is also consistent with the theoretic conclusions of time complexities of Algorithms 6.1 and 6.2

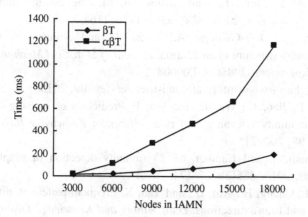

Fig. 6.5. Execution time of β-clique detection and that of $\alpha-\beta$-community detection.

given in Section 6.3. Therefore, the communities could be detected efficiently upon the constructed IAMN, which also verifies that IAMN could be efficiently applied to some social network analysis to a certain extent.

6.5 Summary

Latent links in social media are useful for association analysis, categorization, link prediction, knowledge completion, etc. To discover latent links among users in social networks, we looked upon the behavioral observations as transactions, from which we obtained the frequent itemsets. By focusing on the latent link representation and discovery with uncertainties, we proposed the algorithm for IAMN-based community detection. The most important contribution of this chapter is the latent link discovery from social behavioral interactions instead of social network structures.

References

1. Atzmueller, M., Doerfel, S., and Mitzlaff, F. Description-oriented community detection using exhaustive subgroup discovery. *Information Sciences*, 2015, **329**(1): 965–984.
2. Baralis, E. and Garza, P. I-prune: Item selection for associative classification. *International Journal of Intelligent Systems*, 2012, **27**(3): 279–299.
3. Behrens, T., Hunt, L., and Rushworth, M. The computation of social behavior. *Science*, 2009, **324**(5931): 1160–1164.
4. Danon, L., Diaz-Gwilera, A., Duch, J., and Arenas, A. Comparing community structure identification. *Journal of Statistical Mechanics: Theory and Experiment*, **2005**(9): P09008.
5. DBLP, http://www.informatik.uni-trier.de/~ley/db/, 2015.
6. Ding, J., Jiao, L., Wu, J., and Liu, F. Prediction of missing links based on community relevance and ruler inference. *Knowledge-Based Systems*, 2016, **98**: 200–215.
7. Fortunato, S. and Kamber, M. Community detection in graphs. *Physics Reports*, 2010, **486**(3): 75–174.
8. Han, J., Cheng, H., Xin, D., and Yan, X. Frequent pattern mining: Current status and future directions. *Data Mining and Knowledge Discovery*, 2007, **15**(1): 55–85.

9. Han, J. and Kamber, M. *Data Mining: Concepts and Techniques.* 1st edn. Morgan Kaufmann, California, 2000.

10. Ibrahim, N. and Chen, L. Link prediction in dynamic social networks by integrating different types of information. *Applied Intelligence*, 2015, **42**(4): 738–750.

11. Jiang, J., Wilson, C., Wang, X., Sha, W., Huang, P., Dai, Y., and Zhao, B. Understanding latent interactions in online social networks. *ACM Transactions on the Web*, 2013, **7**(4), **18**:1–18:39.

12. Kadushin, C. *Understanding Social Networks: Theories, Concepts, and Findings.* Oxford University Press, Oxford, 2012.

13. Kannan, R., Vempala, S., and Vetta, A. On clusterings: Good, bad and spectral. *Journal of the ACM*, 2004, **51**(3): 497–515.

14. Koelle, D., Pfautz, J., Farry, M., Cox, Z., Catto, G., and Campolongo, J. Applications of bayesian belief networks in social network analysis. *Proc. UAI Workshops*, 2006.

15. Lazer, D., Pentland, A., Adamic, L., *et al.* Social science: Computational social science. *Science*, 2009, **323**(5915): 721–723.

16. Leskovec, J., Lang, K., and Mahoney, M. Empirical comparison of algorithms for network community detection. *Proc. WWW*, 2010, pp. 631–640.

17. Li, Z., He, L., and Li, Y. A novel multiobjective particle swarm optimization algorithm for signed network community detection. *Applied Intelligence*, 2016, **44**(3): 621–633.

18. Li, Z., Zhang, S., Wang, R., Zhang, X., and Chen, L. Quantitative function for community detection. *Physical Review E*, 2008, **77**(3), doi: 10.1103/PhysRevE.77.036109.

19. Liu, W., Yue, K., Liu, H., Zhang, P., Luo, Y., Liu, S., and Wang, Q. Associative categorization of frequent patterns based on the probabilistic graphical model. *Frontiers of Computer Science*, 2014, **8**(2): 265–278.

20. Liu, W., Yue, K., Wu, H., Fu, X., Zhang, Z., and Huang, W. Markov-network based latent link analysis for community detection in social behavioral interactions. *Applied Intelligence*, 2018, **48**(8): 2081–2096.

21. Newman, M. The structure and function of complex networks. *SIAM Review*, 2003, **45**: 167–256.

22. Newman, M. and Girvan, M. Finding and evaluating community structure in networks. *Physical Review*, 2004, E69(026113): 2.

23. Ostergard, P. A fast algorithm for the maximum clique problem. *Discrete Applied Mathematics*, 2002, 120: 197–207.

24. Palla, G., Derenyi, I., Farkas, I., *et al.* Uncovering the overlapping community structure of complex networks in nature and society. *Nature*, 2005, **435**(7043): 814–818.

25. Pearl, J. *Probabilistic Reasoning in Intelligent System: Network of Plausible Inference.* Morgan Kaufmann, Publishers, San Mateo, CA, 1988.

26. Shen, H., Cheng, X., and Guo, J. Quantifying and identifying the overlapping community structure in networks. *Journal of Statistical Mechanics: Theory and Experiment*, 2009(7): P07042.

27. Wan, H., Lin, Y., Wu, Z., and Huang, H. Discovering typed communities in mobile social networks. *Journal of Computer Science and Technology*, 2012, **27**(3): 480–491.

28. Xie, J., Kelley, S., and Szymanski, B. Overlapping community detection in networks: The state-of-the-art and comparative study. *ACM Computing Surveys*, 2011, **45**(4): 115–123.

29. Yang, T., Jin, R., Chi, Y., and Zhu, H. A Bayesian framework for community detection integrating content and link. *Proc. UAI*, 2012, pp. 615–622.

30. Yang, X., Guo, Y., and Liu, Y. Bayesian-inference based recommendation in online social networks. *IEEE Transactions on Parallel and Distributed Systems*, 2013, **24**(4): 642–651.

31. Yang, Z., Algesheimer, R., and Tessone, C. A comparative analysis of community detection algorithms on artificial networks. *CoRR*, 2016, abs/1608.00763.

32. Yue, K., Wu, H., Fu, X., Yin, Z., and Liu, W. A data-intensive approach for discovering user similarities in social behavioral interactions based on the bayesian network. *Neurocomputing*, 2017, **219**: 364–375.

33. Zhao, Z., Feng, S., Wang, Q., Huang, J. Z., Williams, G., and Fan, J. Topic oriented community detection through social objects and link analysis in social networks. *Knowledge-Based Systems*, 2012, **26**: 164–173.

Chapter 7

Probabilistic Inferences of Latent Entity Associations in Textual Web Contents

Latent entity associations (EA) represent that two entities associate with each other indirectly through multiple intermediate entities in different textual Web contents (TWCs) including e-mails, Web news, social network pages, etc. In our study, Bayesian network (BN) is adopted as the framework to represent and infer latent EAs as well as the probabilities of the associations. In this chapter, we give the concept of entity association Bayesian network (EABN), and then focus on the algorithms to construct EABN efficiently. To guarantee the efficiency of EABN learning from massive TWCs, we employ self-organizing map (SOM) for TWC dataset division to make the co-occurrence-based dependence of each pair of entities concern just a small set of documents. To evaluate and rank EAs in all possible pairs of entities, we incorporate probabilistic inferences of EABN, such that novel latent EAs could be found effectively. Experimental results show the effectiveness and efficiency of our method.

7.1 Motivation and Basic Idea

Including e-mails, Web news, social network pages, etc., textual Web content (TWC) is composed of words, some of which refer to entities. Figure 7.1 shows an example of entity associations (EAs) in TWC documents, where rounded rectangles representing entities and edges indicate that two entities co-occur in the same TWC document. Intuitively, EAs could be divided into two categories: direct EAs and latent EAs. The former represents that two entities co-occur in the same TWC document, while the latter represents that two entities associate with each other indirectly through other intermediate entities in different TWC documents.

179

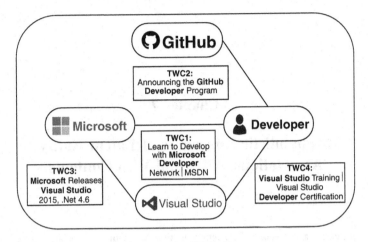

Fig. 7.1. EAs in TWC documents.

As shown in Fig. 7.1, a direct EA exists between "GitHub" and "Developer", while a latent EA exists between "GitHub" and "Microsoft". Both a direct EA and a latent EA exist (through "Visual Studio") between "Microsoft" and "Developer". Actually, in realistic TWC documents, more latent EAs are embodied than direct ones. Expressing latent EAs appropriately is the basis of data acquisition [24], relationship strength estimation [12], and social media analysis [25]. In this chapter, we present the method to find latent EAs from TWCs while focusing on the representation and inference of implied dependencies upon the co-occurrence of entity pairs [10].

From the characteristics of latent EAs in practical applications, several critical challenges are confronted taking as input TWC documents.

(1) Latent EAs are uncertain in general cases. As shown in Fig. 7.1, whether "Microsoft" is associative with "GitHub" is uncertain unless all co-occurrences are discovered already.

(2) Latent EAs are likely to exist between two arbitrary entities. It is necessary to construct a global model that contains most entities in TWC documents while efficiently fulfilling the evaluation of co-occurrences on large volume entities.

(3) Ranking of latent EAs is significant, since not all latent EAs are useful for subsequent tasks with respect to the situations with massive TWC and massive entities.

It is known that Bayesian network (BN) is a well-adopted framework for representing and inferring uncertain knowledge, as well as prediction, diagnosis, and decision [7, 13, 21]. By using BN as the knowledge framework, we propose entity association Bayesian network (EABN), in which entities are regarded as variables, edges describe the associations between entities from the co-occurrence point of view, and conditional probability table (CPT) quantifies the dependencies. By EABN, the dependence relationships among entities could be described from the co-occurrences of pairs of entities, and latent EAs could be inferred by probabilistic inferences of BN.

Self-organizing map (SOM) is a type of artificial neural network trained using unsupervised learning to produce a low-dimensional (typically two-dimensional) and discretized representation of the input space of training samples [9, 11, 19]. To construct the EABN from TWC efficiently, we employ SOM to divide a TWC dataset into several subsets. Most co-occurrences for each entity pair could be found by traversing a TWC subset including much fewer documents. Thus, the execution time of EABN construction will not be increased sharply with respect to the exponential increase of costly traversal on TWC documents even with the linear increase of entities.

Given specific entities, we focus on ranking associative entities based on the latent EAs by probabilistic inferences of EABN [3]. To this end, we translate the task of discovering latent EAs into the computation of conditional probabilities. For example, we regard X as "evidence variables" and Y as "query variables" to discover the latent EA, denoted as $X \rightarrow Y$. The results of probabilistic inferences induce the set Y of entities and corresponding probabilities as the association degree, by which we rank the latent EAs composed of pairs of possibly associative entities in descending order.

Experimental results on real datasets show that our approach could be used to express both direct and latent EAs. It is consistent with practical situations that most EAs are latent EAs but cannot be found by the classic association rule (AR) mining algorithm [1, 4, 6]. Our proposed approach for inferring EAs is effective by comparing the results with those by AR mining. Moreover, novel latent EAs could be discovered by our method. The execution time of EABN has been reduced greatly by using the SOM-based TWC division, and the efficiency of our approach is verified. The capability of inferring latent EAs with probabilistic associations and expressing latent EAs distinguish our approach compared with the classic algorithms for entity association discovery based on Latent Dirichlet Allocation (LDA) [17, 23, 26], and relation extraction (RE) [15, 18, 20], and AR.

The remainder of this chapter is organized as follows: In Section 7.2, we introduce related work. In Section 7.3, we give definitions and problem formalization. In Section 7.4, we present the idea for generating samples of EABN nodes. In Section 7.5, we give the algorithm for EABN learning and EA ranking. In Section 7.6, we show experimental results and performance studies. In Section 7.7, we summarize our work in this chapter.

7.2 Related Work

LDA for TWC analysis: Zhang *et al.* [26] obtained the different topic distributions on different categories in each microblog, and calculated the similarities between users. Wood *et al.* [23] translated knowledge sources into a topic distribution and ensured that the topic inference process is consistent with existing knowledge. Poria *et al.* [17] proposed an LDA method leveraged on the semantics associated with words and multi-word expressions to improve LDA. These methods learn BNs to express the joint probability distribution of entities in TWC documents, while our approach learns an EABN and finds EAs based on probabilistic inferences of EABN.

Relation extraction from TWC: Mintz *et al.* [15] used Freebase, a sizable semantic database of several thousand relations, to provide distant supervision for a relation extraction task. Surdeanu *et al.* [20] proposed a novel approach to multi-instance and multi-label learning for relation extraction. Ren *et al.* [18] proposed a novel domain-independent framework which jointly embeds entity mentions, relation mentions into two low-dimensional spaces, and then estimates the similarity between a new relation and relations in low-dimensional spaces. These methods aim to find instances for a predefined relation type between two entities, but our approach can express latent EAs.

AR mining from TWC: Idoudi *et al.* [6] proposed to enrich existing ontology base by using the discovered ARs. Ahmed and Gargouri [1] introduced an approach for enhanced AR derivation, where two main categories of knowledge are employed in the mining process. Erlandsson *et al.* [4] proposed association learning to detect relationships between users in online social networks. These methods are effective to discover direct EAs. In contrast, our approach is developed to express both direct and latent EAs implied in TWCs.

7.3 Definitions and Problem Formalization

In this section, we give the definition of entity BN based on the idea of a general BN [3], and then formalize our problem to be discussed.

Definition 7.1. An entity association Bayesian network (EABN) is a pair $B_e = (G_e, P_e)$. $G_e = (V, E)$ is a DAG. V is the set of nodes and E is the set of edges in EABN. A node in V represents an entity as a variable in EABN, and V's possible values express frequencies of entities qualitatively. Edges correspond to the dependency of one node (an entity) on another in TWC documents. P_e is specified as a set of CPTs associated with the nodes in G_e.

The problem to be solved is formalized as follows:

(1) Wikidata [5, 8, 22] and supplementary entities are integrated into a knowledge base K to recognize entities in a TWC dataset T. Then, frequent entities are selected to serve as nodes of an EABN, denoted as B_e. Samples of EABN nodes are generated by normalizing frequencies of frequent entities in each TWC document and adopted as the training data for learning B_e.

(2) Learning B_e contains structure selection and parameter estimation. In structure selection, SOM is employed to divide T into multiple subsets, which we choose to provide samples, and thus the time

consumption could be reduced. In parameter estimation, CPTs are generated for each node in the EABN by maximum-likelihood estimation.

(3) For each pair of nodes $\langle X, Y \rangle$ in B_e, we set $X = x$ as the "evidence" and set Y as the "query variables". By probabilistic inferences of EABN, $P(Y \mid X = x)$ could be obtained, as the conditional probability over the values of Y to express frequencies of Y qualitatively. We then provide $W_{Y,x} = \sum y * P(Y = y)$ as the quantitative evaluation for the latent EA of y given x. Finally, we produce $W_{Y,x}$ for all entity pairs $\langle X, Y \rangle$ and rank all $W_{Y,x}$ in descending order.

7.4 Generating Samples of EABN Nodes

Wikidata and supplementary entities could be integrated into a knowledge base K and entity frequencies could be sampled but vary greatly in different TWC documents. To reduce the complexity of EABN construction, entity frequencies will be normalized into bounded values. We check whether each word in TWC documents is an entity (whether the word exists in K) and add it into an entity set. Then, some most frequent entities serve as the EABN nodes. Finally, we record and normalize the frequencies of most frequent entities in each TWC document as integers. Figure 7.2 shows an example, in which we generate two samples from two TWC documents for three most frequent entities.

The above ideas are summarized in Algorithm 7.1.

Suppose the average of $|T_i|$ is C_1, so Step 1 will be executed for MC_1 times. Step 2, 4, and 6 will be executed for $|H| \log |H|$, $|T_i.E|n$, and n times, respectively. Thus, the total number of iterations in Algorithm 7.1 is $MC_1 + |H| \log |H| + M * (|T_i.E|n + n + n)$, and the complexity of Algorithm 7.1 is $O(M|T_i.E|n)$.

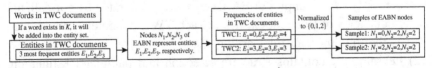

Fig. 7.2. Generating two samples from two TWC documents for three most frequent entities.

Algorithm 7.1 Generating samples of EABN nodes

Input:

$B_e = (G_e, P_e)$, $G_e = (V, E)$, an EABN

$T = \{T_1, \ldots, T_M\}$, a TWC dataset containing M documents

K, a knowledge base consisting of Wikidata and supplementary entities

n, EAs among n entities to be evaluated and ranked

Variables:

$T_i.E$, entity array of T_i; $T_i.E$.append(Ent), the function to append entity Ent into $T_i.E$

H, a hash table storing frequencies of entities (default values are 0)

Output:

$T_i.S$, samples of V in T_i

Steps:

1. For $i \leftarrow 1$ To M Do // find frequent entities
       For $j \leftarrow 1$ To $|T_i|$ Do // $T_{i,j}$ is the j-th word in T_i
         If $T_{i,j} \in K$ Then // words in K serve as nodes of EABN
           $T_i.E$.append($T_{i,j}$)
           If $H[T_{i,j}]$ is undefined Then
             $H[T_{i,j}] \leftarrow 0$
           Else
             $H[T_{i,j}] \leftarrow H[T_{i,j}] + 1$ // frequency of $T_{i,j}$ is increased
           End If
         End If
       End For
     End For
2. Sort H by entity frequencies
3. $V \leftarrow \{$top n frequent entities in $H\}$

Algorithm 7.1 (Continued)

---

4. For $i \leftarrow 1$ To M Do // generating samples for frequent entities

    For $j \leftarrow 1$ To $|T_i.E|$ Do

      For $k \leftarrow 1$ To $|V|$ Do

        If $T_i.E[j] = V[k]$ Then

          If $T_i.S[k]$ is undefined Then

            $T_i.S[k] \leftarrow 0$

          Else

            $T_i.S[k] \leftarrow T_i.S[k] + 1$

          End If

        End If

      End For

    End For

  End For

5. $X_M \leftarrow \text{Max}\{T_i.S[k]\}$

6. For $k \leftarrow 1$ To $|V|$ Do

    $T_i.S[k] \leftarrow \text{Round}[(T_i.S[k]/X_M) \times (Z - 1)]$ //normalization

  End For

7. Return $T_i.S$

7.5 Learning an EABN and Ranking EAs

7.5.1 *BIC metric and division of TWC dataset*

As the classic algorithm for learning a BN from data, scoring and search based structure learning defines a scoring function that measures how well the structure fits samples, and then finds the highest-scoring structure from a hypothesis space of potential models [3]. To exhibit the trade-off between the degree of fitting and structure complexity, the Bayesian Information Criterion (BIC) [3] is employed as the scoring function in our method. The stronger the dependence of an EABN node on its parents, the higher the score will be. The BIC scoring function is given as follows:

$$
\begin{cases}
\text{score}_{\text{BIC}}(G_e : T) = M \sum_{i=1}^{n} I_{\widehat{P}}(X_i; Pa(X_i)) - \dfrac{\log M}{2} |V| \\
I_{\widehat{P}}(X_i; Pa(X_i)) = \sum_{X_i, Pa(X_i)} \widehat{P}(X_i, Pa(X_i)) \log \dfrac{\widehat{P}(Pa(X_i)|X_i)}{\widehat{P}(Pa(X_i))}
\end{cases}
$$

$$(7.1)$$

where G_e denotes an EABN structure and $|V|$ is the number of nodes in G_e. T is a TWC dataset and $\widehat{P}$ is the empirical distribution observed in samples. X_i is a node of G_e and $Pa(X_i)$ is the set of X_i's parents.

In EABN construction, the execution time of BIC evaluation is increased exponentially with the linear increase of entities. To this end, we propose a strategy called subset BIC (SBIC) to reduce the execution time of BIC evaluation so that massive TWC documents from various domains could be leveraged. SBIC consists of two phases. In phase 1, SOM is employed to divide the TWC dataset into several subsets. A unique index is assigned to each entity in the TWC dataset and the indexes of entities are used to build a feature vector for each TWC document. SOM will assign a TWC document into multiple two-dimensional output vectors. Thus, we treat an output vector as a TWC subset containing some documents, where the numbers of entities in each subset are also recorded. The above ideas are given in Algorithm 7.2.

Suppose that the average of $|T_i.E|$ is C_2, so Step 2 is iteratively executed C_2 times. The While loop is executed I_m times and Step 3 is executed $I_m \times 2N_s$ times. Suppose that the average of $|S[i].D|$ is C_3 and the average of $|S[i].D[j].E|$ is C_4, so Steps 4 and 5 will be iteratively executed $N_s C_3 C_4$ times. Thus, the total number of iterations in Algorithm 7.2 is $M \times (C_2 + I_m \times 2N_s) + N_s C_3 C_4$ and the complexity of Algorithm 7.2 is $O(MI_m N_s)$.

Example 7.1. We now give an example in Fig. 7.3 to illustrate the evaluation of SBIC. For demonstration purposes, the learning rate of

SOM is assigned as 1 and output vectors are initialized to [0.5, 0.5, 0.5, 0.5].

In phase 1 of SBIC: (1) We assign 0, 1, 2, and 3 to entities "Microsoft", "Visual Studio", "Developer", and "Github", respectively.

Algorithm 7.2 TWC division by SOM

Input:

T, a TWC dataset

N_s, the number of output vectors in SOM

Variables:

$T_i.E$, the entity array of T_i

$F_i = [0, \ldots, 0]$, the feature vector of T_i, $|F_i| = |V|$

H_I, a hash table storing indexes of entities

I_m, the iteration limit of SOM

Output:

S, the array containing output vectors of SOM;

$S[k]$, the k-th output vector in S; $S[k].D$, the array containing
  TWC documents assigned to $S[k]$; $S[k].H$, the hash table
  containing the number of entities in $S[k]$

Function:

Euc(X_1, X_2), calculating the Euclidean distance
between X_1 and X_2

$S[k].D$.append(doc), appending the TWC document
doc into $S[k].D$

Steps:

1. $I \leftarrow 0$ // number of SOM iterations

2. For $i \leftarrow 1$ To M Do
     For $j \leftarrow 1$ To $|T_i.E|$ Do
       If $H_I[T_i.E[j]]$ is undefined Then
         $I \leftarrow 0$, $I \leftarrow 0$, $C_E \leftarrow 0$
       End If
     End For
   End For

Algorithm 7.2 (Continued)

---

3. For $i \leftarrow 1$ To M Do

    For $j \leftarrow 1$ To $|T_i.E|$ Do

        If $H_I[T_i.E[j]]$ is undefined Then

            $H_I[T_i.E[j]] \leftarrow C_T \leftarrow C_E,\ C_E \leftarrow C_E + 1$

        Else

            $C_T \leftarrow H_I[T_i.E[j]]$

        End If

    End For

    $F_i[C_T] \leftarrow 1$

    While $I < I_m$ Do // assign T_i to an output vector of SOM

        $I \leftarrow I + 1$

        For $k \leftarrow 1$ To N_s Do

            If D_T is undefined Or $\mathrm{Euc}(F_i, S[k]) < D_T$ Then

                $D_T \leftarrow \mathrm{Euc}(F_i, S[k])$

                $k_B \leftarrow k$ // k_B records the index of best matching output vector

            End If

            $S[k_B].D.\mathrm{append}(T_i)$

        End For

    End While

    End For

4. For $k \leftarrow 1$ To N_s Do // updating the output vectors

    $a \leftarrow 1 - I/I_m,\ \theta \leftarrow [(N_s{}^\wedge 0.5)/2] \times a$

    If $\mathrm{Euc}(S[k_B], S[k]) < \theta$ Then

        $S[k] \leftarrow S[k] + \theta a[F_i - S[k]]$

    End If

    End For

5. For $i \leftarrow 1$ To N_s Do // recording the numbers of entities in each subset

    For $j \leftarrow 1$ To $|S[i].D|$ Do

        For $k \leftarrow 1$ To $|S[i].D[j].E|$ Do

            $\mathrm{Ent} \leftarrow S[i].D[j].E[k],\ S[i].H[\mathrm{Ent}] \leftarrow S[i].H[\mathrm{Ent}] + 1$

        End For

    End For

    End For

6. Return S

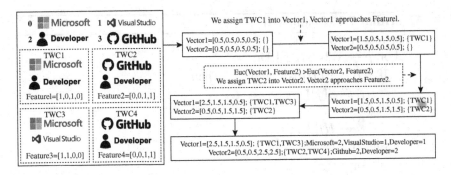

Fig. 7.3. Dividing a TWC dataset into two subsets (output vectors).

(2) Each TWC document produces a feature vector based on corresponding entities. (3) Each feature vector of TWC document is assigned to an output vector with the minimal Euclidean distance. TWC1 and TWC3 are assigned to output Vector1. TWC2 and TWC4 are assigned to output Vector2. (4) We also record the number of entities in each output vector.

In phase 2 of SBIC, we consider a candidate structure "Microsoft→ Developer→GitHub", $I_{\widehat{P1}}$(Developer(i); Microsoft$_{\text{Developer}(i)}$) and $I_{\widehat{P2}}$ (Github(i); Developer$_{\text{Github}(i)}$) need to be computed where Developer(i) represents the i-th value of "Developer". $I_{\widehat{P1}}$ can be computed by the samples in Vector1 since "Developer" and "Microsoft" do not co-occur in Vector2. 50% time consumption is reduced, since only two TWC documents (TWC1 and TWC3) in Vector1 are engaged in computing $I_{\widehat{P1}}$. In practical situations, Vector1 is chosen to compute $I_{\widehat{P1}}$, since it has the maximal sum of frequency of "Developer" and "Microsoft". By SBIC, a subset is chosen to compute each $I_{\widehat{P}}(X_i; Pa(X_i))$ and provides an approximation of BIC by less execution time.

7.5.2 *Scoring-based construction of EABN*

In this section, a heuristic search is used to find the structure of EABN with the highest SBIC score starting from an empty structure G. By applying edge addition, deletion, or edge reversal, we can generate G's neighbors and evaluate their SBIC scores, respectively. Then, we use the change that leads to the best improvement of SBIC scores until no modification could improve the score. The above idea is given in Algorithm 7.3.

EABN includes $|V|$ nodes and $|E|$ edges. Edge addition, deletion, and reversal are made for $|V|(|V| - 1) - |E|$, $|E|$, and $|E|$ times, respectively. The total number of operations of edges is $V|(|V| - 1) + |E|$. Thus, the complexity of Algorithm 7.3 is $O(M|V|^2)$.

Based on the structure G_c generated by Algorithm 7.3, we use Maximum-Likelihood Estimation (MLE) to implement parameter estimation, which satisfies the global decomposition property of the likelihood function [3]. Furthermore, we can decompose the local-likelihood function for a CPT into a product of simple-likelihood function $P(X_i \mid Pa(X_i))$, calculated by Eq. (7.2). For a node X_i and the set of parent nodes

---

Algorithm 7.3 Obtaining an EABN structure with the highest SBIC score

---

Input:

$B_e = (G_e, P_e)$, $G_e = (V, E)$, an EABN

G_c, the empty structure of an EABN B_e

Output:

G_c, the highest-scoring structure of B_e

Steps:

1. $X_S \leftarrow 0$ // X_S record the maximal SBIC score

  $X_B \leftarrow$ TRUE // X_B indicates whether we find a better structure

2. While $X_B =$ TRUE Do

  $X_B \leftarrow$ FALSE

  For each G'_c Do // edge addition, deletion, or edge reversal

  If SBIC(G'_c) $> X_S$ Then

   $X_S \leftarrow$ SBIC(G'_c)

   $X_B \leftarrow$ TRUE

   $G_c \leftarrow G'_c$

  End If

  End For

  End While

3. Return G_c

$Pa(X_i)$, N_{pr} is the number of instances in the TWC dataset T such that $X_i = p$ and $Pa(X_i) = r$, while N_r is the number of instances such that $Pa(X_i) = r$.

$$P(X_i \mid Pa(X_i)) = \frac{N_{\mathrm{pr}}}{N_r} \qquad (7.2)$$

Example 7.2. Now we give an example to show the process of EABN construction. On the generated samples, Eq. (7.2) is employed to generate CPTs for each edge in the DAG of EABN. For instance, we employ *Entity*(i) to represent that an entity in EABN is assigned to its i-th value. The numbers of instances for *Developer*(0) and *Developer*(1) are 4 and 6, respectively, given *Microsoft*(0). There are three instances of *Developer*(0) and seven instances of *Developer*(1), given Microsoft(1). Thus, we could compute the following four conditional probabilities that constitute the CPT for the directed edge from "Microsoft" to "Developer", as shown in Fig. 7.4.

$$P(Developer(0) \mid Microsoft(0)) = 4/(4+6) = 0.4,$$

$$P(Developer(1) \mid Microsoft(0)) = 0.6,$$

$$P(Developer(0) \mid Microsoft(1)) = 0.3,$$

$$P(Developer(1) \mid Microsoft(1)) = 0.7.$$

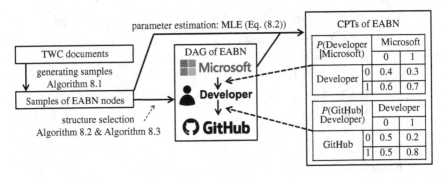

Fig. 7.4.   EABN construction.

7.5.3 Ranking EAs by probabilistic inferences of EABN

To produce the quantitative evaluations of EAs, we set $X = x$ as "evidence" and Y as "query variables" for each pair of nodes $\langle X, Y \rangle$ in B_e. By probabilistic inferences of EABN, we obtain $P(Y \mid X = x)$ as the conditional probability over the value of Y, which expresses frequencies of Y qualitatively. We provide $W_{Y,x} = \sum y * P(Y = y)$ as the quantitative evaluation for $A_{x \to Y}$. Finally, we produce $W_{Y,x}$ for all entity pairs $\langle X, Y \rangle$ and rank all $W_{Y,x}$ in descending order. Top $W_{Y,x}$ indicates significant EAs implied in TWC documents.

To rank EAs effectively, we employ forward sampling [3] to implement efficient approximate inference of EABN, since an exact inference algorithm will be executed in exponential time, which does not work with respect to a large number of entities in TWC documents. M samplings of EABN nodes were generated by assigning values to non-evidence nodes according to the topological order obtained by employing the depth-first search (DFS) [2]. A random value could be generated from the CPT of V_j, since the values of V_j's parent nodes U_j are known according to the topological order.

For instance, $P(V_j = 0 \mid U_j) = 0.2$ and the range from 0 to 0.2 is assigned to $V_j = 0$. $P(V_j = 1 \mid U_j) = 0.8$ and the range from 0.2 to 1.0 is assigned to $V_j = 1$. A random value between 0.0 and 1.0 is generated in the range from 0.2 to 1.0. Thus, we set V_j to be 1. M_y is counted by representing the number of instances for $Y = y$ and then $P(Y = y) = M_y/M$ is calculated. The above ideas are summarized in Algorithm 7.4.

The complexity of producing the topological order of EABN nodes is $O(|V| + |E|)$. We can produce $L_C = |V| \times (|V| - 1)/2$ entity pairs and the number of iterations of Step 3 is $L_C \log(L_C)$. Thus, the complexity of Algorithm 7.4 is $O(M|V|^3)$.

Example 7.3. On the EABN in Fig. 7.4, an example is provided for ranking EAs including EA1 ($A_{Microsoft \to Developer}$), EA2 ($A_{Developer \to Github}$), and EA3($A_{Microsoft \to Github}$), where *val*, *ins*, and *prob* denote the value

---

Algorithm 7.4 Ranking EAs by probabilistic inferences of EABN

Input:
 $B_e = (G_e, P_e)$, $G_e = (V, E)$, an EABN
 M, the number of forward samplings
Variables:
 $F = \{F[1], \ldots, F[M]\}$, the set of forward samplings
 $Y[k]$, the value of Y in $F[k]$
Output:
 R, a ranked list for $W_{Y,x}$
Steps:
1. $V_1, \ldots, V_{|V|} \leftarrow$ a topological ordering of V
2. For $p \leftarrow 1$ To $|V|$ Do
  For $q \leftarrow 1$ To $|V|$ Do
   If $p \neq q$ Then
    $Y \leftarrow \{V_p\}$ // evidence variables
    $X \leftarrow \{V_q = v_q\}$ // query variables
   End If
   For $i \leftarrow 1$ To M Do
    For $j \leftarrow 1$ To $|V|$ Do // forward sampling to obtain $P(Y \mid X)$ ($\times$)
     Find $P(V_j \mid U_j)$ from the CPT of v_j
     $v_j \leftarrow$ a random value according to $P(V_j \mid U_j)$
     If $j = q$ And $v_j \neq v_q$ Then
      Continue // v_j does not match the evidence, goto ($\times$)
     End If
    End For
    $F[i] \leftarrow \{v_1, \ldots, v_n\}$
   End For
$$P(Y = y \mid X = x) \leftarrow \frac{1}{M} \sum_{k=1}^{M} \{Y[k] = y\}$$
   $W_{Y,x} \leftarrow \sum y \times P(Y = y)$
   $R \leftarrow R \cup \{(A_{x \to Y}, W_{Y,x})\}$ // append the pair $(A_{x \to Y}, W_{Y,x})$ into R
  End For
 End For
3. Sort R by $W_{Y,x}$
4. Return R

Table 7.1. Conditional probability distributions and EABN evaluations.

Generating 100 forward samplings for each EA (*val*, *ins*, *prob*)

EA1(*Microsoft* = 1)			EA2(*Developer* = 1)			EA3(*Microsoft* = 1)		
Developer	*val*	0	1	*GitHub*	*val*	0	1	*GitHub*	*val*	0	1
	ins	40	60		*ins*	20	80		*ins*	32	68
	prob	0.4	0.6		*prob*	0.2	0.8		*prob*	0.32	0.68

$W_{Developer,\ Microsoft=1}$ $\quad$ $W_{Github,\ Developer=1}$ $\quad$ $W_{Developer,\ Microsoft=1}$
$= 0 \times 0.4 + 1 \times 0.6 = 0.6$ $\quad = 0 \times 0.2 + 1 \times 0.8 = 0.8$ $\quad = 0 \times 0.32 + 1 \times 0.68 = 0.68$

of entity, instance number of the value, and the conditional probability, respectively. EA1 and EA2 are direct EAs while EA3 is a latent EA. In Table 7.1, 100 forward samplings are generated for EA3 when *Microsoft* is set to 1. Among the 100 forward samplings, we can obtain 32 instances satisfying Github = 0 and 68 instances satisfying Github = 1. Thus, we can compute the conditional probabilities $P(Github = 0 \,|\, Microsoft = 1) = 32/100 = 0.32$ and $P(Github = 1 \,|\, Microsoft = 1) = 68/100 = 0.68$. After all $W_{Y,x}$ were computed, we can rank EAs in descending order as [EA2(0.8), EA3(0.68), EA1(0.6)].

7.6 Experimental Results

7.6.1 *Experiment setup*

Configuration: Python 2.7 is employed to implement all the aforementioned algorithms. All algorithms are executed by a machine with Intel Xeon CPU (4 × 3.6 GHz) and 128 GB RAM.

Datasets: "Groceries dataset" [14] serves as the standard data, which contains 1 month (30 days) of real-world point-of-sale transaction data from a typical local grocery outlet with 9835 transactions and the items are aggregated to 169 categories. The realistic "News Popularity in Multiple Social Media Platforms Dataset" [16] which comprises four topics of news headlines was adopted as our test dataset. The topic "Microsoft" with 21858 documents is abbreviated as the "Microsoft dataset".

Metrics: The effectiveness of our method is tested by two aspects. First, two rankings produced by EABN and Apriori, respectively, for the same EA is compared. Second, we divide a TWC dataset equally into several subsets and propose a metric named consistency of ratio (COR) as follows:

$$COR(A_{X \to Y}) = STDEV(N_Y/N_X) \qquad (7.3)$$

where N_Y is an array of Y's number in each TWC subset and $N_{Y,i}$ represent Y's number in the i-th subset. STDEV is the function to compute a standard deviation.

The efficiency of our method is tested by the execution time of learning and inferences of the EABN, including the total time of model learning by BIC and SBIC, respectively, the total time and average time of probabilistic inference with respect to each EA.

7.6.2 *Effectiveness*

AR (Apriori algorithm with *minSupport* = 0.04 and *minConfidence* = 0.2) and EABN (top 32 frequent entities in Groceries dataset as nodes) are employed to find EAs in the Groceries dataset. We summarized the results of AR and EABN in Table 7.2 (a). AR (the Apriori algorithm with *minSupport* = 0.013 and *minConfidence* = 0.2) and EABN (top 20 frequent entities in Microsoft dataset as nodes) are employed to find EAs in the Microsoft dataset. The results are summarized in Table 7.2(b).

It can be noted from Table 7.2 that the order of EAs obtained by the EABN-based ranking is consistent with that by the Apriori-based ranking. EABN could be used to infer latent EAs, and thus more EAs could be found upon EABN than those found by Apriori (just direct EAs). The rank of a direct EA is greater than that by Apriori, since latent EAs do not exist in the latter.

COR is used to express whether the ratio $N_{Y,i}/N_{X,i}$ remains consistent in different TWC subsets. If the ratio $N_{Y,i}/N_{X,i}$ remains consistent while $N_{Y,i}$ and $N_{X,i}$ change randomly in different TWC subsets, then

Table 7.2. EAs found by EABN and AR in Groceries dataset and Microsoft dataset: (a) Groceries dataset; (b) Microsoft dataset.

(a)

$A_{X \to Y}$		EABN ranking	Apriori ranking
X	Y		
Root vegetables	Whole milk	5	1
Root vegetables	Other vegetables	7	2
Tropical fruit	Whole milk	9	3
Other vegetables	Whole milk	14	5
Yogurt	Whole milk	15	4
Whole milk	Other vegetables	30	8
Yogurt	Other vegetables	33	6
Rolls/buns	Whole milk	36	7

(b)

$A_{X \to Y}$		EABN ranking	Apriori ranking
X	Y		
Google	Microsoft	5	1
Apple	Microsoft	6	2
Windows	Microsoft	13	3
Company	Microsoft	14	6
Software	Microsoft	16	5
Users	Microsoft	17	4

the tendencies of N_Y and N_X are similar and COR metric would be relatively small. Thus, we conclude that smaller COR metrics are more valuable for subsequent EA-based tasks.

Our experiments are conducted to test whether EAs could be found by EABN with small COR values. In the Groceries dataset, $A_{e3(root\ vegetables) \to e4(whole\ milk)}$ ranks first in the Apriori ranking and $A_{e1(chicken) \to e2(other\ vegetables)}$ ranks first in the EABN ranking. The statistics of some entities in this dataset are listed in Table 7.3. N_{e1}/N_{e2}, N_{e3}/N_{e4} and corresponding averages are shown in Fig. 7.5(a). Intuitively, we know that the ratio N_{e1}/N_{e2} is more consistent than the ratio N_{e3}/N_{e4}. In fact, $\mathrm{COR}(A_{e1(chicken) \to e2(other\ vegetables)}) = 0.029$

Table 7.3. Statistics of some entities in Groceries dataset.

	Subsets of the Groceries dataset									
	1	2	3	4	5	6	7	8	9	10
N_{e1}	32	40	37	50	42	52	38	37	48	46
N_{e2}	186	197	185	197	201	226	179	156	176	200
N_{e1}/N_{e2}	0.17	0.20	0.20	0.25	0.21	0.23	0.21	0.24	0.27	0.23
N_{e3}	110	117	99	109	140	114	89	104	92	98
N_{e4}	269	248	252	227	284	274	231	262	235	231
N_{e3}/N_{e4}	0.41	0.47	0.39	0.48	0.49	0.42	0.39	0.40	0.39	0.42

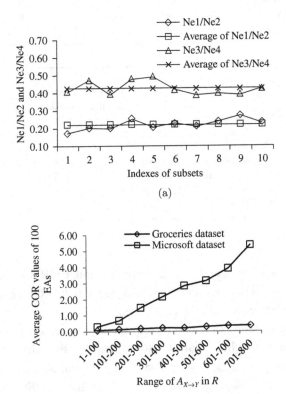

(a)

(b)

Fig. 7.5. COR values: (a) N_{e1}/N_{e2} and N_{e3}/N_{e4}; (b) Average of 100 $COR(A_{X \to Y})$.

is less than $COR(A_{e3(root\ vegetables)\rightarrow e4(whole\ milk)}) = 0.041$. The EA between N_{e1} and N_{e2} has not been found by Apriori, since N_{e1} and N_{e2} do not co-occur frequently. However, N_{e1}/N_{e2} is more consistent than N_{e3}/N_{e4} when N_{e1} and N_{e3} change in different TWC subsets. Thus, $A_{e1(chicken)\rightarrow e2(other\ vegetables)}$ could be found successfully by EABN with smaller COR values for subsequent EA-based tasks than $A_{e3(root\ vegetables)\rightarrow e4(whole\ milk)}$.

$COR(A_{X\rightarrow Y})$ could be computed for each $A_{X\rightarrow Y}$ in the ranked list R obtained by Algorithm 7.4. Figure 7.5(b) shows the average of 100 $COR(A_{X\rightarrow Y})$ values for ranges in the Groceries dataset and Microsoft dataset, since the number of entity Y is usually influenced by many entities rather than only X and $COR(A_{X\rightarrow Y})$ is not strictly ordered. It can be concluded from Fig. 7.5(b) that the COR value is increased generally in ranked by $W_{Y,x}$ in descending order and the Groceries dataset has a smaller average of COR than the Microsoft dataset in the same range of R.

7.6.3 Efficiency

Figure 7.6(a) compares the total time of learning an EABN by BIC metric on the Groceries dataset with various numbers of EABN nodes and various sizes of samples. It can be seen that the total time of EABN learning increases exponentially with the linear increase of the nodes in the EABN on each sample set. Figure 7.6(b) compared the total time of learning an EABN by SBIC metric, and the time consumption on various numbers of nodes and various sized samples is about 30% of that when using the classic BIC metric shown in Fig. 7.6(a). This verifies that our proposed SBIC could greatly reduce the execution time of BIC evaluation in EABN learning, which facilitates the applicability of our method for massive TWC documents from various domains.

Figure 7.7(a) shows the total time of finding all EAs by probabilistic inferences with an EABN with various numbers of EABN nodes and various times of forward sampling. Figure 7.7(b) shows the average time to find an EA by probabilistic inferences. Both the total time and the

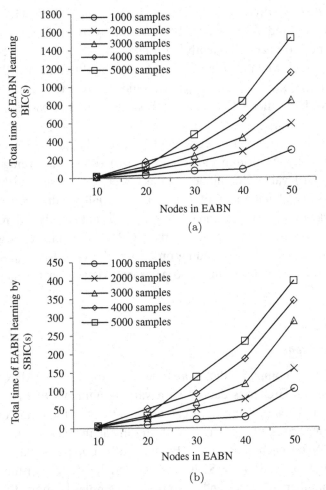

Fig. 7.6. Execution time of EABN learning: (a) Total time of EABN learning by BIC; (b) Total time of EABN learning by SBIC.

time to find an EA are increased with the increase of sampling, while not sensitive to the number of nodes in an EABN. By comparing Figs. 7.7(a) and (b), it can be concluded that the total time of probabilistic inferences may not increase strictly since EABN with fewer nodes may also produce a more complex structure than that with more nodes.

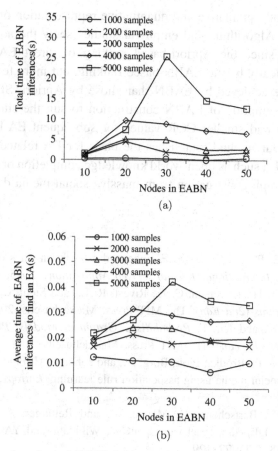

Fig. 7.7. Execution time of EABN inferences: (a) Total time of EABN inferences; (b) Average time of EABN inferences to find an EA.

7.7 Summary

As one of the most important social media data, TWC implies EAs to reflect users' behavioral patterns, critical events, popular news, and debated opinions, etc. Other than direct or straightforwardly observed associations, latent associations are more valuable but challenging. In this chapter, we incorporate EABN, SBIC, and COR to find latent EAs implied in TWCs by making use of the probabilistic inferences with BNs. Both qualitative and quantitative representation of EAs could be provided. Algorithms and empirical studies show the advantages of our method, since the Apriori-based ranking of direct EAs could be achieved basically by the EABN-based ranking, but more feasible latent EAs could be achieved by EABN than those by Apriori. SBIC reduces the time consumption of EABN construction to suit the situations with more entities and smaller COR values for subsequent EA-based query processing. Our method establishes the basis for EA-related knowledge discovery tasks, such as open-world knowledge completion or incremental knowledge graph construction from massive social media data.

References

1. Ahmed, E. B. and Gargouri, F. Enhanced association rules over ontology resources. *International Journal of Web Applications*, 2015, **7**(1): 10–22.
2. Cormen, T. H., Leiserson, C. E., Rivest, R. L., and Stein, C. *Introduction to Algorithms (2nd Edn)*. The MIT Press, Massachusetts, 2001.
3. Daphne, K. and Nir, F. *Probabilistic Graphical Models: Principles and Techniques (1st edn)*. The MIT Press, Massachusetts, 2009.
4. Erlandsson, F., Bródka, Piotr, Borg, A., and Johnson, H. Finding influential users in social media using association rule learning. *Entropy*, 2016, **18**(5): 164–178.
5. Färber, M., Bartscherer, F., Menne, C., and Rettinger, A. Linked data quality of DBpedia, Freebase, OpenCyc, Wikidata, and YAGO. *Semantic Web*, 2018, **9**(1): 77–129.
6. Idoudi, R., Ettabaâ, K. S., and Solaiman, B. Association rules-based ontology enrichment. *International Journal of Web Applications*, 2016, **8**(1): 16–25.
7. Ishak, R., Messaouda, F., and Hafida, B. Toward a general formalism of fuzzy multi-entity bayesian networks for representing and reasoning with uncertain knowledge. *Proc. ICEIS*, 2017, Vol. 1, pp. 520–528.
8. Ismayilov, A., Kontokostas, D., Auer, S., and Lehmann, J. Wikidata through the Eyes of DBpedia. *Semantic Web*, 2018, **9**(4): 493–503.
9. Kuo, R. J., Rizki, M., Zulvia, F. E., and Khasanah, A. U. Integration of growing self-organizing map and bee colony optimization algorithm for part clustering. *Computers & Industrial Engineering*, 2018, **120**: 251–265.

10. Li, L., Yue, K., Zhang, B., and Sun, Z. A probabilistic approach for inferring latent entity associations in textual web contents. *Proc. DASFAA Workshops*, 2018, pp. 3–18.

11. Li, Z., Fang, H., Huang, M., Wei, W., and Zhang, L. Data-driven bearing fault identification using improved hidden Markov model and self-organizing map. *Computers & Industrial Engineering*, 2018, **116**: 37–46.

12. Liao, C., Xiong, Y., Kong, X., Zhu, Y., and Li, S. Functional-oriented relationship strength estimation: From online events to offline interactions. *Proc. DASFAA*, 2018, pp. 442–459.

13. Liu, W., Yue, K., Yue, M., Yin, Z., and Zhang, B. A Bayesian network-based approach for incremental learning of uncertain knowledge. *International Journal of Uncertainty, Fuzziness and Knowledge-Based Systems*, 2018, **26**(1): 87–108.

14. Machine-Learning-with-R-datasets/groceries.csv, https://github.com/stedy/Machine-Learning-with-R-datasets/blob/master/groceries.csv, 2018.

15. Mintz, M., Bills, S., Snow, R., and Jurafsky, D. Distant supervision for relation extraction without labeled data. *Proc. ACL/IJCNLP*, 2009, pp. 1003–1011.

16. News Popularity in Multiple Social Media Platforms Data Set, http://archive.ics.uci.edu/ml/datasets/News+Popularity+in+Multiple+Social+Media+Platforms, 2018.

17. Poria, S., Chaturvedi, I., Bisio, F., and Bisio, F. Sentic LDA: Improving on LDA with semantic similarity for aspect-based sentiment analysis. *Proc. IJCNN*, 2016, pp. 4465–4473.

18. Ren, X., Wu, Z., He, W., Qu, M., Voss, C. R., Ji, H., Abdelzaher, T. F., and Han, J. Cotype: Joint extraction of typed entities and relations with knowledge bases. *Proc. WWW*, 2017, pp. 1015–1024.

19. Saraswati, A., Nguyen, V. T., Hagenbuchner, M., and Tsoi, A. C. High-resolution self-organizing maps for advanced visualization and dimension reduction. *Neural Networks*, 2018, **105**: 166–184.

20. Surdeanu, M., Tibshirani, J., Nallapati, R., and Manning, C. Multi-instance multi-label learning for relation extraction. *Proc. EMNLP-CoNLL*, 2012, pp. 455–465.

21. Teye, M., Azizpour, H., and Smith, K. Bayesian uncertainty estimation for batch normalized deep networks. *Proc. ICML*, 2018, pp. 4914–4923.

22. Wikidata Homepage, https://www.wikidata.org/wiki/Wikidata:Main_Page, 2018.

23. Wood, J., Tan, P., Wang, W., and Corey, A. Source-LDA: Enhancing probabilistic topic models using prior knowledge sources. *Proc. ICDE*, 2017, pp. 411–422.

24. Yin, Z., Yue, K., Wu, H., and Su, Y. Adaptive and parallel data acquisition from online big graphs. *Proc. DASFAA*, 2018, pp. 323–331.

25. Zhang, J., Tan, L., Tao, X., Zheng, X., Luo, Y., and Lin, C. W. SLIND: Identifying stable links in online social networks. *Proc. DASFAA*, 2018, pp. 813–816.

26. Zhang, W., Pan, T., Wang, Y., Wang, Z., and Xu, L. UT-LDA based similarity computing in microblog. *Proc. QRS*, 2015, pp. 197–201.

Chapter 8

Containment of Competitive Influence Spread on Social Networks

To contain the competitive influence spread in social networks is to maximize the influence of one participant and contain the influence of its opponent. It is desirable to develop effective strategies for influence spread of the participants themselves instead of blocking the influence spread of their opponents. In this chapter, we incorporate the realistic specialties and characteristics of the containment of competitive influence spread and extend the linear threshold (LT) model to establish the diffusion–containment model with probabilistic measurements, abbreviated as D–C model. Then, we discuss the influence spread mechanism for the D–C model, and give the algorithm for the propagation of the diffusion influence (D-influence) and containment influence (C-influence). Further, we define the submodular set function of the C-influence in the D–C model and consequently give a greedy algorithm for solving the problem of maximizing the competitive influence containment approximately. Experimental results show the feasibility of our method.

8.1 Motivation and Basic Idea

Social network has become an important medium for information propagation among its members. With the increasing popularity of social media, such as Facebook, Twitter, LinkedIn, etc., ideas, opinions, news, and product information are spread upon online social networks [29]. In recent years, there has been increasing interest in the topic of influence diffusion [12, 27], and many researchers focus on influence maximization to find a set of seed nodes that maximize the spread of influence. Kempe *et al.* [17, 18] formulated influence maximization as a discrete optimization problem and proposed two classic influence diffusion models: linear threshold (LT) model and independent cascade

(IC) model upon the early work. The seminal work given by Kempe *et al.* [17] motivates various studies on influence maximization in social networks [6, 13, 14, 18, 20, 22, 30].

In view of the situations with positive and negative influence simultaneously, the influence maximization problem is more challenging but frequently experienced in the real world, where how to limit the misinformation spread or maximize the overall influence is paid much attention [3, 5, 7, 23, 28]. Specifically, Bharathi *et al.* [1] extended the IC model to capture the existence of competition in social networks, and studied the competitive influence spread. For example, an advertising strategy will take advantage of the effect of "word-of-mouth" among the relationships of individuals to promote a product by some social networking websites, such as *orkut.com* and *facebook.com*. In reality, there exist two or more products competing with one another. For example, the introduction of *Apple phone* competes with *Samsung phone*, both of which want to attract people's attention and spread their influence as much as possible in a social network [32].

Actually, in the competitive situations, each of the competing participants aims to make its influence spread as maximal as possible and make that of its opponents as minimal as possible. To this end, a straightforward idea is to block the spread of its opponents' influence, such as the methods for link or influence blocking [15, 19]. However, from the perspective of realistic situations, blocking the opponents' influence spread does not always make sense, since it is impossible for one enterprise to interfere with the legal marketing strategies of others upon online social networks. Meanwhile, from the perspective of underlying techniques, blocking the opponents' influence spread is not always feasible, since it will take great computation cost when confronted with the large number of opponent seeds. Therefore, we will have to consider developing effective strategies of the participants themselves.

Naturally, from the above statement, the question arises how can a participant use its influence spread strategy to contain and thus minimize the spread of its opponents' influence? In this chapter, we focus on finding a seed set such that its influence spread contains the spread of the competing influence maximally and breaks the rules of the opponent influence propagation [25]. For this purpose, we consider the following problems:

(1) How to establish the model for the diffusion and containment of the competitive influence as the basis for developing the above propagation mechanism? For this problem, it is natural to consider the classic LT model [17, 18], a popular influence diffusion model that describes how influence is propagated throughout the network, starting from the initial seed vertices. The LT model is also typically extended with respect to the competitive influence maximization [2]. Thus, it is necessary to establish the model by incorporating the realistic characteristics of the containment of competitive influence spread.

(2) What is the mechanism of the D-influence and C-influence propagation, and then how to evaluate the propagation effects of the containment? For this problem, it is necessary to consider the probabilities of the D-influence and C-influence propagation and then develop the measurement of the propagation effects.

(3) How to find the seed set for maximally containing the spread of the competing influence? It is straightforward that the optimization problem for selecting the most effective C-seed vertices is NP-hard. Thus, it is necessary to develop the approximation algorithm correspondingly.

Aiming at the above three problems, the contributions of this chapter are summarized as follows:

- We extend the LT model to establish the Diffusion–Containment model (D–C model), abbreviated as D–C model. In the D–C model, we first define the activated threshold and the infected degree of influence propagation based on the payoffs dependent on different competing strategies. Then, we extend the certain active states (or inactive states) of vertices in the LT model into uncertain active states with probability estimation.
- We discuss the mechanism of influence spread for the D–C model. Then, we use the activation probability to describe the state of a vertex and give the algorithm for activation probability propagation

of the D-influence and C-influence. In the following, we measure the propagating effects of D-activation probabilities in the network.

- We define the submodular set function of the C-influence in the D–C model and consequently give a greedy algorithm for approximately solving the problem of competitive influence containment maximally, which has the efficient approximation with a ratio of $(1 - 1/e)$.

- We implement our algorithms and make corresponding experiments to test the feasibility of our method.

Generally speaking, the D-competitive situations are handled by the strategies for containing the influence diffusion, instead of blocking the influence propagation of opponents.

The remainder of this chapter is organized as follows. In Section 8.2, we survey the related work. In Section 8.3, we define the D–C model. In Section 8.4, we give our algorithm for the propagation of vertex activation probabilities. In Section 8.5, we define the problem for minimizing D-influence and prove its submodularity under the D–C model, and then give the greedy algorithm. In Section 8.6, we present experimental results. In Section 8.7, we summarize our work in this chapter.

8.2 Related Work

Social influence diffusion problem: The problem of influence diffusion in social networks has been paid much attention in recent years [29]. Guille *et al.* [12] surveyed the techniques for information diffusion in online social networks. Kempe *et al.* [17, 18] formally defined influence maximization as an optimization problem and gave LT and IC models for influence diffusion, as the basis of later research on influence propagation. Rodriquez and Song [27] surveyed various diffusion methods for fine-grained large-scale diffusion and social event data. The problem of influence maximization was pointed out to be NP-hard and a greedy approximation algorithm was proposed [17]. In particular, He and Kempe [14] discussed the effect of noise on the performance of influence maximization algorithms and showed that the objective function is NP-hard to approximate to within a factor of $O(n^{1-\varepsilon})$ for any $\varepsilon > 0$.

Hajian and White [13] presented the measurement of influence in social networks. As for the social network structure, the algorithm in [17] was based on multiple local tree structures, while the method in [20] used a tree structure to make the computation tractable. Lin *et al.* [24] proposed the method for label propagation for community detection in large-scale social networks.

Influence maximization without competitions: Many researchers proposed various methods of influence maximization from various perspectives. For example, Lappas *et al.* [20] and Chen *et al.* [6] tried to solve the influence maximization problem more efficiently and proposed some approximation algorithms. Wang *et al.* [30] gave the method for mining influential nodes in social networks and the community-based greedy algorithm for influence maximization. Li *et al.* [22] proposed the conformity aware cascade and context-specific model, as well as the partition-based greedy algorithm to generate the high-quality seed set efficiently in large-scale social networks. Chen *et al.* [5] extended the IC model and proposed an influence cascade model with negative opinions. As the application or extension of influence maximization, Embar *et al.* [8] defined various functional and usability criteria that social scores should satisfy and identified influencers by aspect-specific influence analysis. Embar *et al.* [9] gave the method for estimating or evaluating such latent variables by connection length and diffusion path in network diffusion by capturing the posterior distribution in a Bayesian framework.

Influence spread with opposite players: With respect to the situation with opposite relationships, Li *et al.* [23] proposed the method for finding the seed set to maximize the short-term influence coverage or long-term steady-state influence coverage with friend and foe relationships. Budak *et al.* [3] gave the method to minimize the number of people that adopt the bad campaign to limit the spread of misinformation. Datta *et al.* [7] defined the seed selection problem for multiple products to maximize the overall influence.

Competitive influence maximization: Shirazipourazad *et al.* [28] gave the strategy for influencing the nodes in a competitive fashion with multiple players. Bharathi *et al.* [1] discussed the problem of competitive influence maximization in online social networks. Carnes *et al.* [4] presented the competitive extensions of the IC model from the perspective of followers. Borodin *et al.* [2] extended the LT model for competitive influences and made the greedy algorithm applicable accordingly. Wu *et al.* [32] extended the LT model with respect to viral marketing, and discussed the submodularity and approximation degree of the algorithm for competitive influence maximization.

Influence blocking or containment: Considering the influence diffusion of the current player and its opponents simultaneously, it is natural to maximize the influence propagation of the current player by containing those of its opponents. Kimura *et al.* [19] gave the method for blocking links to minimize the contamination spread in a social network for the competitive situation. He *et al.* [15] proposed a competitive LT model for solving the problem of influence blocking maximization.

Then, we compare the above existing work and the study in this chapter from the following aspects:

(1) The methods for influence maximization without competitions give the roadmap based on the classical LT or IC model and the greedy algorithm.

(2) The methods for influence spread with opposite players cannot suit the competitive situations, since the mutual interactions between players with competitions is more complex and challenging to describe than those between opposite players.

(3) The methods for competitive influence maximization were not well generalized, since the strategies for containing the influence diffusion of opponents are not concerned.

(4) The models for influence blocking or containment have not considered the interaction of the strategies for competitive influence spread, which is exactly the focus of this chapter. Furthermore, blocking the influence propagation of opponents is not always feasible for influence containment, since it will require great computation cost when confronted with the large number of opponent seeds.

Therefore, in this chapter, we extend the LT model, widely used for influence maximization, by considering the practical demands and inherent characteristics of competitive influence spread. Different from the models and methods mentioned above, we are to contain the influence spread of the opponent by considering the interaction of the strategies instead of influence blocking. That is, we discuss the strategy for containing the spread of the competing influence maximally and breaking the propagation rules of the opponent influence.

8.3 Diffusion–Containment Model

The LT model [17] is widely used for modeling influence diffusion in a network. In this model, a network is considered as a graph $G = (V, E)$, where V is the set of vertices and E is the set of edges. Each edge $e(v_i, v_j) \in E(v_i, v_j \in V, i \neq j)$ has a weight $w_{ij} \geq 0$ indicating the importance of the vertex v_j affected by v_i. For each v_j, we have $\sum_{v_i \in N(j)} w_{ij} \leq 1$, where $N(j)$ is the set of neighbors of v_j. Each vertex is either active or inactive, and once it is active, it stays active forever. Each vertex v_j chooses a threshold θ_j uniformly from the interval $[0, 1]$ randomly. v_j is activated if and only if $\sum_{v_i \in N_a(j)} w_{ij} > \theta_j$, where $N_a(j)$ is the set of active vertices in $N(j)$.

As has been mentioned above, the classic LT model is not suitable for the competitive situation where both the diffusion and containment of the influence are concerned, since only the influence diffusion is considered in the LT model. In this section, we develop the D–C model as a natural extension of the classic LT model for competitive influence spread. Relatively, we use D-influence and C-Influence to represent the influence that will be diffused and contained, respectively. The idea of influence containment is to propagate another C-influence to block the spread of the D-influence. To extend the classic LT model, we are to reconsider the vertex states given the diffusion and containment seeds. Meanwhile, the possible interaction strategies of players are also critical to determine the propagation direction and rules of influences.

8.3.1 *Graph model*

First, similar to the LT model, we model a social network as a graph $G = (V, E)$, where each edge $e(v_i, v_j) \in E$ has a weight $w_{ij} \geq 0$.

For each vertex v_j, we have $\sum_{v_i \in N(j)} w_{ij} \leq 1$. Given the set D^* of the diffusion seeds and C^* of the containment seeds, each vertex v_j has three possible states: D-state, C-state, and I-state (inactive-state) by the influence spread of D^* and C^*, in which each state has different probability distributions.

8.3.2 *Interaction strategy*

Second, each vertex v_j is affected by both D-influence and C-influence, and v_j has three possible actions: D (choosing D-influence), C (choosing C-influence), and I (choosing inactive state).

We consider the distribution over v_j's actions to the influence spread as the payoff of v_j. Note that the payoffs of v_j are affected by the strategies of the neighbors of v_j in G, in which v_i and v_j are the players and D, C, and I are the possible strategies. The payoffs are defined as follows:

- If one of v_i and v_j adopts the inactive behavior, each of them gets a payoff of 0.
- If v_i and v_j adopt opposite behaviors, each of them gets a payoff of 0.
- If v_i and v_j adopt behavior D, each of them gets a payoff of $u_D > 0$.
- If v_i and v_j adopt behavior C, each of them gets a payoff of $u_C > 0$.

It is worth noting that if v_i and v_j adopt opposite (or inactive) behaviors, their distribution to the influence spread will be very small. If D-influence is easier to propagate than C-influence, then $u_D > u_C$ will hold. We can write the above combination of actions and the corresponding payoffs in terms of a payoff matrix in Table 8.1.

If v_j has many neighbors, then the payoff of v_j will be the sum of the payoffs over each neighbor. Intuitively, when $\sum_{v_i \in N_d(j)} w_{ij} \times u_D > \sum_{v_k \in N_c(j)} w_{kj} \times u_C$, v_j is more easily infected by D-influence than

Table 8.1. Payoff matrix.

v_j \ v_i	D	C	I
D	u_D, u_D	$0, 0$	$0, 0$
C	$0, 0$	u_C, u_C	$0, 0$
I	$0, 0$	$0, 0$	$0, 0$

C-influence. The larger the payoff of D (i.e., U_D), the more easily this vertex will be infected and thus the smaller the threshold θ_j^D, which is the contrary of the situation of θ_j^C. Thus, similar to the threshold θ_j in the LT model, we give the threshold rule of the D–C model as follows:

$$
\theta_j^D = \frac{q' \times u_C}{q \times u_D + q' \times u_C}, \quad \theta_j^C = \frac{q \times u_D}{q \times u_D + q' \times u_C}, \tag{8.1}
$$

where $q = \sum_{v_i \in N_d(j)} w_{ij}$, $q' = \sum_{v_k \in N_C(j)} w_{kj}$, and $\theta_j^D (0 \le \theta_j^D \le 1)$ and $\theta_j^C (0 \le \theta_j^C \le 1)$ are the threshold of the D-influence and the C-influence of v_j, respectively.

8.3.3 *D-State probability and C-State probability*

The probability that v_j is in D-state after the influence spread from D^* and C^* is called the D-state probability of v_j, denoted as $P(v_j = d)$ and computed by the following linearity expectation:

$$
P(v_j = d) = \begin{cases} \sum_{v_i \in N_d(j)} P(v_i = d) \times w_{ij} & \sum_{v_i \in N_d(j)} P(v_i = d) \times w_{ij} \ge \theta_j^D \\ 0 & \sum_{v_i \in N_d(j)} P(v_i = d) \times w_{ij} < \theta_j^D \end{cases}
$$

$$\tag{8.2}$$

where d represents v_j's state in D-state. Similarly, $P(v_j = c)$ and $P(v_j = i)$ represent the C-state probability and I-state probability, respectively.

Now we consider the propagation capability of the D-influence and C-influence itself, also a weight of the D-influence or C-influence propagation, except the weights on edges. We use ξ_D and ξ_C to denote the infected degree of D-influence and that of C-influence, respectively. Intuitively, based on the payoff matrix in Table 8.1, we have

$$
\xi_D = \frac{u_D}{u_C + u_D}, \quad \xi_C = \frac{u_C}{u_C + u_D} \tag{8.3}
$$

Actually, ξ_D is the function of u_D and u_C, and reflects the capability of D-influence propagation quantitatively. ξ_D and ξ_C describe the property of ease of propagation of the D-influence and C-influence, respectively. For example, the value of ξ_D of product A will be larger than that of B, if A is cheaper and better than B. When v_j is affected by v_i with D-influence, the probability that v_j is affected by v_i should be $P(v_j = d) = P(v_i = d) \times w_{ij} \times \xi_D$. When v_j is affected by v_i with C-influence, the probability that v_j is affected by v_i should be $P(v_j = c) = P(v_i = c) \times w_{ij} \times \xi_C$. When v_j is affected by different vertices with D-influence and C-influence, respectively, the ratio of the D-state probability to the C-state probability is denoted by ξ_D/ξ_C.

It can be seen that the LT model is extended in the D–C model, where the larger the value of $\sum_{v_i \in N(j)} [P(v_i = d) \times w_{ij}]$, the larger the D-state probability of v_j when $\sum_{v_i \in N(j)} [P(v_i = d) \times w_{ij}] \geq \theta_j^D$. However, in the LT model, v_j is certainly activated when $\sum_{i \in N(j)} w_{ij} \geq \theta_j$. Therefore, the proposed D–C model is more consistent with the actual situation of competitive influence spread than the LT model. In the D–C model, we regard $\left[\sum_{v_j \in V} P(v_j = d) \right]/|V|$ as the evaluation function of the D-influence spread and $\left[\sum_{v_j \in V} (1 - P(v_j = d)) \right]/|V|$ as the evaluation function of the D-influence containment.

In the following, we give an example to illustrate the above concepts on the social network in Fig. 8.1, where vertex C is affected by A with D-influence (horizontal shadow) and B with C-influence (vertical shadow). We suppose $P(A = d) = 1$, $P(B = c) = 1$, $w_{AC} = 0.4$, and $w_{BC} = 0.3$. According to the definition of the D-state probability and infected degree, we have $P(C = d) = P(A = d) \times 0.4 \times \xi_D$ and $P(C = c) = P(B = c) \times 0.3 \times \xi_C$. We regard that vertex C will be D-activated if $P(C = d) \geq \theta_C^D$ after the influence propagation.

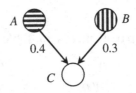

Fig. 8.1. A social network where one vertex is affected by different vertices with D-influence and C-influence, respectively.

8.3.4 *Influence propagation rules*

Compared to the LT model where each vertex can only accept one kind of influence, each vertex in the D–C model can accept different kinds of influences from D-seeds and C-seeds. In the LT model, a vertex can only be in active or inactive state, which can be changed only from the former to the latter by single-direction manner. However, in the D–C model, the state of a vertex is described by the activation probability, and each vertex only accepts the influence from the neighbor with higher probability, where the sum of the probabilities of possible states is not larger than 1. Based on the above ideas, we discuss the rules of influence propagation.

For the D-influence, if $P(v_j = d) < P(v_i = d)$ holds, then v_j is affected by v_i but v_j does not affect v_i. Similarly, for every vertex v_j, we have the following propagation rule of the C-influence:

$$P(v_j = d) + P(v_j = c) \leq 1 \qquad (8.4)$$

In summary, Table 8.2 shows the comparison between the classic LT model and the D–C model given in this chapter, where $|V|$ denotes

Table 8.2. Comparison between LT model and D–C model.

	LT model	D–C model
Types of seeds	Seeds of D-influence	Seeds of D-influence and seeds of C-influence
Activation probability of vertices	$P(v_j = d) = 0$ or $P(v_j = d) = 1$	$P(v_j = d) = 0$ or $0 < P(v_j = d) \leq 1$
Propagating direction of influence	From $P(v_j = d) = 1$ to $P(v_j = d) = 0$	From $P(v_i = d)$ to $P(v_j = d)$, if $P(v_i = d) > P(v_j = d)$
Evaluation function of the spread of influence	$\left[\sum_{v_j \in V} P(v_j = d) = 1 \right] / |V|$	$\left[\sum_{v_j \in V} P(v_j = d) \right] / |V|$

the number of nodes in G. It can be seen easily that the D–C model is the natural extension of the LT model, and D–C can be regarded as the generalized LT.

8.4 Propagation of Vertex Activation Probabilities

For a given network, the D-activation (or C-activation) probability of a vertex v_j at time $t + 1$ is affected by the D-activation (or C-activation) probability of its neighbors at time t. Meanwhile, by the influence propagation rule in Eq. (8.4), we know that the D-influence (C-influence) is spread by one-way manner. Algorithm 8.1 describes the above ideas for the propagation of vertex activation probabilities.

Algorithm 8.1 Propagation of activation probabilities

Input:

$G = (V, E)$, an undirected graph, where V is the set of vertices and E is the set of undirected edges

$w_{ij} \geq 0$, the weight of edge $e(v_i, v_j) \in E$

θ_j^D, the D-influence threshold of v_j

θ_j^C, the C-influence threshold of v_j

ξ_D, the infected degree of D-influence

ξ_C, the infected degree of C-influence

D^*, the set of D-seeds

C^*, the set of C-seeds

T, the upper time limit

Output:

Q, the evaluation function of the D-influence containment

Variables:

$N(v_j)$, the set of neighbors of v_j

temp_D^j, a temporary value of the D-activation probability of v_j

temp_C^j, a temporary value of the C-activation probability of v_j

λ, the flag of stop running

t, the time step

F_j, the free range of v_j

Algorithm 8.1 (Continued)

Steps:

1. Initialization

   $t \leftarrow 0, \lambda \leftarrow 1$

   For each v_j in D^* Do

   $\quad P(v_j = d) \leftarrow 1$

   End For

   For each v_j in C^* Do

   $\quad P(v_j = c) \leftarrow 1$

   End For

   For each v_j in $V \backslash \{C^* \cup D^*\}$ Do

   $\quad P(v_j = d) \leftarrow 0, P(v_j = c) \leftarrow 0$

   End For

   $\text{temp}_D^t j \leftarrow 0, \quad \text{temp}_C^t j \leftarrow 0$

2. From time 1 to T, calculate the D-activation probability and
   C-activation probability of every vertex v_j in V

   While $\lambda > 0$ and $t < T$ Do

   $\quad$ For$_1$ each $v_j \in V - D^* - C^*$ Do

   $\quad\quad$ For$_2$ each $v_i \in N(v_j)$ Do

   $\quad\quad\quad F_j \leftarrow 1 - \text{temp}_D^t j - \text{temp}_C^t j$

   $\quad\quad\quad$ If $P^t(v_i = d) > P(v_j = d)$ Then

   $\quad\quad\quad\quad \text{temp}_D^t j \leftarrow \text{temp}_D^t j + P^t(v_i = d) \times w_{ij} \times F_j \times \xi_D$

   $\quad\quad\quad$ If $P^t(v_i = c) > P(v_j = c)$ Then

   $\quad\quad\quad\quad \text{temp}_C^t j \leftarrow \text{temp}_C^t j + P^t(v_i = c) \times w_{ij} \times F_j \times \xi_C$

   $\quad\quad$ End For$_2$

   $\quad\quad \text{temp}_D^{t+1} j \leftarrow \text{temp}_D^t j, \quad \text{temp}_C^{t+1} j \leftarrow \text{temp}_c^t j$

   $\quad\quad P^{t+1}(v_j = d) \leftarrow \text{temp}_D^{t+1} j, \quad P^{t+1}(v_j = c) \leftarrow \text{temp}_C^{t+1}$

   $\quad\quad t \leftarrow t + 1$

   $\quad$ End For$_1$

   $$\lambda \leftarrow \sum_{v_k \in V} (P^t(v_k = d) - P^{t-1}(v_k = d))$$

   $$+ \sum_{v_k \in V} (P^t(v_k = c) - P^{t-1}(v_k = c))$$

   End While

Algorithm 8.1 (Continued)

---

3. Output the value of evaluation function, the D-activation probability, and the C-activation probability of each vertex v_j in V

$Q \leftarrow 0$

For$_3$ each v_j in V Do

   If $P^t(v_j = d) < \theta_j^D$ Then $P^t(v_j = d) \leftarrow 0$

   If $P^t(v_j = d) < \theta_j^C$ Then $P^t(v_j = d) \leftarrow 0$

   $Q \leftarrow Q + (1 - P^t(v_j = d))$

End For$_3$

$Q \leftarrow Q/|V|$

4. Return Q

In Algorithm 8.1, by the T iterations in Step 2, we calculate the D-activation probability and the C-activation probability of every vertex v_j in V. Step 2 in the algorithm is executed $t(0 < t < T)$ times or until no more changes can be made on the activation probability. Mainly depending on the calculation of the vertex's activation probability, the time complexity of Algorithm 8.1 is $O(|\bar{e}| \times |V| \times T)$, where $|\bar{e}|$ is the average degree of all vertices in G.

In the following, we give an example to illustrate the execution of Algorithm 8.1 on the social network in Fig. 8.2. We suppose v_1 and v_3 are D-seeds while v_2 is a C-seed, that is, $P(v_1 = d) = 1$, $P(v_3 = d) = 1$, and $P(v_2 = c) = 1$. The weights on edges are as follows: $w_{14} = 0.3$, $w_{24} = 0.4$, $w_{35} = 0.8$, $w_{46} = 0.4$, and $w_{56} = 0.4$, and we suppose $\xi_D = \xi_C = 0.5$.

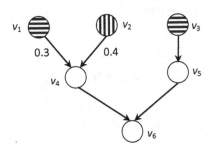

Fig. 8.2. A social network with six vertices.

(1) At time 1, v_4 and v_5 are affected. Thus, $P(v_4 = d) = P(v_1 = d) \times w_{14} \times \xi_D = 1 \times 0.3 \times 0.5 = 0.15$, $P(v_4 = c) = P(v_2 = c) \times w_{24} \times \xi_C = 1 \times 0.4 \times 0.5 = 0.2$, $P(v_4 = i) = 1 - 0.15 - 0.2 = 0.65$, $P(v_5 = d) = P(v_3 = d) \times w_{35} \times \xi_D = 1 \times 0.8 \times 0.5 = 0.4$, $P(v_5 = c) = 0$, $P(v_5 = i) = 1 - 0.4 - 0 = 0.6$.

(2) At time 2, v_6 is affected. Thus, $P(v_6 = d) = P(v_4 = d) \times w_{46} \times \xi_D + P(v_5 = d) \times w_{56} \times \xi_D = 0.15 \times 0.4 \times 0.5 + 0.4 \times 0.4 \times 0.5 = 0.11$, $P(v_6 = c) = P(v_4 = c) \times w_{46} \times \xi_C = 0.2 \times 0.4 \times 0.5 = 0.04$, $P(v_6 = i) = 1 - 0.11 - 0.04 = 0.85$.

(3) According to the evaluation function of the D-influence containment, we know $Q = \sum_{v_j \in V} (1 - p(v_j = d))/|V|$.

Thus, $Q = \{(1 - 1) + (1 - 0) + (1 - 1) + (1 - 0.15) + (1 - 0.4) + (1 - 0.11)\}/6 = 3.34/6 = 0.556$.

8.5 Finding C-Seeds for D-Influence Minimization

In the competitive situation with two participants, one with C-influence will adopt the strategy of seed distribution as its own decision to contain the D-influence of the others to minimize the influence spread. Based on the D–C model, we describe the problem of D-influence minimization as follows. For the given network $G = (V, E)$, at the first step $t = 0$, we give the set D^* of diffusion seeds (D-seeds) in which $P^{t=0}(v_i = d) = 1$ for any v_i in D^* and the size of C-seed set C^* is denoted as k (i.e., $k = |C^*|$). We are to find the seed set C^* such that the D-activation probability in G leads to the smallest expectation value at the final step $t = T$ (i.e., to maximize $\sum_{v_j \in V} [1 - P^T(v_j = d)]$). By Algorithm 8.1 given in Section 8.4, for each vertex v_j in V, we have

$$P^T(v_j = d) = \sum_{0}^{T} \sum_{v_i \in N(j)} P^t(v_i = d) \times w_{ij}$$
$$\times (1 - \text{temp}_D^t j - \text{temp}_C^t j) \times \xi_D \qquad (8.5)$$

where $P^T(v_j = d)$ is the function of C^*, since $\text{temp}_C^t j$ has an effect on $P^T(v_j = d)$.

We rewrite $P^T(v_j = d)$ as $\sum_{l \in Pa(D^* \to v_j)} P_l(v_j = d) \times I_l(C^*)$. We use $Pa(D^* \to v_j)$ to denote the set of paths from those in D^* to v_j, and

$P_l(v_j = d)$ to denote the D-activation probability of v_j affected by the D-seeds through the path l in $Pa(D^* \to v_j)$. In the path l of $D^* \to v_j$, $I_l(C^*)$ is used to denote whether the D-influence is contained by the C-influence. $I_l(C^*) = 1$ if the spread of $D^* \to v_j$ is not contained, and $I_l(C^*) < 1$ if there are some intersection edges between l and l' ($l \in Pa(D^* \to v_j)$ and $l' \in Pa(C^* \to v_j)$).

To minimize the D-influence is to maximize the part unaffected by the D-influence. Thus, we can reduce $\min\left(\sum_{v_j \in V}(P^T(v_j = d))\right)$ to $\max\left(\sum_{v_j \in V}(1 - P^T(v_j = d))\right)$. Since $P^T(v_j = d) = \sum_{l \in Pa(D^* \to v_j)} P_l(v_j = d) \times I_l(C^*)$, the D-influence minimization can be described as follows:

$$\arg\max_{C^*} \left\{ \sum_{v_j \in V} 1 - \left(\sum_{l \in Pa(D^* \to v_j)} P_l(v_j = d) \times I_l(C^*) \right) \right\} \quad (8.6)$$

For this purpose, we are to find the C^* satisfying Eq. (8.6). We know that influence maximization under the LT model is NP-hard [5, 17], and consequently the D-influence minimization is also NP-hard under the D–C model. To overcome the NP-hardness, we are to explore an approximation algorithm upon the submodularity property based on that given in [11]. We define the submodularity in D-influence minimization as follows.

Definition 8.1. Let $f : 2^V \to R$ be a set function on vertices of $G = (V, E)$. f is monotone if $f(S) \leq f(T)$ for all $S \subseteq T \subseteq V$ and f is submodular if $f(S \cup \{u\}) - f(S) \geq f(T \cup \{u\}) - f(T)$ for all $S \subset T$ and $u \in V \backslash T$.

We regard $\sum_{v_j \in V} 1 - \left(\sum_{l \in Pa(D^* \to v_j)} P_l(v_j = d) \times I_l(C^*)\right)$ in Eq. (8.6) as a set function of C^*, denoted as $f(C^*)$, and

$$f(C^*) = \sum_{v_j \in V} 1 - \sum_{l \in Pa(D^* \to v_j)} [P_l(v_j = d) \times I_l(C^*)] \quad (8.7)$$

In the following, we first show that $f(C^*)$ on C^* is a monotone increasing function.

Lemma 8.1. *Given a network $G = (V, E)$ and the set D^* of D-seeds and the set C^* of C-seeds on G, the function $f(C^*)$ in Eq. (8.7) is monotone.*

Proof. Let C_1^* and C_2^* be two sets of C-seeds and $C_2^* \supseteq C_1^*$. □

For each vertex v_j in V, we have $Pa(C_2^* \to v_j) \supseteq Pa(C_1^* \to V_j)$, since $C_2^* \supseteq C_1^*$. Thus, the set of intersection edges of $Pa(D^* \to v_j)$ and $Pa(C_2^* \to v_j)$ includes the set of intersection edges of $Pa(D^* \to v_j)$ and $Pa(C_1^* \to v_j)$. Therefore, we have

$$\sum_{l \in Pa(D^* \to V_j)} P_l(v_j = d) \times I_l(C_2^*)$$

$$\leq \sum_{l \in Pa(D^* \to v_j)} P_l(v_j = d) \times I_l(C_1^*), \quad \text{i.e.,}$$

$$f(C_2^*) = \sum_{v_j \in V} 1 - \left(\sum_{l \in Pa(D^* \to v_j)} P_l(v_j = d) \times I_l(C_2^*) \right) \geq f(C_1^*)$$

$$= \sum_{v_j \in V} 1 - \left(\sum_{l \in Pa(D^* \to v_j)} P_l(v_j = d) \times I_l(C_1^*) \right)$$

Then, we show that $f(C^*)$ is a submodular set-function.

Theorem 8.1. *Given a network $G = (V, E)$ and the set D^* of D-seeds on G, let C_1^* and C_2^* be two sets of C-seeds on G and $V \supseteq C_2^* \supseteq C_1^*$. For any vertex $u \in V/C_2^*$, $f(C_2^* \cup u) - f(C_2^*) \leq f(C_1^* \cup u) - f(C_1^*)$.*

Proof. According to the submodularity property in Definition 8.1, the possible spread paths for any vertex $v_j \in V/D^*$ include $D^* \to v_j$, $C_1^* \to v_j$, $u \to v_j$, and $C_2^* \to v_j$. Thus, we use Fig. 8.3 to show the set of paths from various seed-sets to v_j, where $S_1 = Pa(D^* \to v_j)$, $S_2 = Pa(C_1^* \to v_j)$, $S_3 = Pa(u \to v_j)$, and $S_4 = Pa(C_2^* \to v_j)$. It can be seen that the set $S_1 = Pa(D^* \to v_j)$ is partitioned into $w_1, w_2, \ldots, w_6$, that is, $w_1 \cup w_2 \cup \cdots \cup w_6 = S_1$ and $w_i \cap w_j = \emptyset$ $(i, j = 1, \ldots, 6)$. w_2 is the subset of paths in $Pa(D^* \to v_j)$, in which each path

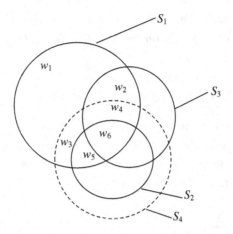

Fig. 8.3. Sets of paths from various seed-sets to v_j.

contains intersection edges of $l \in Pa(D^* \to v_j)$ and $l' \in Pa(C* \to v_j)$. $w_3, w_4, w_5,$ and w_6 can be described analogously. □

Let $Pa_c * (D^* \to v_j)$ be the subset of paths in $Pa(D^* \to v_j)$, in which each path is affected by C^*, respectively, that is, each path in $Pa_{c*}(D^* \to v_j)$ contains the intersection edges of $l \in Pa(D^* \to v_j)$ and $l' \in Pa(C^* \to v_j)$. It can be seen from Fig. 8.3 that

$$Pa_{(C_1^*)}(D^* \to v_j) = w_5 \cup w_6$$

$$Pa_{(c_1^* \cup u)}(D^* \to v_j) = w_2 \cup w_4 \cup w_5 \cup w_6$$

$$Pa_{(c_2^*)}(D^* \to v_j) = w_3 \cup w_4 \cup w_5 \cup w_6$$

$$Pa_{(c_2^* \cup u)}(D^* \to v_j) = w_2 \cup w_3 \cup w_4 \cup w_5 \cup w_6$$

Thus, we have

$$Pa_{(c_1^* \cup u)}(D^* \to v_j) - Pa_{(c_1^*)}(D^* \to v_j)$$

$$\supseteq Pa_{(c_2^* \cup u)}(D^* \to v_j) - Pa_{(c_2^*)}(D^* \to v_j)$$

That is, $I_l(C_1^* \cup u) - I_l(C_1^*) \geq I_l(C_2^* \cup u) - I_l(C_2^*)$.

By the definition of $f(C^*)$, we have

$$f(C_1^* \cup u) - f(C_1^*)$$

$$= \left[\sum_{v_j \in V} 1 - \left(\sum_{l \in Pa(D^* \to v_j)} (P_l(v_j = d) \times I_l(C_1^* \cup u)) \right) \right]$$

$$- \left[\sum_{v_j \in V} 1 - \sum_{l \in Pa(D^* \to v_j)} (P_l(v_j = d) \times I_l(C_1^*)) \right]$$

$$= \sum_{l \in Pa(D^* \to v_j)} (P_l(v_j = d) \times (I_l(C_1^*) - I_l(C_1^* \cup u))$$

Similarly, we have

$$f(C_1^* \cup u) - f(C_1^*) = \sum_{l \in Pa(D^* \to v_j)} (P_l(v_j = d) \times (I_l(C_2^*) - I_l(C_2^* \cup u))$$

$$[I_l(C_1^*) - I_l(C_1^* \cup u)] \le [I_l(C_2^*) - I_l(C_2^* \cup u)]$$

This means that the containment effect on $P_l(v_j = d)$ of $I_l(C_1^*) - I_l(C_1^* \cup u)$ is less than that of $I_l(C_2^*) - I_l(C_2^* \cup u)$. Then, we have

$$\sum_{l \in Pa(D^* \to v_j)} (P_l(v_j = d) \times (I_l(C_1^*) - I_l(C_1^* \cup u))$$

$$\ge \sum_{l \in Pa(D^* \to v_j)} (P_l(v_j = d) \times (I_l(C_2^*) - I_l(C_2^* \cup u))$$

Therefore, $f(C_1^* \cup u) - f(C_1^*) \ge f(C_2^* \cup u) - f(C_2^*)$, and $f(C^*)$ is submodular.

Kempe *et al.* [17] pointed out that effective approximate solutions can be achieved by a greedy algorithm for the optimization problem with submodular set functions. Consequently, we adopt the greedy algorithm to solve the D-influence minimization problem approximately based on the submodularity conclusion in Theorem 8.1. Algorithm 8.2 selects a currently best C-seed u iteratively from $V - D^* - C^*$, which maximally contains the D-influence spread into the seed set C^* starting from an empty set, until k seeds are selected.

Algorithm 8.2 Greedy Algorithm for finding the set C^*

Input:

  $G = (V, E)$, the undirected graph in Algorithm 8.1

  D^*, the set of D-seeds

  $k = |C^*|$, the number of C-seeds

Output:

  C^*, the set of C-seeds

Steps:

1. Initialization: $C^* \leftarrow \emptyset$
2. Select C-seeds one by one
   For $i \leftarrow 1$ to k Do
      Select $v^* = \underset{u \in V \setminus (D^* \cup C^*)}{\arg\max} \ (f(C^* \cup u))$ //Executing Algorithm 8.1
      for each vertex
      $C^* \leftarrow C^* \cup \{v^*\}$
   End For
3. Return C^*

According to the conclusion in [11, 17], Algorithm 8.2 can achieve the approximation ratio of $(1 - 1/e)$ for the D-influence minimization problem, since $f(C^*)$ in the D–C model is submodular. It is worth noting that the critical step of Algorithm 8.2 is the execution of Algorithm 8.1, that is, for each time of selecting a C-seed, the computation in Algorithm 8.1 will be executed once for each vertex in V to compute the evaluation function of the D-influence containment. Therefore, the time complexity of Algorithm 8.2 is $O(K \times |V| \times R)$, where K, $|V|$, and R are the number of C-seeds, the number of vertices in G, and the execution time of Algorithm 8.1, respectively.

8.6 Experimental Results

8.6.1 Experiment setup

It is well known that NetworkX [26] is the widely adopted toolkit for the creation, manipulation, and study of the structure, dynamics, and functions of complex networks. It has the highest level of functionality in terms of producing high-quality networks with various distributions. To test the effectiveness of our algorithms under the D–C Model, we adopted the power–law social networks generated by the NetworkX toolkit randomly when the power value is 3, and generated the social network with 2268 edges on 1000 vertices and that with 382 edges on 200 vertices. We also adopted the Wikipedia-who-votes-on-whom (abbreviated as Wiki-vote) network [21], including 7115 nodes and 103689 edges, to test the feasibility of our algorithms. In the experiments, the subnetworks with various numbers of nodes were used.

The experiments were conducted on a machine with Intel Core i5-3470 CPU and 4GB main memory running Windows 8.1 operating system. The codes were written in JAVA 1.8 by Eclipse Luna Release 4.4.0.

It is intuitive that the general metric of average number of infected nodes [17] is not suitable for our method, since the nodes are infected probably in the context of this chapter. Thus, we adopted the evaluation function (i.e., Q in Algorithm 8.1) value, the average probability of the infected nodes, as the metric to test the feasibility of the D–C model-based greedy algorithm for C-seed selection. In the experiments, we compared the value of the evaluation function Q obtained when selecting the seeds by our greedy algorithm (denoted as Greedy), the random algorithm (denoted as Random, selecting the seeds randomly), and MaxDegree algorithm (denoted as MaxDegree, selecting the seeds with the largest degree) [31], which is well regarded as the effective algorithm for the networks with power law distributions. Then, we further showed the functionality and relationships of relevant parameters in Algorithms 8.1 and 8.2.

8.6.2 *Feasibility*

On the social network with 1000 nodes generated by NetworkX, we recorded the values of the evaluation function Q when selecting C-seeds by Greedy, Random, and MaxDegree, respectively, with the increase of D-seeds, where we assigned the upper time limit $T = 75$, $|U_C|/|U_D| = 1/3$ (i.e., $U_C = 0.25$, $U_D = 0.75$), and $|C^*|/|D^*| = 1$.

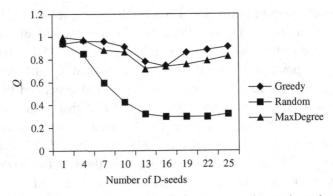

Fig. 8.4. Value of evaluation function Q with the increase of D-seeds on the generated network.

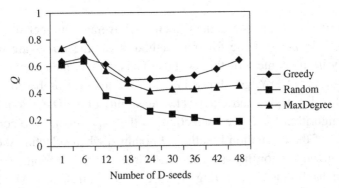

Fig. 8.5. Value of evaluation function Q with the increase of D-seeds on the Wiki-vote network.

MaxDegree was adopted as the criterion of comparisons shown in Fig. 8.4. Meanwhile, we compared the values of Q by these three methods on the Wiki-vote network with 2000 nodes, shown in Fig. 8.5.

It can be seen that the more the D-seeds, the more advantageous the Greedy and MaxDegree for the competitive situation with more than one D-seed. The results of D-influence containment by our greedy algorithm are better than those by Random and MaxDegree. The values of Q by Greedy and MaxDegree are basically consistent, and moreover the value of Q by the former algorithm is a little larger than the latter for each number of D-seeds, although the value of Q on the actual Wiki-vote

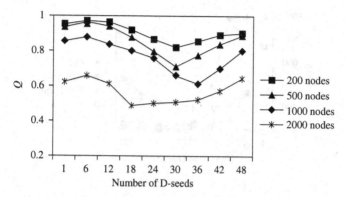

Fig. 8.6.   Value of evaluation function Q with the increase of D-seeds on the Wiki-vote network with various numbers of nodes.

network is smaller than that on the generated network for the same number of D-seeds. The above experimental results hold on the generated and actual networks, and this means that the D–C model given in this chapter is feasible.

Further, we tested the values of Q with the increase of D-seeds on the Wiki-vote networks with 200, 500, 1000, and 2000 nodes, respectively, shown in Fig. 8.6. It can be seen that the more the nodes in the Wiki-vote network, the smaller the value of Q with respect to the same number of D-seeds. This means that the larger the social network, the harder the effective containment of competitive influence spread, which is consistent with the definition of Q. However, the value of Q is increased steadily when the number of D-seeds is larger than 36 for various sized Wiki-vote networks.

It is straightforward that the better the D-influence containment strategy, the more the vertices that are not activated by the D-influence, denoted as ND, consisting of the vertices contained by the C-seeds and not activated by either the D-seeds or C-seeds. Therefore, we further compared the number of ND (denoted as |ND|) by Greedy, MaxDegree, and the mechanism with no influence containment (denoted as NC) to verify the feasibility of our containment strategy based on the D–C model. To count |ND|, we pick a D-state threshold β, for all $v_i \in V$, if $P(v_i = d) >= \beta$, then v_i is in the D-state. In this experiment, we assigned the upper time limit $T = 75$, $|U_C|/|U_D| = 1/3$, $|C^*|/|D^*| = 1$,

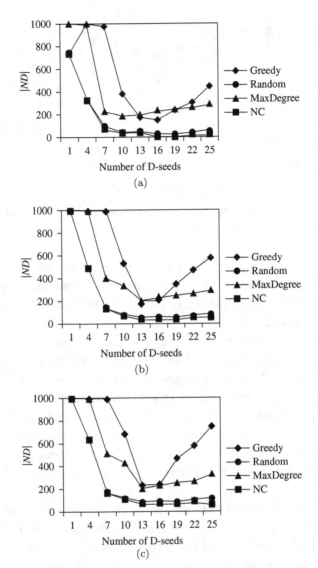

Fig. 8.7. Vertices not activated by D-influence on the generated network: (a) $\beta = 0.9$; (b) $\beta = 0.85$; (c) $\beta = 0.8$.

and the D-state threshold β as 0.9, 0.85, and 0.8, respectively. The comparisons are shown in Figs. 8.7(a)–(c), respectively.

It can be seen that |ND| by our greedy algorithm is larger than those by the other three strategies under various D-influence threshold values for most cases with various number of D-seeds. This means that our greedy algorithm can lead to the best result of D-influence containment by selecting C-seeds appropriately. Meanwhile, it can be seen that the smaller the D-influence threshold value, the better the results obtained by our greedy algorithm. This means that the D-influence can be contained by our greedy algorithm with higher probabilities than the MaxDegree algorithm.

Under the current experiment setup, |ND| achieves the minimal value when the number of D-seeds is between 13 and 16, and it becomes larger with the increase of the number of D-seeds. The influence is weakly diffused when the D-seeds is less than 12, which makes less vertices activated with large |ND| values. When the D-seeds is more than 16, the containment of the C-seeds will appear, which makes less vertices activated with large |ND| values as well. Meanwhile, the smaller the D-influence threshold value, the faster the diffusion of the D-influence itself, when the C-seed selection is relatively more important than the situation with larger D-influence threshold values. It is natural that the D-state threshold β should be larger than 0.5 if a vertex is infected, so β should be about 0.8 in general cases.

Then, we compared the number of ND by Greedy, Random, MaxDegree, and NC when $T = 75$, $|U_C|/|U_D| = 1/3$, $|C^*|/|D^*| = 1$, $\beta = 0.8$ on the Wiki-vote subnetwork with 2000 nodes shown in Fig. 8.8. The results are consistent with those in Fig. 8.7.

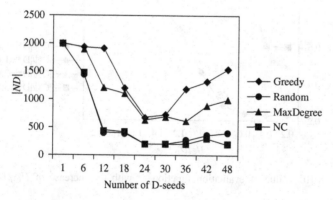

Fig. 8.8. Vertices not activated by D-influence on the Wiki-vote network.

8.6.3　*Functionality and relationship of relevant parameters*

In this experiment, we show the functionalities and relationships of relevant parameters in the D–C model and the consequent greedy algorithm on the generated social network with 200 vertices. First, we recorded the values of the evaluation function with the increase of $|C^*|/|D^*|$ under various U_C/U_D, shown in Fig. 8.9. Then, we recorded the values of the evaluation function with the increase of U_C/U_D under various $|C^*|/|D^*|$, shown in Fig. 8.10.

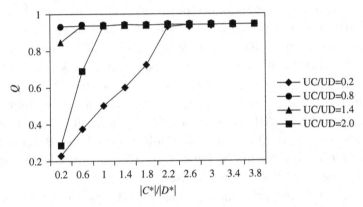

Fig. 8.9.　Value of evaluation function Q with the increase of $|C^*|/|D^*|$.

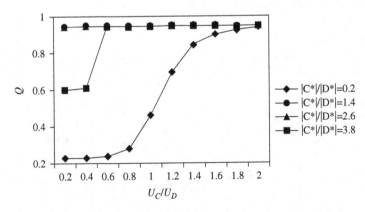

Fig. 8.10.　Value of evaluation function Q with the increase of U_C/U_D.

First, we can see that the higher the ratio $|C^*|$ to $|D^*|$, or the higher the ratio U_C to U_D, the better the results of the D-influence containment, which is consistent with the intuition and the real-world situations. In Fig. 8.9, almost all the D-influence under various U_C/U_D will be contained when $|C^*|/|D^*|$ reaches 2, which means that the assignment of $|C^*|$ in Algorithm 8.2 makes sense when $|C^*|/|D^*|$ is not larger than 2. In Fig. 8.10, the D-influence will be contained when U_C/U_D reaches 2, which means that the assignment of ξ_D and ξ_C in Algorithm 8.1 makes sense such that U_C/U_D is not larger than 2 as well. Accordingly, we conclude that the result of influence containment can be improved by increasing C-seeds under the certain U_C/U_D or increasing the U_C/U_D under the certain C-seed set.

From Figs. 8.9 and 8.10, the relationship of relevant parameters, which hold both in Greedy and MaxDegree, can be summarized as follows. First, the containment of C-seeds is influenced by $|C^*|/|D^*|$ and $|U_c|/|U_d|$. Relative to the D-seeds, the more the C-seeds (i.e., the larger the value of $|C^*|/|DD^*|$), the better the result of the C-seeds' containment. Then, the larger the value of U_c, the larger the C-seeds' infected degree (i.e., ξ_c); meanwhile, the smaller the C-influence's threshold (i.e., θ_c), the more easily the C-influence is propagated. Thus, the larger the value of $|U_c|/|U_d|$, the better the result of the C-seeds' containment.

8.7 Summary

Aiming at the effective strategies of participants themselves for competitive influence spread, this chapter extended the LT model to establish the D–C model by incorporating the realistic specialties and characteristics of the containment of competitive influence spread. As the general extension of the classic LT model, the presented D–C model accepts different kinds of influence from D-seeds and C-seeds, and the state of a vertex described by the activation probability. The D–C model and corresponding strategies for influence spread containment can provide underlying techniques for decision-making, customer marketing/targeting, disease prevention, etc.

References

1. Bharathi, S., Kempe, D., and Salek, M. Competitive influence maximization in social networks. *Proc. WINE*, 2007, pp. 306–311.
2. Borodin, A., Filmus, Y., and Oren, J. Threshold models for competitive influence in social networks. *Proc. WINE*, 2010, pp. 539–550.
3. Budak, C., Agrawal, D., and Abbadi, A. E. Limiting the spread of misinformation in social networks. *Proc. WWW*, 2011, pp. 665–674.
4. Carnes, T., Nagarajan, C., Wild, S. M., and van Zuylen, A. Maximizing influence in a competitive social network: A follower's perspective. *Proc. ICEC*, 2007, pp. 351–360.
5. Chen, W., Collins, A., Cummings, R., Ke, T., Liu, Z., and Rincón, D. Influence maximization in social networks when negative opinions may emerge and propagate. *Proc. SDM*, 2011, pp. 379–390.
6. Chen, W., Yuan, Y., and Zhang, L. Scalable influence maximization in social networks under the linear threshold model. *Proc. ICDM*, 2010, pp. 88–97.
7. Datta, S., Majumder, A., and Shrivastava, N. Viral marketing for multiple products. *Proc. ICDM*, 2010, pp. 118–127.
8. Embar, V., Bhattacharya, I., Pandit, V., and Vaculin, R. Online topic-based social influence analysis for the Wimbledon championships. *Proc. KDD*, 2015, pp. 1759–1768.
9. Embar, V., Pasumarthi, R., and Bhattacharya, I. A Bayesian framework for estimating properties of network diffusions. *Proc. KDD*, 2014, pp. 1216–1225.
10. Fan, L., Wu, W., Zhai, X., Xing, K., Lee, W., and Du, D. Z. Maximizing rumor containment in social networks with constrained time. *Social Network Analysis and Mining*, 2014, **4**(1): 214.
11. Fujishige, S. *Submodular Functions and Optimization (2nd Edn)*. Elsevier, 2005.
12. Guille, A., Hacid, H., Favre, C., and Zighed, D. A. Information diffusion in online social networks: A survey. *SIGMOD Record*, 2013, **42**(2): 17–28.
13. Hajian, B. and White, T. On measurement of influence in social network. *Proc. ASONAM*, 2012, pp. 101–105.
14. He, X. and Kempe, D. Stability of influence maximization. *Proc. KDD*, 2014, pp. 1256–1265.
15. He, X., Song, G., Chen, W., and Jiang, Q. Influence blocking maximization in social networks under the competitive linear threshold model. *Proc. SDM*, 2012, pp. 463–474.

16. Kan, Z., Klotza, J. R., Pasiliao Jr, E. L., and Dixon, W. E. Containment control for a social network with state-dependent connectivity. *Automatica*, 2015, **56**: 86–92.

17. Kempe, D., Kleinberg, J. M., and Tardos, E. Maximizing the spread of influence through a social network. *Proc. KDD*, 2003, pp. 137–146.

18. Kempe, D., Kleinberg, J., and Tardos, E. Influential nodes in a diffusion model for social networks. *Proc. ICALP*, 2005, pp. 1127–1138.

19. Kimura, M., Saito, K., and Motoda, H. Blocking links to minimize contamination spread in a social network. *ACM Transactions on Knowledge Discovery from Data*, 2009, **3**(2): 1–23.

20. Lappas, T., Terzi, E., Cunopulos, D., and Mannila, H. Finding effectors in social networks. *Proc. KDD*, 2010, pp. 1059–1068.

21. Leskovec, J. and Krevl, A. SNAP Datasets: Stanford large network dataset collection. Available at http://snap.stanford.edu/data, 2016.

22. Li, H., Bhowmick, S. S., Sun, A., and Cui, J. Conformity-aware influence maximization in online social networks. *The VLDB Journal*, 2015, **24**(1): 117–141.

23. Li, Y., Chen, W., Wang, Y., and Zhang, Z. Influence diffusion dynamics and influence maximization in social networks with friend and foe relationships. *Proc. WSDM*, 2013, pp. 657–666.

24. Lin, Z., Zhang, X., Xin, N., and Chen, D. CK-LPA: Efficient community detection algorithm based on label propagation with community kernel. *Physica A: Statistical mechanics & Its Applications*, 2014, **416**(C): 386–399.

25. Liu, W., Yue, K., Wu, H., Li, J., Liu, D., and Tang, D. Containment of competitive influence spread in social networks. *Knowledge-Based Systems*, 2016, **109**: 266–275.

26. NetworkX. http://networkx.github.io/documentation/latest/reference/generators.html, 2015.

27. Rodriquez, M. and Song, L. Diffusion in social and information networks: Research problems, probabilistic models, and machine learning methods. *Proc. KDD*, 2015, pp. 2315–2316.

28. Shirazipourazad, S., Bogard, B., Vachhani, H., Sen, A., and Horn, P. Influence propagation in adversarial setting: How to defeat competition with least amount of investment. *Proc. CIKM*, 2012, pp. 585–594.

29. Trprevki, D., Tang, W. K. S., and Kocarev, L. Model for rumor spreading over networks. *Physical Review E*, 2010, **81**(5 Pt 2): 056102.

30. Wang, Y., Cong, G., Song, G., and Xie, K. Community-based greedy algorithm for mining top-*k* influential nodes in mobile social networks. *Proc. KDD*, 2010, pp. 1039–1048.

31. Wasserman, S. and Faust, K. *Social Network Analysis: Methods and Applications*. Cambridge University Press, 1994.

32. Wu, H., Liu, W., Yue, K., Huang, W., and Yang, K. Maximizing the spread of competitive influence in a social network oriented to viral marketing. *Proc. WAIM*, 2015, pp. 516–519.

Chapter 9

Locating Sources in Online Social Networks via Random Walk

To locate source nodes of influence propagation given an observation set in online social networks is the source location problem. It is increasingly critical to control the diffusion of malicious information in terms of source nodes with the popularity of online social networks. In this chapter, we focus on multi-source location with incomplete information on active nodes and network structures. First, to track the causes to activate nodes, we give the Bayes backtracking model (BBM), where the posterior probabilities of activation causes are formulated. Then, we employ random walk to represent the source backtracking process and present the corresponding backtracking algorithm for source location by taking the posterior probability in BBM as the transition probability in random walk. Finally, we test the effectiveness of our method on real online social networks and make performance studies.

9.1 Motivation and Basic Idea

Nowadays, online social network has become the important media of information dissemination due to the convenience and rapid propagation. Upon online social networks, news can spread quickly and advertising can reach potential users efficiently. Parallely, some malicious information, such as rumors and computer virus, may also be diffused uncontrollably [24, 25, 28]. Therefore, how to control the propagation of harmful information to reduce the corresponding loss is also an important subject in the paradigm of influence diffusion. To prevent the diffusion of harmful information, we could locate source nodes of influence spread. In real online social networks, the diffusion process and network structure are observed incompletely, under which we consider how to identify source nodes of information diffusion.

In recent years, there have been many efforts on influence diffusion in social networks. Researchers mainly focus on understanding and modeling the diffusion process and solving the influence maximization problem [2, 10, 14–16]. As for the diffusion process, the susceptible–infected-recovered (SIR) model was proposed to represent the disease propagation, which could also be used to model the influence diffusion on social networks [3]. Kempe *et al.* [14] proposed two classic models to describe the diffusion process: Independent Cascade (IC) model and Linear Threshold (LT) model. Based on the diffusion models, many studies on influence diffusion have been conducted, such as influence maximization and source location. In this work, we employ IC model to simulate the influence diffusion process followed by the source location, since the IC model is concise and could reflect the randomness of diffusion.

The problem of source location is to locate possible source nodes of influence spread based on an observation about network structure and diffusion details. Recently, researchers have made a lot of efforts on this problem. For example, Dong and Vincezo proposed the heuristic algorithms [8, 9] and Zang *et al.* proposed the reverse propagation model [27]. These approaches mainly focus on estimating the single source node according to the diffusion result with complete network information. However, there may be more than one source node frequently in real social networks. Furthermore, it is impossible to obtain the complete information about the global network structure and diffusion details due to the large scale of online social networks. In this work, we aim to propose a multi-source locating solution based on incomplete observation information on the diffusion process and network structure [29].

Actually, there may be more than one source node of influence diffusion with a partial observation of propagation results in large-scale online social networks. In this chapter, we are to locate the multi-source nodes. In other words, we are to find out possible source nodes after the diffusion has occurred. It is known that Bayes model [20] is a classic method in probability theory and formulates the posterior probability of causes when the results have occurred. However, when we use the Bayes model to formulate the posterior probabilities of activation causes, it is hard to compute the posterior probability of a source node with incomplete information on active nodes and the network structure.

To this end, we first consider locating the possible node that activates the observed active node instead of the possible source node based on the Bayes model. The possible parent node which activates the observed active node indicates the possible direction that the influence comes from. Then, we consider how to track the possible source nodes reversely, step by step. It is known that random walk constitutes a finite Markov chain and has been wildly used in graph research for a long time [17]. Unlike the spreading in the diffusion process, backtracking to source nodes is just an opposite process similar to a random walk in a graph. In our work, we regard the backtracking process as random walk based on the posterior probability of activation formulated by the Bayes model. Compared with the maximum-likelihood estimation, random walk reflects the randomness of the activation process of nodes in social networks.

Generally speaking, the contribution of this chapter is summarized as follows.

First, we propose a Bayes backtracking model (BBM) to identify the possible node, which spreads influence to other nodes in the activation process. Since the locating process starts from an observation node, we try to find out the node which activates this observation node, instead of locating source nodes immediately. A node is activated if this node is a source node or it is activated by one of its active parent nodes. In the BBM, we define the probability that the node activates itself and use the Bayes model to formulate the posterior probability of causes that activate the node.

Second, we propose a random walk based backtracking algorithm (RWBA) to locate the source nodes via posterior probabilities in BBM. Different from the diffusion process, the activation process could be simulated by random walk in a graph. By RWBA, we could backtrack to the source nodes by crawling the parent nodes of passing nodes in an online social network with incomplete network structures starting from partial observation of active nodes.

Finally, we implement our algorithms and conduct performance studies. Experiment results show that our proposed method is effective for the situation with multiple source nodes as well as that with just a single source node.

The reminder of this chapter is organized as follows. In Section 9.2, we introduce related work. In Section 9.3, we state the problem of source location in social networks. In Sections 9.4 and 9.5, we give the BBM and RWBA, respectively. In Section 9.6, we show experimental results. In Section 9.7, we summarize our work in this chapter.

9.2 Related Work

Influence propagation in online social networks has received more and more attention. Many researchers focus on propagation modeling and influence maximization. In terms of propagation modeling, Kempe *et al.* [14] proposed two classic models: IC model and LT model. Following their work, many researchers presented some extended models [5, 11, 16] and formalized the influence maximization problem accordingly. Goyal *et al.* [11] proposed three models: static model, continuous time model, and discrete time model, in which the influence probabilities are relative to the action log instead of the discrete time step. Chen *et al.* [5] extended the IC and LT models by incorporating the time-delay aspect of influence diffusion. Most of these models describe the diffusion process of influence propagation globally instead of the activation process of a single node.

Recently, various studies were conducted for source location [1, 6, 7, 13, 19, 23, 26, 27, 31]. For example, Zang *et al.* [27] proposed a reverse propagation model and identified sources in a community using the maximum-likelihood estimation. Jiang *et al.* [13] adopted a reverse dissemination strategy to specify a set of suspects of the real rumor source and employed a novel microscopic rumor spreading model to calculate the maximum-likelihood for each suspect. The randomness, the key characteristic of influence propagation, has not been well incorporated in the maximum-likelihood method. Zhu and Ying [31] developed a reverse infection algorithm to find the sample path-based estimator in general graphs. In these methods, the complete information about activation is required. Xu and Chen [26] proposed an algorithm to compute rumor quantifier, a reachability based score for ranking the importance of nodes as the rumor source, but the monitor's position is critical. By contrast, we consider the location of multiple source nodes without complete observations.

Many random walk based methods have been proposed to effectively solve the social network analysis problems that are independent of the process of influence propagation, such as sampling [12, 18, 22, 30] and recommending systems [4]. Differently, we employ random walk to simulate the activation process of nodes in a social network.

9.3 Influence Propagation Model and Source Location Problem

9.3.1 *Influence propagation model*

A social network is denoted as a directed graph $G = \langle V, E \rangle$, where V is the set of nodes, $v_i \in V$ represents individuals, and E is the set of edges. An edge $e_{ij} \in E$ represents the influence spread node v_i to node v_j. We use IC model [14] to simulate the influence diffusion process, in which a node is either active or inactive. We use symbol s_i to represent the state of node v_i.

$$s_i = \begin{cases} 1, & v_i \text{ is active} \\ 0, & v_i \text{ is inactive} \end{cases} \tag{9.1}$$

Once an inactive node v_i is activated, v_i stays active. The node activates its inactive neighbor v_j only once independently with the active probability p_{ij}, which is initialized randomly in the IC model.

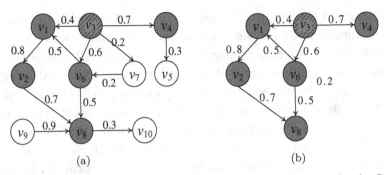

Fig. 9.1. An example of influence propagation: (a) Influence propagation in G; (b) Active subgraph G_a.

For convenience, we give the definitions of active set, inactive set, and active subgraph.

Definition 9.1. V_a is the active set containing all active nodes in G. V_i is the inactive set containing all inactive nodes in G. E_a is the set of edges connecting active nodes. The active subgraph $G_a = \langle V_a, E_a \rangle$ is a subgraph of G containing only active nodes and corresponding edges. That is, $V_a = \{v_i \mid v_i \in V, \text{ and } s_i = 1\}$ and $V_i = \{v_i \mid v_i \in V, \text{ and } s_i = 0\}$, such that $V_a \cap V_i = \phi$, $V_a \cup V_i = V$.

Example 9.1. Figure 9.1(a) shows an example of influence propagation, where source node v_3 activates its neighbor v_1, v_4, and v_6. v_1 activates v_2 and v_6 activates v_8. v_5, v_7, v_9, and v_{10} are inactive nodes. The active subgraph is showed in Fig. 9.1(b).

9.3.2 *Source location problem*

The set of source nodes is a subset of active nodes, which originate the influence or initiate the diffusion. Thus, the problem of source location is to locate the influence sources in propagation starting from a sampling set of active nodes, also called observation set. Given a partial observation set $O \subseteq V_a$ in a graph G, we are to locate the most probable source nodes based on the observation set.

For instance, if we suppose that the observation node v_8 is active in the example shown in Fig. 9.1(a), then the task of source location is to find out the possible source nodes starting from v_8, such as v_3.

9.4 Bayes Backtracking Model

In this section, we give the BBM to model the backtracking process of node activation. According to the influence propagation process, v_i itself is a source node or v_i is activated by one of its active parent nodes, which activates v_i.

As we know, the number of source nodes is ordinarily small relative to the number of nodes in graph G. If a node is active while its parent nodes have a small chance to activate it, then this node is more likely to be a source node. In order to describe the possibility of a source node, we define the probability that a node activates itself.

Definition 9.2. The probability that node v_i activates itself is denoted as p_{ii} and described as follows:

$$p_{ii} = 1 - \max_{j \in \mathrm{AP}_i} p_{ji} \qquad (9.2)$$

where AP_i is the set of active parent nodes of v_i, specified as

$$\mathrm{AP}_i = \{v_j \,|\, e_{ji} \in E,\, s_j = 1\} \qquad (9.3)$$

We suppose that there is no distinction between different parent nodes when they are trying to activate the same child node. This means that the activation attempts from these nodes are uniform. Thus, we have the probability that v_j tries to activate v_i as follows:

$$P(A_{j \to i}) = \frac{1}{1 + |AP_i|} v_j \in \mathrm{AP}_i \cup \{v_i\} \qquad (9.4)$$

where $A_{j \to i}$ means that v_j tries to activate v_i.

$P(s_i = 1 \mid A_{j \to i})$ denotes the conditional probability that v_i is activated while the parent node v_j tries to activate v_i. In the IC model, $P(s_i = 1 \mid A_{j \to i})$ is equal to the active probability p_{ji} and $P(s_i = 1 \mid A_{i \to j})$ is equal to the probability of v_i that activates itself, denoted as p_{ii}. That is

$$P(s_i = 1 \mid A_{j \to i}) = p_{ji} v_j \in \mathrm{AP}_i; \quad P(s_i = 1 \mid A_{i \to j}) = p_{ij} v_j = v_i$$

$$(9.5)$$

Then, the posterior probability of node v_i is activated by its active parent node $v_j \in \mathrm{AP}_i$, when the activation state of v_i is observed. Based on the Bayes model, the posterior probability is computed as follows:

$$P(A_{j \to i} \mid s_i = 1)$$

$$= \frac{P(s_i = 1 \mid A_{j \to i}) P(A_{j \to i})}{P(s_i = 1 \mid A_{j \to i}) P(A_{i \to i}) + \sum_{k \in \mathrm{AP}_i} P(s_i = 1 \mid A_{j \to i}) P(A_{j \to i})}$$

$$= \frac{p_{ji} \times \frac{1}{1+|\mathrm{AP}_i|}}{p_{ii} \times \frac{1}{1+|\mathrm{AP}_i|} + \sum_{k \in \mathrm{AP}_i} p_{ki} \times \frac{1}{1+|\mathrm{AP}_i|}} = \frac{p_{ji}}{p_{ii} + \sum_{k \in \mathrm{AP}_i} p_{ki}}$$

$$(9.6)$$

The posterior probability of node v_i activated by itself can be computed as follows:

$$P(A_{i \to i} \mid s_i = 1)$$

$$= \frac{P(s_i = 1 \mid A_{j \to i}) P(A_{i \to i})}{P(s_i = 1 \mid A_{j \to i}) P(A_{i \to i}) + \sum_{k \in \mathrm{AP}_i} P(s_i = 1 \mid A_{j \to i}) P(A_{j \to i})}$$

$$= \frac{p_{ii} \times \frac{1}{1+|\mathrm{AP}_i|}}{p_{ii} \times \frac{1}{1+|\mathrm{AP}_i|} + \sum_{k \in \mathrm{AP}_i} p_{ki} \times \frac{1}{1+|\mathrm{AP}_i|}} = \frac{p_{ii}}{p_{ii} + \sum_{k \in \mathrm{AP}_i} p_{ki}}$$

$$(9.7)$$

Here, we have

$$P(A_{i \to i} \mid s_i = 1) + \sum_{j \in AP_i} P(A_{j \to i} \mid s_i = 1) = 1 \qquad (9.8)$$

Thus, $P(A_{j \to i} \mid s_i = 1)$ presents the possibility of the direction from which the influence spreads as the probability of activation causes.

Example 9.2. In the example shown in Fig. 9.1(a), if we know v_8 is active, then one of its active parent nodes, v_2 and v_6, is capable of activating v_8, or v_8 itself is a source node. By Eq. (9.2), the probability that v_2 activates v_8 is $p_{28} = 0.7$, the probability that v_6 activates v_8 is $p_{68} = 0.5$, and the probability that v_8 activates itself is $p_{88} = 0.3$, shown in Fig. 9.2(a). Based on the BBM, we could compute the probability that v_8 is activated by v_2 as follows:

$$P(A_{2 \to 8} \mid s_8 = 1) = \frac{p_{28}}{p_{88} + p_{28} + p_{68}} = \frac{0.7}{0.3 + 0.7 + 0.5} \approx 0.47$$

Similarly, we have $P(A_{6 \to 8} \mid s_8 = 1) \approx 0.33$ and $P(A_{8 \to 8} \mid s_8 = 1) = 0.2$, shown in Fig. 9.2(b). According to the above posterior probabilities, we know that v_2 is most likely to activate v_8.

Based on the BBM, we could theoretically formulate the posterior probability that a node is activated in graph G as well as all active nodes.

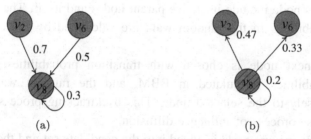

(a)   (b)

Fig. 9.2. Bayes analysis for backtracking: (a) Probability that v_8 activates itself; (b) Probabilities of the three causes.

However, it is obviously impossible to compute the posterior probability of a node as source node in a real online social network, which motivates the idea for source location by using random walk.

9.5 Random Walk Based Sources Location

A random walk on graph G denotes the following process. Given a starting node v_i, we select a neighbor node of v_i randomly to be the next node [17]. The transition probability 'is not uniform and related to the active probability in terms of source location, different from the normal random walk with uniformly distributed transition probabilities. In our method, the transition probability is determined by the posterior probability in BBM.

First, we obtain the observation set by randomly selecting some nodes and checking their state. If a selected node is active (inactive), then we add (do not add) it into the observation set. This process will be repeated until the default number of observation nodes is reached. Then, we start the backtracking process based on random walk from the nodes in the observation set, which is called candidate set and is denoted as C. The observation set is copied to the candidate set initially, and then a random walk is started from every active node in C. The random walk processes should be started n times, if there are n active nodes in C. The process of each random walk is as follows:

(1) An edge is added from the node to itself. The next possible nodes of this node include its active parent nodes and itself. The transition probabilities in the random walk are calculated by Eqs. (9.6) and (9.7).
(2) The next node is chosen with transition probabilities, posterior probabilities formulated in BBM, and the random walk moves reversely to the selected node. This backtracking process is just a reverse process of influence diffusion.
(3) A new arriving node is added into the candidate set and the previous one is removed. Then, the next random walk step will be moved from the updated candidate set repeatedly.

The above steps are repeated until the default number of random walks is reached or the candidate set is not changed anymore. The nodes remaining in the candidate set are regarded as candidate source nodes.

We repeat the backtracking experiments independently and record the number of each selected candidate source node, which is also called hit frequency. Naturally, the hit frequency will be close to its real distribution if as many repetitions as possible are conducted. When locating the source nodes in a real online social network (e.g., locating a rumor source in Weibo), we could observe active nodes and backtrack to its parent nodes. Suppose that a node is aware of the state of its parent nodes as well as corresponding activation probabilities, we need not know the whole structure of the network or the state of each node.

In the following, we summarize the above ideas in Algorithm 9.1.

Clearly, the time complexity of Algorithm 9.1 is $O(T \times S \times OC)$. When we add the arriving node to the candidate set, the starting node

---

Algorithm 9.1 RWBA

Input:
   G_a, active subgraph with active probabilities,
   OC, upper bound of observation size,
   T, upper bound of number of experiments,
   S, upper bound of number of random walk steps
Output:
   Hit frequency of each node in the candidate set
Steps:

1. Initialization:
       Freq[i] $\leftarrow$ 0 // hit frequency of the i-th candidate source node
       NE $\leftarrow$ 0 // number of experiments done
       NR $\leftarrow$ 0 // number of random walk steps done
2. While NE $<$ T Do
       $O \leftarrow \phi$ // observation set
       $OS \leftarrow$ 0 // size of the observation set
       While $OS < OC$ do
       Select a node v randomly

Algorithm 9.1 (Continued)

If v is active Then

$\qquad O \leftarrow O \cup \{v\}$

$\qquad OS \leftarrow OS + 1$

End If

End While

$C \leftarrow O$ // assign observation set O to candidate set C

While NR $< S$ Do

For each $v_i \in C$ Do

$\qquad$ 1) Find all active parent nodes of v_i and add them to AP$_i$

$\qquad$ 2) Compute the probability that v_i activates itself:

$$p_{ii} = 1 - \max_{j \in \text{AP}_i} p_{ji} \ // \text{ by Eq. (9.2)}$$

$\qquad$ 3) Compute transition probabilities: // by Eqs. (9.6)
and (9.7)

$$P(A_{j \to i} \mid s_i = 1) \leftarrow \frac{p_{ji}}{p_{ii} + \sum_{k \in \text{AP}_i} p_{ki}},$$

$$P(A_{i \to i} \mid s_i = 1) \leftarrow \frac{p_{ii}}{p_{ii} + \sum_{k \in \text{AP}_i} p_{ki}}$$

$\qquad$ 4) Select the next node v_k among v_i and its
parent nodes with the above transition probabilities

$\qquad$ 5) Update the candidate set: $C \leftarrow C \backslash \{v_i\}$, $C \leftarrow C \cup v_j$

End For

$\qquad$ NR $\leftarrow$ NR $+ 1$

End While

NE $\leftarrow$ NE $+ 1$

For each $v_i \in C$ Do //update Freq[] according to the result C

$\qquad$ Freq[i] $\leftarrow$ Freq[i] $+ 1$

End For

End While

3. Return Freq[]

---

of random walk is removed, so the number of candidate sets does not change. If the random walks from different nodes in the candidate set move to the same node, $|C|$ will be decreased. Furthermore, the random walk is a backtracking process leading to the source node. At each step, we track the suspicious node according to the posterior probability in BBM, which means that the next node in random walk is more unreliable than the previous one.

9.6 Experimental Results

9.6.1 *Experiment setup*

We implemented our algorithm on the real Twitter dataset,[a] crawled from public sources, containing 81306 nodes and 2420766 edges, where a node represents a user in the social network and edges indicate the friend relationships between users.

First, we simulated the influence diffusion process. We set the active probabilities on edges randomly and implemented the IC model. Running the diffusion simulation on the Twitter dataset with different random source nodes, we obtained different diffusion results, on which we tested our RWBA.

To compare our method with the reverse propagation model and maximum-likelihood estimation method [13, 27, 31], we compared our RWBA with the Maximum Likely Greedy Algorithm (MLGA), where we made greedy selection of the suspicious nodes at every backtracking step via the maximum-likelihood estimation [27] instead of random walk. When tracking source nodes from node v_i in the candidate set, we selected node v_j as the next candidate node with the maximal posterior probability. More specifically in the backtrack process, the next node v_j is determined by the following idea:

$$v_j = \underset{v_k \in AP_i \cup \{v_i\}}{\arg\max} \ P(s_i = 1 \mid A_{k \to i}) \tag{9.9}$$

---

[a]http://snap.stanford.edu/data/egonets-Twitter.html.

9.6.2 *Performance studies*

According to Algorithm 9.1, the node with higher hit frequency is more likely to be a source node. Therefore, we compared the hit frequency of source node(s) with the average hit frequency of other nodes in different diffusion cases to test the effectiveness of our method.

The backtracking results in diffusion cases with one source node are shown in Figs. 9.3–9.5, where there are 24283 and 2209 active

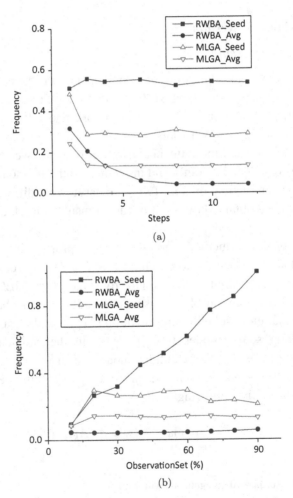

(a)

(b)

Fig. 9.3. Hit frequency with one source node and 24 active nodes: (a) Different backtracking steps; (b) Different sizes of observations.

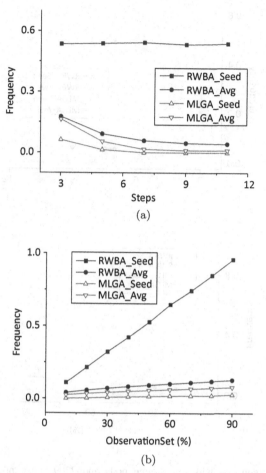

Fig. 9.4. Hit frequency with one source node and 283 active nodes: (a) Different backtracking steps; (b) Different sizes of observations.

nodes, respectively. For the diffusion case in Fig. 9.5, we selected the source node (ID = 361349552) randomly, and obtained the diffusion result which contains 2209 active nodes by simulating the spreading process based on IC model. Figures 9.3(a), 9.4(a), and 9.5(a) show the hit frequency with different random walk steps. Figures 9.3(b), 9.4(b), and 9.5(b) show the hit frequency with different sizes of the observation set. It can be seen that the hit frequency of a source node is much

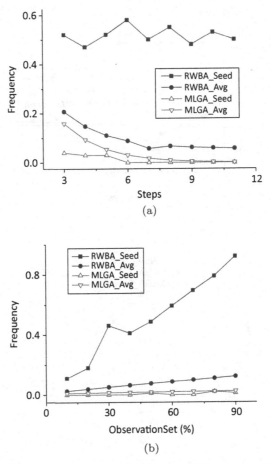

Fig. 9.5. Hit frequency with one source node and 2209 active nodes: (a) Different backtracking steps; (b) Different sizes of observations.

higher than the average hit frequency by Algorithm 9.1, which means that our method is effective for source location in the situation with one source node. When random walk moves more steps, the average hit frequency decreases since the backtracking process is more likely to leave non-source nodes and concentrate on the source node.

Meanwhile, the hit frequency of source node is increased remarkably with the increase of the observation nodes, since more activation information could be helpful to improve the precision of location results

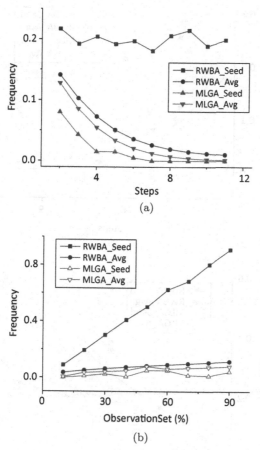

Fig. 9.6. Hit frequency with two source nodes: (a) Different backtracking steps; (b) Different sizes of observations.

by our method. It can also be seen that the results by our proposed RWBA are much better than those by MLGA. The hit frequency of source node in MLGA is too close to the average frequency to distinguish the source node from others.

In the situation with multiple source nodes (2, 3, 4, and 5), the results of hit frequency with different numbers of random walk steps and different sizes of observation sets are shown in Figs. 9.6–9.9, respectively. It can be seen that the increase of source nodes brings the instability

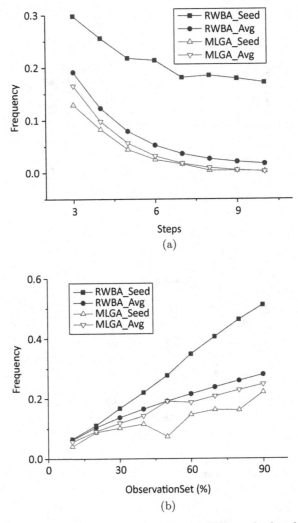

Fig. 9.7. Hit frequency with three source nodes: (a) Different backtracking steps; (b) Different sizes of observations.

of source average hit frequency, which is still higher than that of other nodes obviously. Therefore, our proposed RWBA is effective to solve the source location problem not only for the situation with single source but also the situation with multiple sources. In almost all cases, our proposed

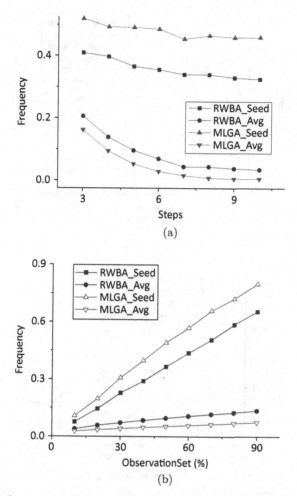

Fig. 9.8. Hit frequency with four source nodes: (a) Different backtracking steps; (b) Different sizes of observations.

RWBA outperforms MLGA, which is just effective for the partial cases such as those in Fig. 9.6(c).

In Table 9.1, we set the number of random walk step to 5 and the size of observation set to 50%. Then, we compared the hit frequency of seed(s), average frequency of other nodes, and standard deviation in different cases. It can be seen that the average frequency concentrates

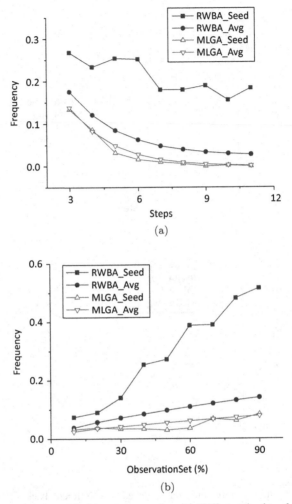

Fig. 9.9. Hit frequency with five source nodes: (a) Different backtracking steps; (b) Different sizes of observations.

on a lower level and the hit frequency of seed(s) is larger than the average hit frequency. Therefore, the suspicious source nodes could be identified by using our proposed method and adopting the metric of hit frequency.

Table 9.1. Hit frequency and standard deviation.

Cases	Hit frequency of seed(s)	Average hit frequency	Standard deviation
Fig. 9.3	0.553	0.142272727	0.121125351
Fig. 9.4	0.3214	0.069946099	0.077356819
Fig. 9.5	0.52	0.110443841	0.168462551
Fig. 9.6	0.501	0.08169562	0.108401997
Fig. 9.7	0.218	0.07931155	0.09613003
Fig. 9.8	0.365333333	0.096039216	0.139261481
Fig. 9.9	0.272	0.097221099	0.135516986

9.7 Summary

Aiming at source location of influence diffusion in online social networks, we give a random walk based method to solve the multi-source location problem with incomplete information. Our method makes full use of the observed information about network and diffusion. In particular, our proposed RWBA performs better than MLGA in almost all cases to maintain the randomness of activation in diffusion.

References

1. Alsudais, A., Leroy, G., and Corso, A. We know where you are tweeting from: Assigning a type of place to tweets using natural language processing and random Forests. *Proc. BigData Congress*, 2014, pp. 594–600.
2. Altarelli, F., Braunstein, A., Dall'Asta, L., Lage-Castellanos, A., and Zecchina, R. Bayesian inference of epidemics on networks via belief propagation. *Physical Review Letters*, 2014, **112**(11): 118701.
3. Anderson, R. M. and May, R. M. Population biology of infectious diseases: Part I. *Nature*, 1979, **280**: 361–367.
4. Backstrom, L. and Leskovec, J. Supervised random walks: Predicting and recommending links in social networks. *Proc. WSDM*, 2010, pp. 635–644.
5. Chen, W., Wei, L., and Zhang, N. Time-critical influence maximization in social networks with time-delayed diffusion process. *Chinese Journal of Engineering Design*, 2015, **19**(5): 340–344.

6. Chen, I. X., Yang, C. Z., Lu, T. K., and Jaygarl, H. Implicit social network model for predicting and tracking the location of faults. *Proc. COMPSAC*, 2008, pp. 136–143.

7. Chen, Z., Zhu, K., and Ying, L. Detecting multiple information sources in networks under the SIR model. *IEEE Transactions on Network Science & Engineering*, 2016, **3**(1): 17–31.

8. Dong, W., Zhang, W., and Tan, C. W. Rooting out the rumor culprit from suspects. *Proc. ISIT*, 2013, pp. 2671–2675.

9. Fioriti, V. and Chinnici, M. Predicting the sources of an outbreak with a spectral technique. *Computer Science*, 2012, pp. 6775–6782.

10. Freeman, L. C. Centrality in social networks conceptual clarification. *Social Networks*, 1978, **1**(3): 215–239.

11. Goyal, A., Bonchi, F., and Lakshmanan, L. V. S. Learning influence probabilities in social networks. *Proc. WSDM*, 2010, pp. 241–250.

12. Hardiman, S. J. and Katzir, L. Estimating clustering coefficients and size of social networks via random walk. *Proc. WWW*, 2013, pp. 539–550.

13. Jiang, J., Wen, S., Yu, S., Xiang, Y., and Zhou, W. Rumor source identification in social networks with time-varying topology. *IEEE Transactions on Dependable & Secure Computing*, 2018, **15**(1): 166–179.

14. Kempe, D., Kleinberg, J., and Tardos, É. Maximizing the spread of influence through a social network. *Proc. KDD*, 2003, pp. 137–146.

15. Kitsak, M., Gallos, L. K., Havlin, S., Liljeros, F., and Muchnik, L., *et al.* Identification of influential spreaders in complex networks. *Nature Physics*, 2010, **6**(11): 888–893.

16. Liu, B., Cong, G., Xu, D., and Zeng, Y. Time constrained influence maximization in social networks. *Proc. ICDM*, 2012, pp. 439–448.

17. Lovász, L., Lov, L., and Erdos, O. P. Random walks on graphs: A Survey. *Combinatorics*, 1993, **8**(4): 1–46.

18. Lu, J. and Li, D. Sampling online social networks by random walk. *Proc. HotSocial*, 2012, pp.33–40.

19. Luo, W., Tay, W. P., and Leng, M. Infection spreading and source identification: A hide and seek game. *IEEE Transactions on Signal Processing*, 2015, **64**(16): 4228–4243.

20. Neal, R. M. *Bayesian Learning for Neural Networks.* Springer, 1996, **8**(2): 456–456.

21. Pinto, P. C., Thiran, P., and Vetterli, M. Locating the Source of Diffusion in Large-Scale Networks. *Physical Review Letters*, 2012, **109**(6): 068702.

22. Ribeiro, B. and Towsley, D. Estimating and sampling graphs with multidimensional random walks. *Proc. IMC*, 2010, pp. 390–403.

23. Salih, B. A., Wongthongtham, P., Beheshti, S. M. R., and Zhu, D. A preliminary approach to domain-based evaluation of users' trustworthiness in online social networks. *Proc. BigData Congress*, 2015, pp. 460–466.

24. Shah, D. and Zaman, T. Rumor centrality: A universal source detector. *Proc. SIGMETRICS*, 2012, pp. 199–210.

25. Shah, D. and Zaman, T. Rumors in a network: Who's the culprit? *IEEE Transactions on Information Theory*, 2011, **57**(8): 5163–5181.

26. Xu, W. and Chen, H. Scalable rumor source detection under independent cascade model in online social networks. *Proc. MSN*, 2015, pp. 236–242.

27. Zang, W., Zhang, P., Zhou, C., and Guo, L. Locating multiple sources in social networks under the SIR model: A divide-and-conquer approach. *Journal of Computational Science*, 2015: 278–287.

28. Zhang, Z., Liu, L., Yue, K., and Liu, W. An estimation framework of node contribution based on diffusion information. *Proc. APWeb/WAIM(1)*, 2018, pp. 130–137.

29. Zhang, Z., Yue, K., Sun, Z., Liu, L., and Liu, W. Locating sources in online social networks via random walk. *Proc. BigData Congress*, 2017, pp. 337–343.

30. Zhong, M. and Shen, K. Random walk based node sampling in self-organizing networks. *ACM SIGOPS Operating Systems Review*, 2006, **40**(3): 49–55.

31. Zhu, K. and Ying, L. Information source detection in the SIR model: a sample-path-based approach. *IEEE/ACM Transactions on Networking*, 2016, **24**(1): 408–421.

Chapter 10

Conclusion

Knowledge discovery is an everlasting and challenging subject with great interest in various paradigms including data science, artificial intelligence, machine learning, information retrieval, etc. Following the tendency of data socialization, computational or intelligent social science has been developed rapidly in recent years. Analysis of social media data facilitates knowledge discovery, behavioral preference/profile modeling, personalized services, sentiment monitoring, society governance, etc. The methodology of data-intensive social media analysis also accelerates the improvement of research and development of traditional social science.

Both in academic and industry paradigms, social media analysis is the subject with many research contents and fruitful findings, which could not be included totally in this book definitely. The massive, heterogeneous, dynamic characteristics of social media data, the large volume and incomplete topology of social network, and the unobservable, nonlinear, and uncertain characteristics of behavioral association motivate our proposed methods. Undoubtedly, it is neither feasible nor possible to provide universal methodologies for social media analysis driven by specific applications. Upon social behavioral interactions and social networks, in this book we mainly focus on behavioral associations and inferences based on probabilistic models.

As the basis of data analysis, we give a parallel and incremental method to acquire and update online big graphs, including social networks, linked Webpages, and knowledge graphs, so the user-generated data and social behavioral interactions could be collected. As the underlying knowledge framework, we give the method for incremental learning of Bayesian network (BN) in response to the dynamically changing characteristics of social media. Then, we give the data-intensive method to measure user similarities based on BN. Meanwhile, we give the Markov network (MN)-based method to represent user associations from frequent patterns in behavioral interactions, which also establishes the relationship between frequent patterns, association rule, and MN. Consequently, we give the method to discover latent links and communities from behavioral interactions instead of social network topologies. Meanwhile, to limit the misinformation spread or maximize the overall influence, we give the methods to contain influence spread and locate influence sources by the graph model with state probabilities and random walk with transition probabilities.

The contents in this book also leave open many challenging problems that are worth following and studying further.

- Upon the acquired heterogeneous social media data and incrementally revised probabilistic models, various tasks of social media analysis and consequent information services could be conducted. The incremental learning of BN in time-series social media environments could be considered by extending our approach with temporal specialties. The algorithm for incremental learning of BNs from data streams could be developed by extending our proposed algorithm in terms of the specialties of data streams and incorporating online learning techniques.

- Our proposed approach for modeling user similarities based on BN provides the idea for inferring indirect similarities. However, user similarities not only depend on the social behavioral interactions but also the contents involved in the interactions (e.g., blogs, comments, and paper titles), which makes us further consider user behaviors and contents simultaneously.

- The methods for MN-based associative categorizations, latent link analysis, community detection, and entity association could be further extended by adding directions of edges to fulfill inferences of associations with uncertainty. Thus, any form of queries of user associations could be evaluated by computing forward conditional probabilities, reverse posterior probabilities, and marginal probabilities.

- Knowledge graph, as a typical online big graph and a representation of domain knowledge, could be incorporated into the method for data acquisition to improve the effectiveness of the collected social media data, and incorporated into influence spread on social networks to fulfill domain-specific influence containment.

- Knowledge graph could be extended by incorporating BN to make associations among entities described with uncertainties quantitatively. Thus, the novel mechanisms for fusing knowledge graphs in multiple domains and BNs learned from corresponding data could be studied, where the strategies for processing big graphs and massive data should be addressed accordingly.

- The associations and latent links among users could be further used for link prediction on social networks. The acquired social media data also facilitate the open world completion of knowledge graphs.

Index

A

activation probability, 207, 215
active set, 240
active subgraph, 240
adaptive data collection, 16
association degree, 162
association rule, 2, 110
associative categorization, 6, 110

B

backtracking process, 244
Bayes backtracking model (BBM), 237
Bayesian Information Criterion (BIC), 186
Bayesian network (BN), 181
behavior association, 110
behavioral interaction, 79
Berk-Stan, 26
branch and bound, 16

C

$\alpha-\beta$-community, 166
C-activation probability, 218
C-influence, 211
C-seed, 219
chain rule, 79
Chest-clinic network, 59
chordal, 52, 123
community detection, 7, 154
competitive influence containment, 9
conditional independence, 40, 116
conditional probability table (CPT), 4

conflict efficiency, 22
containment of competitive influence, 207
Cooper–Herskovits scoring function, 43

D

D-activation probability, 218
D-influence, 211
D-influence containment, 224
D-seeds, 219
data acquisition, 11
data updating, 24
data-intensive computation, 83
dependency model, 116
Diffusion–Containment model (D–C model), 9, 207, 211
directed acyclic graph (DAG), 4

E

entity association Bayesian network (EABN), 183
entity association (EA), 7, 179
Euclidean distance, 190

F

forward sampling, 193
frequent itemset, 155
frequent pattern, 2, 110

G

greedy algorithm, 223
Groceries dataset, 195

H

HDFS, 92
hierarchical categorization, 126, 143
hill-climbing, 43, 56
hit frequency, 245

I

IAMN-based community detection, 157
incremental learning, 40
incremental maintenance, 23
Independency map (I-map), 116
Independent Cascade (IC), 236
infected degree, 213
influence blocking, 206
influence degree, 42, 49
influence maximization, 206
information diffusion, 236
item-association Markov network
  (IAMN), 6, 114, 117, 156

J

joint probability distribution (JPD), 79

K

k-clique, 160
K-fork tree, 16
k-nearest neighbor set, 161
knowledge base, 183

L

L1-Norm, 101
latent link analysis, 154
latent social link, 154
linear threshold (LT), 205
logarithmic CH function, 55

M

β-maximum-clique, 162
MapReduce, 5, 74
Markov blanket (MB), 43, 54, 74
Markov equivalence, 42, 52
Markov network (MN), v, 112, 155
microblog network, 138
microblog user categorization, 144
minimal I-map, 119
mutually similar subgraph, 85

N

News Popularity dataset, 195
normalized mutual information (NMI),
  174

O

online big graph (OBG), 2, 12
overlapping community structures, 156

P

partially directed acyclic graphs, 46
Poisson process, 14, 23–24
posterior probability, 242
probabilistic graphical model (PGM), vi,
  112
probabilistic inference, 87, 193

Q

Quasi-Monte Carlo (QMC) sampling, 13

R

random walk, 237, 244
reversible confidence, 161

S

scoring and search, 58
self-organizing map (SOM), 8, 181
similarity degree, 81, 87
Sina Weibo, 92
social behavioral interaction, 71
social media, v
social network, v
source location, 236, 240
Spark, 14
submodularity, 220

T

textual Web content (TWC), 7, 179
threshold rule, 213
Twitter, 247

U

uncertain knowledge, 40
user Bayesian network, 80
user behavioral data, 1

user similarity, 5, 72
user-generated data, 1, 71

V

V-structure, 46, 50
variation degree, 47

W

Weibo, 26
Wiki-vote, 225
Wikidata, 26, 183
window factor, 24

East China Normal University Scientific Reports
Subseries on Data Science and Engineering

Published (continued from page ii)

Vol. 8   *Network Data Mining and Analysis*
          by Ming Gao (East China Normal University, China),
          Ee-Peng Lim (Singapore Management University, Singapore) and
          David Lo (Singapore Management University, Singapore)

Vol. 7   *Time-Aware Conversion Prediction for E-Commerce*
          by Wendi Ji (East China Normal University, China),
          Xiaoling Wang (East China Normal University, China) and
          Aoying Zhou (East China Normal University, China)

Vol. 6   *Discovery and Fusion of Uncertain Knowledge in Data*
          by Kun Yue (Yunnan University, China), Weiyi Liu
          (Yunnan University, China), Hao Wu (Yunnan University, China),
          Dapeng Tao (Yunnan University, China) and
          Ming Gao (East China Normal University, China)

Vol. 5   *Review Comment Analysis for E-commerce*
          by Rong Zhang (East China Normal University, China),
          Aoying Zhou (East China Normal University, China),
          Wenzhe Yu (East China Normal University, China),
          Yifan Gao (East China Normal University, China) and
          Pingfu Chao (East China Normal University, China)

Vol. 4   *Opinion Analysis for Online Reviews*
          by Yuming Lin (Guilin University of Electronic Technology, China),
          Xiaoling Wang (East China Normal University, China) and
          Aoying Zhou (East China Normal University, China)

Vol. 3   *Querying and Mining Uncertain Data Streams*
          by Cheqing Jin (East China Normal University) and
          Aoying Zhou (East China Normal University

Vol. 2   *School Mathematics Textbooks in China:*
          Comparative Study and Beyond
          by Jianpan Wang (East China Normal University)

Vol. 1   *High-Frequency Trading and Probability Theory*
          by Zhaodong Wang (East China Normal University) and
          Weian Zheng (East China Normal University)

Printed in the United States
By Bookmasters